SCHOOL SOCIAL SYSTEMS AND STUDENT ACHIEVEMENT

Schools Can Make a Difference

SCHOOL SOCIAL SYSTEMS AND STUDENT ACHIEVEMENT

Schools Can Make a Difference

WILBUR BROOKOVER
CHARLES BEADY
PATRICIA FLOOD
JOHN SCHWEITZER
JOE WISENBAKER

PRAEGER SPECIAL STUDIES • PRAEGER SCIENTIFIC
A J.F. BERGIN PUBLISHERS BOOK

Library of Congress Cataloging in Publication Data

Brookover, Wilbur B
  School social systems and student achievement.

  A. J.F. Bergin Publishers Book
  Bibliography: p.
  Includes index.
  1. Educational sociology—United States.
2. Education, Elementary—United States.
I. Title
LC191.B687   370.19'3   79-10758
ISBN 0-03-052721-X

Published in 1979 by Praeger Publishers
A division of Holt, Rinehart and Winston/CBS, Inc.
383 Madison Avenue, New York, New York 10017 U.S.A.

J.F. Bergin Publishers, Inc.
65 South Oxford Street, Brooklyn, New York 11217 U.S.A.

9 056 987654321

Printed in the United States of America

The research reported here was supported in part by Grant
NIE-G-74-0020 from the National Institute of Education,
Department of Health, Education and Welfare. The Michigan
Department of Education assisted in the research by providing
access to the School Assessment data and jointly requesting
cooperation of the schools.

Preface

This volume is the report of a major study of the relation of elementary school social systems to educational outcomes. The title emerges from evidence that school social-cultural variables may significantly affect the learning of students. This is in contrast to some indication that only the family background explains the differences in educational outcomes. Although variation in the socio-economic status and racial composition of schools' student bodies are related to reading and mathematics achievement, this study of random samples of Michigan elementary schools indicates that school social climate and social structure variables explain the differences between schools in achievement as well. Furthermore, school social climate variables explain much more of the differences in mean self-concept of academic ability and mean student self-reliance than the student body composition.

This, like any study of similar magnitude, could only be completed through the cooperation of many people. The major research staff personnel are identified on the title page. All these have made major contributions at various stages of the research process. Carol Conn, Joseph Passalacqua, Jeffrey Schneider and Arthur Tabachneck made significant contributions to the data processing and analysis. Numerous other people assisted in the field work, and we wish to recognize them and express our appreciation for their fine work. They were: Charlotte Bain, Gerald Bennett, Edna Brookover, Francis Dean, Vinson Dudley, Letta Green, Barbara Gunnings, Joanie Hall, Kathie Morland, Connie O'Neal, Dorothy Sachse, Elizabeth Schweitzer and Jay Van Hoven. Holly Mikel, Cindy Alspaugh, Pearl Dawodu, and Cindy Russell have all gone beyond the call of duty in carrying out the multitude of clerical tasks invoved in the project.

The National Institute of Education grant to the senior author made this project possible and Michael Cohen of the Institute staff has been extremely helpful in all stages of the research. Michigan State University and more specifically, the College of Urban Development, has supported this project in many ways including much time of the research staff. Dr. Robert Green, Dr. Lawrence Lezotte, and Dr. L. Eudora Pettigrew in their administrative roles have assisted at every stage. Mr. Thad Twarozynski of the Research and Contract Office has always been most helpful in facilitating the project.

The cooperation of Dr. John Porter, Superintendent, and Dr. David Donovan of the Michigan Department of Education, were absolutely essential to the project. They have always been both helpful and supportive of our endeavors.

Most important of all was the cooperation of the students, teachers, principals and central administrators of the schools that participated in the study. Without the help of these unnamed people, this research could not have been done. We thank them and assure that they have contributed to the further understanding of the educational process.

Although many have assisted, this report is the product of the authors and they are responsible for it. More specifically, the senior author, who prepared this preface, is responsible for any errors or inadequacies in the report. Further analysis and perhaps other publications will follow this report. Hopefully any corrections that need to be made can appear in subsequent work. The criticisms and suggestions of readers are, therefore, welcomed.

Wilbur Brookover

Contents

Tables

SCHOOL SOCIAL SYSTEMS AND STUDENT ACHIEVEMENT

Schools Can Make a Difference

1

The Problem,
Theory and Method

In recent years a great deal of research investigating the relationship between school characteristics and student achievement has failed to find school-related variables beyond those of racial and socio-economic composition which distinguish between schools having high and low student achievement or other outcomes. This failure has promoted a council of despair ranging from the policy implication drawn by Jencks (1972) to the identification of school social systems as a fruitless area of research (Hauser, Sewell, and Alwin, 1976). The senior author and his associates hold the belief that school social systems may indeed offer a potent source of explanation for school level differences in achievement. What follows is a summary of some results from a two-pronged research program, funded in part by the National Institute of Education. This research examined the relationships between social system variables and school outcomes. The reported results are of two types—the first being the results from a study of a random sample of Michigan elementary schools and the second being drawn from an observational study of four of these schools intended to supplement the findings of the first section. While the latter section does not and was not intended to conform to strict experimental-correlational methodology, its anthropological approach goes a long way in concretizing the concepts involved and suggesting alternatives by which schools can be improved.

The research reported here examines the thesis that characteristics of the school social system explain much of the between-school variance in school achievement and other outcomes. We ask what, if any, difference in school level achievement do school cultural or normative social-psychological variables account for? Is school social-psychological climate an alternative to social composition as an explanation of between school differences in achievement? Do structural characteristics of the school social system explain any of the differences in outcomes between schools? To what extent do social structure and school climate combined explain the differences in outcomes between schools? And what is the relative contribution of each set of school variables in explaining difference in outcomes?

There is much evidence that the level of academic achievement varies greatly from one school to another and that this variance is associated with the socio-economic and racial composition of schools (Coleman et al., 1966). The between-school differences in such possible outcomes of education as students' mean self-concept or mean self-reliance are not nearly as well established. There is some evidence of differences in self-concept between schools (St. John, 1975), but the relationship between this outcome and school composition is not consistently established. Some have concluded that the school makes little or no contribution to the differences in outcomes such as cognitive achievement and self-concept. Such differences have rather been attributed to the differences in family background identified by socio-economic and racial composition variables. Although the correlation between these social composition characteristics of the school student body and school achievement is clearly significant, such composition variables do not explain all of the variance in achievement between schools. Neither do they explain the differences in other outcomes such as student self-concept of ability, and students' self-reliance. It seems likely, therefore, that other characteristics of schools may contribute to the variance between schools in these outcome variables. Furthermore, the family background and composition variables may be masking other school variables which may be associated with them. The purpose of the study reported here, therefore, is to ask what else about schools may explain the difference in outcomes between schools.

RELATED RESEARCH

While we cannot review all the research relevant to this study, we shall mention that most directly related to its development.

The Equality of Educational Opportunity study has contributed to this line of research on two scores (Coleman et al., 1966). First, the study indicated that the traditional inputs such as reported teacher qualifications, facilities and expenditures did not explain much of the variance between schools or individuals. At the same time, the Coleman analysis and subsequent re-analyses of the Coleman data (Smith, 1972) suggest that perceptions of the school may contribute significantly to the variables in achievement. The student's sense of control and the students' self-concept as well as the teachers' perception of the nature of the school seem to contribute significantly to the variations in student achievement. Although the original analysis of the Equality of Educational Opportunity data is concerned with individual student variation in achievement, analyses by Mayeske and others (1969) suggest that similar variables may explain some of the variance between schools.

The original Equality of Educational Opportunity report and the re-analyses of that data offer purely correlational evidence relating school characteristics to student achievement. Evidence of a more quasi-experimental nature is provided by studies of the patterns of achievement in schools undergoing desegregation since these studies involve changes in school composition.

Nancy St. John (1975) has provided a comprehensive review and analysis of the findings of a wide range of desegregation studies. After careful evaluation of the effect on academic achievement, she concludes, "In sum, adequate data have not yet been gathered to determine a causal relation between school racial composition and academic achievement" (St. John, 1975, page 36). Various studies produce varied and sometimes opposite findings. The effect of desegregation on the achievement of black students has, in some cases, been found to be very beneficial and, in other cases, non existent. However, there is little evidence that the addition of black students to predominantly white schools significantly affects the achievement of the white students. Although school racial and socio-economic composition are confounded with other variables, the inconsistent results of these studies suggest the possibility that other variables, associated with student body composition, are important contributors to school academic outcomes.

In summarizing the effect of school desegregation on self-concept, St. John says, "The evidence of these studies considered as a group, is that the effect of school desegregation on the general or academic self-concept of minority group members tends to be negative or mixed more often than positive. . .this conclusion, however, must remain tentative in view of the fact that none of these studies combine an experimental design, the matching of control and experimental groups on all relevant variables, and the use of scales validated on a black population" (St. John, 1975, page 54). Since differences in the social composition of the student body do not consistently explain differences in self-concept, other school social characteristics may affect the self-concept outcomes of schooling.

The study of academic climate in a small number of high schools (McDill, Rigsby, and Meyers, 1967, and McDill and Rigsby, 1973) is quite directly related to this research. It suggested that much of the variance in academic achievement may be explained by the academic norms and expectations which characterized the student body. This general hypothesis was applied to the elementary school climate in this research. Our research on elementary school climate is directly related to the McDill et al. study of high school climates, but is based on random samples of Michigan elementary schools and uses measures of climate appropriate for elementary schools.

In both the study of Wisconsin high school graduates and Hauser's earlier work (1971), the authors disparage the probability of finding school contextual effects on student outcomes.* Hauser, however, acknowledges that the problem may result from the use of socio-economic composition or other composition variables as a proxy for the total school environment:

> Insofar as the normative or educational processess supposedly indexed by the school's socio-economic level actually do vary within schools, contextual analyses understate their importance. Finally in as far as socio-economic context is used as an index of the residual effects of the school attended, without regard to the mechanisms by which that influence takes place, the use of socio-economic classifications of schools also understates those effects just as it understates gross school effects. (Hauser, 1971, page 45)

His comments suggest that normative characteristics of the school subculture and social-psychological processes may indeed have significant impact on school academic outcomes. Such variables are the foci of this research.

There are not many studies of self-reliance as an outcome of schools, but many educators in recent years have emphasized the importance of such outcomes. In a recent study of the effects of open-school organization

---

* An extensive literature on contextual effects has appeared in recent years (Hauser, 1971 and Farkas, 1974 with Hauser's reply, 1974). These references analyze the issues and give other essential references.

on student outcomes, Epstein and McPartland (1975, Report No. 194) examine the effect of one kind of school variable on self-reliance. Although they find that family type is a more powerful influence on student self-reliance, the degree of openness in the school social structure is positively related to self-reliance. One purpose here is to examine further whether this, as well as other characteristics of the school social system contribute significantly to the between-school variance in student self-reliance.

This research is a direct outgrowth of a preliminary study which focused on the identification of normative social-psychological variables that might distinguish between elementary schools having similar socio-economic and racial composition but significantly different levels of academic achievement (Brookover et al., 1973 and Brookover and Schneider, 1975). Atypical schools, low SES with high achievement or high SES with low achievement, were matched with schools having similar racial and socio-economic composition but significantly different levels of achievement. The twenty-four schools provided the basis for identifying normative social-psychological variables that distinguished between high and low achieving schools. The desire to test the validity of the findings of the preliminary study prompted us to study a random sample of Michigan elementary schools.

While the present study differs in many important methodological aspects from previous research in this area, there are several points which need to be emphasized. First, rather than relying upon socio-economic status and school racial composition or other school variables as proxies for climate, we have endeavored to identify and measure specific social-psychological indices of school climate. In similar fashion, we have identified specific characteristics of the school social structure rather than assuming that composition is the appropriate measure of these aspects of the school social system. Second, our research focuses upon elementary schools—a level where it might be expected that schools could have the greatest incremental impact on outcomes, but one about which we know relatively little. Third, we have employed stratified random samples of elementary schools thereby extending the generality of our results. We have also analyzed the data from separate random majority black and majority white school subsamples in addition to the representative state sample, thereby allowing us to search for potential differences in the subgroups of schools *vis-a-vis* the impact of school climate.

This study concentrates on explaining the variance in achievement, self-concept of ability, and self-reliance between schools rather than the variance among individual students. We recognize that there is additional in-school variance in outcomes as well as differences between large organizational units such as school districts, but our concern is with the differences between elementary schools as social units. As will be noted in a subsequent section, there is much variance in mean school achievement, self-concept, and self-reliance between schools. Since our concern is with these differences, we have used the school as the unit of analysis rather than the individual, the classroom, or the school district.

THEORETICAL FRAMEWORK

The basic theory underlying this research is that the behavior of children in school, especially their achievement in academic subjects, is partly a function of the social and cultural characteristics of the school social system. The children take their cues from those important to them and with whom they interact, attending carefully to their expectations and definitions of appropriate behavior in the student role. In the context of the school social system, students come to perceive the role definitions, the norms, expectations, values, and beliefs that others hold for them and act accordingly. We hypothesize that each school has a set of student status-role definitions, norms, evaluations, and expectations characterizing the behavior expected of students in general and various student subgroups in particular. Although different norms, expectations, and evaluations applied to various groups and individual students account for some variation within the school, we hypothesize that there are also differences in school social systems which explain differences in student outcome among schools.

The basic premise of this research is, therefore, that the school social system or social environment affects school learning outcomes. Simply stated, the guiding hypothesis is that members of a school social system become socialized to behave differently in a given school than they would in another school. These patterns of behavior are acquired in interaction with other members of the social system which we call the school.

Although there is not an extensive body of research from which to specify particular theoretical models, a general model of the following sort guides this research (see Figure 1). The general nature of the inputs into the school system are seen as the first set of variables which may affect the outcomes of the school system. Athough there are many social characteristics of the student body and the adult members of the school, we have identified two sets of variables which may influence the nature of social structure and climate of the school and, primarily through structure and climate, the cognition and affective outcomes. These are first, the socio-economic and racial composition of the student body, and second, a set of other personnel variables. The latter include the school size and average daily attendance, the number of professional personnel per 1,000 students, and the teachers' qualifications in terms of experience, tenure in the particular school, training, and salaries. We hypothesize that the nature of the student body and the adult members of the school social system may affect the schools' social structure and academic climate as well as the level of student achievement, self-concept, and self-reliance in a school.

Figure 1

**General Model of School Social System Variables
with Hypothesized Relation to Student Outcomes**

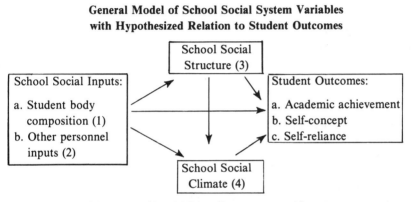

(1)   measured by mean school SES and percentage white.
(2)   measured by standard scores of school size, average daily attendance, professionals per 1,000 students, average years teaching experience, average tenure in school, percentage of teachers with advanced degrees, and mean teacher salary.
(3)   measured by teacher satisfaction with school structure, parent involvement, differentiation in student programs, principal's report of time devoted to instruction, open-closed classroom.
(4)   measured by 14 variables derived from student, teacher and principal reports of the norms, expectations, and feelings about the school.

As indicated in the model, we further hypothesize that the special structure which defines the patterns of interaction that occur within the school has an impact on the social-psychological climate as identified by the perceptions of appropriate behavior, expectations, evaluations, and feelings which members of the social system have of their role and the roles of other school members. Both the social structure variables and the social-psychological climate variables are hypothesized to affect the outcomes as identified by students' cognitive achievement, their self-concepts of ability, and their self-reliance. Through interaction, students, teachers, administrators, and others in the school social system communicate to each other conceptions of the role behaviors and expectations proper for students. The students thus come to perceive their place in the social structure, and the norms and expectations of teachers, principals, and others in the school community. In this way, students develop their own definitions of their place in the social structure, and their norms and beliefs about what is appropriate and possible for them in the school social system. Through this process of interaction, the nature of the students' achievement, and their self-concepts of ability and self-reliance are significantly affected.

We know from previous research that students' individual self-concepts of ability are related to their individual levels of achievement (Brookover et al., 1962, 1965, and 1967). We also hypothesize that this is an interactive process in which students' achievement may modify their self-concepts of ability and vice versa. Although research evidence is not available, we hypothesize a similar interaction among self-reliance and self-concept of ability and cognitive achievement. We therefore seek to determine the extent to which some characteristics of the school social structure and social-psychological climate explain the between-school differences in mean student outcomes. We further hypothesize that these factors—social structure and social climate—explain much of the variance in outcomes frequently attributed to the input variables.

Our focus is on three sets of student outcomes. The key one of these is the most commonly and generally accepted goal of the elementary school system—the acquisition of reading and arithmetic competencies—which we have identified as cognitive school achievement. The second is the academic self-concepts of the students. A third outcome is the degree of students' self-reliance. Although little research has been done on this variable, we have examined a limited conception of students' willingness and desire to depend on their own resources, particularly in the school.

In brief, the theory that guides this research holds that the behavior learned by students will vary between schools and that this variance between schools can be explained by characteristics of the school social system. First, the nature and characteristics of the students, teachers, and other members of the system which are indentified as inputs may affect the student outcomes. These inputs, however, are modified in the processes of interaction which are structured by some characteristics of the school social structure and by the social-psychological norms, expectations, and feelings which characterize the patterns of interaction within the system.

The school social structure and the subculture or climate of the school are thus perceived as intervening variables between the input and outcome variables.

RESEARCH PROCEDURES

This study developed out of the desire to test in a representative sample of public schools some hypotheses generated in previous research (Brookover et al., 1973). The schools studied were randomly sampled from the universe of public elementary schools in Michigan. Michigan may not be representative of the nation, but it is a widely varied state. It includes a large industrial urban area in the southern portion of the state, particularly in the southeast, where Detroit is located. It also includes an extensive rural agricultural area in the southern half of the state, and has a more sparsely populated rural and small-town area in the Upper Peninsula and upper half of the Lower Peninsula. A number of smaller but significant industrial centers are included in addition to the Detroit metropolitan area. These include such cities as Grand Rapids, Flint, Pontiac, Lansing and a number of other smaller cities with major industries.

Michigan was chosen as the site of this research for two reasons. First, it was convenient as the state in which the research team was located. More important, however, was the fact that the State Department of Education, under legislation requiring statewide school assessment, has for several years administered a common test of achievement in reading and arithmetic to all fourth- and seventh-grade public school students. This provided a common measure of cognitive achievement outcomes which could be used as an appropriate comparable measure throughout the state.

The Samples

There are three groups of schools on which our analysis has focused: the state sample, the black school sample, and the white school sample. The 68 schools in the state sample constitute a random sample of Michigan public schools containing fourth- and fifth-grade students.

The 61 schools in the white school sample are those schools contained in the state sample whose student population is more than 50 percent white. These schools, therefore, constitute a random sample of the majority white Michigan public schools containing fourth- and fifth-grade students. For some analyses, this white school sample is divided at the median of the mean SES distribution so that high SES white schools and low SES white schools may be examined separately.

The black school sample is composed of the 7 majority black schools contained in the representative state sample along with 23 additional majority black schools randomly selected from the population of majority black Michigan public schools containing fourth and fifth grades.

Table I contains appropriate population and sample size data for each group. As noted in Table I, a small number of schools drawn in the sample did not participate in the study. The list of schools in the universe from which the samples were drawn was based upon the prior-school-year list available from the State Department of Education. Two schools drawn in the sample had been closed because of reduction in enrollment. The other schools did not participate for a variety of reasons, some of which were not available to the research staff. All of the schools in operation that did not participate were located in the southwest portion of the state. These schools were compared with the cooperating schools in the same section of the state. Analysis carried out using the State Assessment data revealed no significant differences between the cooperative and noncooperative schools on achievement, racial composition, or community type. In view of these facts, we feel a strong case can be made to generalize the results of this study to the relevant population of Michigan public schools containing fourth- and fifth-grade students.

Data Gathering
The data for this study were obtained from four sources: (1) the Michigan School Assessment reports, (2) student questionnaires administered to fourth- and fifth-grade students, (3) teacher questionnaires administered to the teachers of the fourth- and fifth-grade students, and (4) the school principal. The questionnaires will be found in Appendix A.

A computer tape of the school level data included in the Michigan Assessment Report was obtained with the cooperation of the Michigan Department of Education. As indicated below, the data included the percentage of students achieving various levels of performance on 49 objectives in reading and arithmetic. In addition, the average salary paid to the teachers, the number of professionals per thousand students, and the percentage of whites in the student body, were obtained from the school level assessment tape. The tape which was available to the research team contained school level and not individual student achievement data. Therefore, no analysis in this report is based upon individual student achievement. All achievement analyses utilize aggregate school data.

The student questionnaires were administered in each school by a trained staff of research personnel. Each fourth- and fifth-grade classroom teacher was asked to respond to the teacher questionnaire during the time that the student questionnaires were being administered. To avoid any potential interaction between teacher and pupils, the teachers were asked to leave the room during student questionnaire administration. The principal was given a questionnaire when the research team arrived at the school and was asked to respond during the time the field team was there. In a few instances, the principal could not complete the questionnaire during the time and returned it by mail. As indicated in Table I, 100 percent of the principal questionnaires were returned. Less than one percent of the student questionnaires was unusable and approximately 2 percent of the teachers failed to return completed questionnaires.

TABLE 1

Population Data Concerning Three Random Samples of Public Elementary Schools in Michigan with Fourth- and Fifth-Grade Students			
	State Sample	Black Sample	White Sample
Schools in Universe	2,226	225	2,001
Sampled Schools Participating	68	30	61
Sampled Schools Not Participating	10	7	7
Students Participating	8,078	4,737	6,729
Teachers Participating	327	177	276
Principals Participating	68	30	61

2

The School
Variables Studied

As noted in the previous section, we have examined the relation between three sets of school social system variables and three school outcome variables. The data on which each set is based are identified in Appendix B. We have classified the independent variables as (1) input, (2) social structure, and (3) school climate. The dependent variables are (1) mean school achievement, (2) mean student self-concept of academic ability, and (3) mean student self-reliance.

INPUT VARIABLES

The input variable set is composed of (1) the social composition of the student body and (2) characteristics of teacher and other personnel inputs into the social system.

Social Composition of the Student Body
The social composition of the student body is identified in this research by two variables—the mean socio-economic status of the school and the

percentage of white students in the school.

The mean socio-economic status of a school is the mean rating of the family occupational status of fourth- and fifth-grade students in the school. In all the schools outside the city of Detroit, the students were asked to identify the occupation of the family's main breadwinner. Members of the research staff who administered the questionnaires provided assistance, when needed, in identifying occupations. The occupation data were scored using the Duncan Occupational Scale with the resulting scores being averaged across all students within a school who responded to our questionnaire. This provided a basis for a mean school SES score. For the schools in the Detroit school system, a sample of 50 fourth- and fifth-grade students in each school was selected at random by the principal or his designated assistant. The occupational data for the parents of the students in this sample were then obtained from the enrollment files maintained in each school. These data were given to the research team without identifying information so as to preserve the anonymity of the students. Mean school SES was calculated from this sample of parents' occupation data in the same manner as the student data obtained in the other schools.

The racial composition in each school was obtained from enrollment data provided by each school to State Board of Education. The percentages of whites calculated from these data are recorded in the State Assessment Report to the schools which were available to us. The field workers also identified the minority group members of the fourth- and fifth-grade students from whom we obtained questionnaires. These data provided a basis for checking validity of the reported racial composition. There were no significant discrepancies between the two indicators, so the first was used because it represented the total school student body rather than only the fourth and fifth grades.

In some analyses reported here the socio-economic composition and the racial composition are combined in a single standardized index of school student body composition. This was computed after expressing both mean school socio-economic composition and the percentage of whites in standard score form.

Other School Personnel Inputs

A second set of school inputs used in this analysis is sometimes identified as other personnel inputs. This measure is composed of seven variables combined by standardized scores. Three of the measures are related to the number of members in the school social system. The first is the size of the school student body, the second is the average daily attendance of the student body, and the third is the ratio of the number of professional personnel per 1,000 students. Three measures are concerned with the qualifications and characteristics of the teachers in the school. First is the mean number of years of teaching experience of the teachers in the school, second is the mean length of time that the teachers have taught in the particular school, and the third is the percentage of teachers in the school with graduate degrees. The seventh variable is the mean teachers' salary in the school. The standardized scores of these seven variables are combined into a single measure of school personnel inputs for much of the analysis in this report. The inclusion of these seven variables in an input index is based on correlations of the variables and the relationship of each variable to school outcomes as well as the variables' common usage as a measure of school inputs.

The mean teacher salary, professional personnel-pupil ratio and school size were obtained from the State Assessment reports. The teachers' experience and teachers' time in the particular school were reported on the teacher questionnaire; the average daily attendance and the percentage of teachers with graduate degrees were obtained from the principal of each school. Questions on which the latter four items are based are shown in Appendix B.

SCHOOL SOCIAL STRUCTURE

The social structure of the school involves many different variables. Among them are the pattern of relationships between students and teachers, the formalized administrative structure, the categories of personnel and other characteristics of the social stratification and status-role definitions within the school. We have made no attempt to identify or measure all dimensions of the school social structure, but have developed five indices of variables which may contribute to differences in school outcomes. The five variables used to characterize the social structure of interaction among school personnel are described in the following paragraphs.

Parent Involvement in the School

The interaction of the members in the school social system may be characterized in part by the degree to which the children's parents are involved in the school social system. We developed an index of parent involvement based upon two items in the teacher questionnaire and two in the principal questionnaire which are also shown in Appendix B. The first is the teachers' report on the percent of parents who want feedback concerning their students' work. The measure for each school is the mean of the teachers' reported percentages. The second is the mean percent of parents known to the teachers. The percentage of parents that the principal and the teachers have contact with is the third variable. The teachers' report of the amount of contact they have with parents during the year is the fourth. The mean school response on each of these four questions was computed and converted to a standard score. The standard scores were combined into a single measure of parent involvement in the school social system.

Differentiation Among Student Programs

A widely discussed variable in the social structure of schools is the degree to which students are classified or differentiated in order to provide different types of instructional programs to students in different categories. The responses to seven questions asked of teachers and principals were used to formulate an index of differentiation or grouping of students in a particular school.

Four responses to items in the principals' questionnaire were included in this measure. The first of these is the response to, "In general, what grouping procedure is practiced across sections of particular grade levels in this school?" Responses were: homogeneous grouping according to ability, heterogeneous grouping according to ability, random grouping, or no intentional grouping. Responses were coded so that homogeneous grouping was differentiated from the other three responses; thus it measures the differences in school practice with regard to homogeneous grouping according to ability in contrast with other grouping practices. The principals' report of the extent to which objectives for students were the same for all students, or, generally different for the students was also included as a measure of the extent to which differentiated programs for different students were characteristic of the school. The third principal question included in this index was, "Which of the following do you think best predicts a pupil's success or failure in higher education?" Responses indicating (a) group or individual intelligence or aptitude test scores and (b) other standardized test scores were included as an indication of differentiated program planning.

Three items from the teacher questionnaire were also included in the index of differentiation. The first was the teachers' report of the extent to which their teaching objectives were the same for all or different for each student. A "different for each student" response was indicative of differentiated programs. A second measure was the teachers' report of the importance of students' interest in determining teaching objectives for students. The third is the teachers' report of the frequency with which they refer to their students' IQ scores for information upon which to base plans for their work. Teachers' frequent reference to IQ test scores in planning a student's work was used as an indicator of differentiated programs.

Standard scores of these seven responses were combined to provide a measure of the degree to which students are differentiated and different programs are planned for them.

Open and Closed Classroom Organization
The third variable designed to measure the social structure of the school was derived from the concept of open and closed classroom organization. Six items in the teacher questionnaire and six parallel items in the student questionnaire were designed to determine (1) the extent to which students are encouraged to talk to each other, (2) the extent to which they are permitted to move about without permission, (3) the teacher's practices with regard to assigning seats to the students, (4) the frequency with which seat assignments are changed, (5) the degree to which the teacher teaches the class as a whole or has different instructional activities for various groups and individual students, and (6) the extent to which the students work on the same or different lessons. Factor analysis indicated that the six items in each questionnaire loaded heavily on a single factor. Responses to two principal questions were also included in this measure. These are the principals' judgment of the extent to which the teachers have seats assigned for the students and the extent to which the teachers let the students talk without permission. The standard scores of the responses to these fourteen items were combined as a measure of the degree of open or closed classroom organization in each school. The specific items are shown in Appendix B and are found in the questionnaires in Appendix A.

Time Allocation
Another structural variable potentially relevant in the consideration of school performance is the structuring of the school day. Many different activities occur in school and the classroom. The school social structure is affected in a significant manner by the time allocated to various activities such as instruction, play, the checking of attendance and other record-keeping functions, teacher interaction with parents, dealing with personal concerns of the students, and discipline.

The teachers were asked to indicate the percentage of their time allocated to various activities (see teacher question 67, Appendix A), but these data have not been used in this analysis because we are convinced that the teachers' time reports cannot be validly compared across schools.

Participant observation of four schools (reported later), revealed that teachers in schools devoting a very high proportion of their time to instructional activities reported only a moderate amount of time devoted to instruction. On the other hand, teachers in schools in which we observed a very low proportion of time devoted to instruction, tended to report a relatively high proportion of their time spent on instruction. It appears from these observations that the teachers' perceptions of time allocation are not comparable in different schools.

We found the principals' reports of teachers' time allocated to instruction and their own time allocated to supervision more in accord with our observations. Although we do not have a high level of confidence in the principals' reports of time devoted to academic activites in their school classrooms, we have included their reports as one criterion of the time devoted to various activites in the school social system. Since time devoted to the instructional tasks may contribute significantly to school outcomes, we developed an index from the principals' reports as a tentative measure of this variable. The index of time allocation is based on four items. The first one is the principals' report of the percentage of a typical school day that the average teacher spends in conferring with individual students about academic progress; the second is the percentage of time the average teacher devotes to classroom and small group instruction. In addition to these items, the principal's report of the percentage of his time devoted to supervision of the instructional staff are included and the proportion of time that he deals with parents and community concerns. Standard scores of responses to these four items are combined as an index of the school's allocation of time to academic instructional activities and parent concerns.

Staff Satisfaction with the School Structure

Although not directly a measure of the social structure of the school, we have included a measure of teacher satisfaction with the structure and composition of the school and the principals' judgment of the teachers' satisfaction with the school. Five of the eight items included in this index are measures of the teachers' satisfaction with their relationships with parents, other teachers, administrators, and students. Responses to these five questions indicate the teachers' satisfaction with parent-teacher relationships, teacher-teacher relationships, teacher-administration relationships, the degree of teacher autonomy, and the teachers' authority over students. In addition to these five items, the teachers' degree of satisfaction with student achievement and measure of the difference between the racial composition of the school the teacher would prefer to teach in and the percentage of whites in the school in which he or she is teaching are included. The eighth item in the index of satisfaction is the principal's report of the percent of teachers in this school that he believes would prefer to teach in some other school. The standard scores of these items (shown in Appendix B) are combined to give us a measure of the teachers' satisfaction with the kind of social relationships and school characteristics indicated.

We have examined the relation of each of the five social structure variables described above to school outcomes, but in much of the analysis the five variables are combined as a measure of the school social structure. This, of course, is not a complete description of a school's social structure or organizational characteristics, but the set includes a number of variables that have been hypothesized to affect the outcomes of the schools. Although we identify them as social structure variables, they are not completely independent of the school authority patterns and the relationships with other participants in the school might be conceived as a climate variable as well as a reaction to social structure. In similar fashion, some may consider time allocation to instructional activities to be a climate variable similar to one discussed below, the teachers' commitment to doing the instructional job. Examination of the sample correlation coefficients indicates that the relationships between these variables and the climate variable is for the most part rather slight. The intercorrelations of the structure and the climate variables are shown in Appendix C, Tables 1 and 3.

SCHOOL CLIMATE VARIABLES

The concept of school climate has been used in many different ways. The composition of the study body as measured by socio-economic status, race, or other composition variables has frequently been used as a measure for school climate. Others have used measures of student personality or characteristics of school organization as proxies for school climate (Anderson, 1970; O'Reilly, 1975). Our conception of school academic climate may be expressed as follows:

> The school social climate encompasses a composite of variables as defined and perceived by the members of this group. These factors may be broadly conceived as the norms of the social system and expectations held for various members as perceived by the members of the group and communicated to members of the group. (Brookover and Erickson, 1975)

The   two   general   dimensions—norms   and   expectations—are theoretically highly related. Norms tend to be expressed in the common beliefs concerning the appropriate forms of behavior for members of the social system. Norms and expectations involve both the definitions of appropriate behavior expressed by others in the system, and the perceptions of these expectations as understood by members of the group. These definitions of appropriate behavior which characterize a social system, in this instance the school, are no doubt related to the composition of the membership. However, we hypothesize that a school's academic norms, expectations, and beliefs, which we call climate, are not synonymous with the social composition of its student body, and therefore, climate is not adequately measured by composition variables. In the following paragraphs, we discuss the operationalization of the school climate variables involved in this research.

Since school social climate is identified as the composite of norms, expectations, and beliefs which characterize the school social system as perceived by members of the social system, we asked members of each school to report their perceptions of such characteristics of the school. We assume that students, teachers, and principal are the most relevant participants in the school social system. That does not exclude the possible effect that others including parents or other persons who interact with the members of the school society may have. But we assume that the students, teachers, and principal are better informants concerning the norms and expectations that are relevant to student academic behavior in the school than other participants in the social system might be. In any case, a part of our effort was to identify and measure this complex of feelings, attitudes, beliefs, values, expectations, and norms of the school more directly than have other studies using social composition, personality traits, or organizational characteristics as proxies for school climate.

The instruments developed to identify school climate variables in this research are essentially new and result from these stages of development: (1) the pretesting of a large number of items, (2) analysis of data in a preliminary study, and (3) analysis of data from the current study.

Developmental Stage I
A series of questionnaires were pretested in elementary schools of a middle sized midwestern city. The items included in the questionnaire, originally administered to third-, fourth-, fifth-, and sixth-grade students in several schools largely composed of lower socio-economic black and white students, were constructed with general foci upon concepts of norms, perceived evaluations, perceived expectations, and sense of control of students. These items were then modified in the light of problems found in

communication, meaning and readability. Modified instruments were readministered to students in other schools. Various clusters of items were subjected to scalogram analysis to identify scales measuring students' perceived expectations and evaluations, school norms, students' sense of control, and perception of teachers' academic norms. Items of low utility were eliminated.

Developmental Stage II
The student questionnaires developed in the pretest process were used in a preliminary study designed to identify variables that might distinguish between high and low achieving schools with similar composition (Brookover, Gigliotti, Henderson, and Schneider, 1953).

The climate variables did distinguish between high and low achieving schools with similar composition. Thus, the predictive validity of climate variables was demonstrated and further study of the contribution of school normative climate to achievement was justified. The climate variables identified in the preliminary study were the primary source of items for the instruments used in the research involving random samples of Michigan elementary schools reported here. A few items were added to the questionnaires to explore areas of climate that were not adequately covered in the previous research.

Developmental Stage III
The data obtained from the random sample of Michigan elementary schools were factor-analyzed. Three separate factor analyses were carried out using all the school climate items contained in the student, teacher, and principal questionnaires respectively. Since the focus of this research was on the social system of school, the school was the unit of analysis in the factor analysis for both student and teacher climate data. The results of the factor analyses and the content of the items were taken into consideration when placing items in scales. No item was included that did not have a loading of at least .30 on that factor. A small number of items with reasonably high loadings were not included in any climate variable in the final analysis because they did not have appropriate content validity in the independent judgment of the members of the staff. Scale values were calculated by calculating the total item score based on the particular response chosen on a five-point scale response.

The final items for each of the climate variables are shown in Appendix B and may also be located in questionnaires in Appendix A. The student climate variables were identified as: Student Climate 1— Student Sense of Academic Futility; Student Climate 2—Student Perceived Future Evaluations and Expectations; Student Climate 3—

Student Perceived Present Evaluations and Expectations; Student Climate 4—Student Perception of Teacher Push and Teacher Norms; and Student Climate 5—Student Academic Norms. The teacher climate variables were identified as: Teacher Climate 1—Ability, Evaluations, Expectations and Quality of Education for College; Teacher Climate 2—Teacher Present Evaluations and Expectations for High School Completion; Teacher Climate 3—Teacher-Student Commitment to Improve; Teacher Climate 4—Teacher Perception of Principal's Expectations; Teacher Climate 5— Teacher Academic Futility. Principal climate variables that emerged from this analysis were identified as: Principal Climate 1—Parent Concern and Expectations for Quality Education; Principal Climate 2—Principal's Efforts to Improve; Principal Climate 3—Principal and Parent Evaluation of Present School Quality; Principal Climate 4—Principal's Present Expectations and Evaluations of Students.

An examination of the items in the several climate measures suggests that the variables measured are at least reasonably close to our theoretical conception of school climate. The relevance and significance of school climate as a factor in school achievement ultimately depends, of course, on the predictive validity of these instruments.

Although individual student or teacher perceptions may vary within a school society, it is clear from Table 2 that significant between-school variance exists in most of the climate variables. We believe that the differences in climate between schools are important aspects of the school social environment. Further analysis will demonstrate that such differences are predictive of the differences in mean school achievement.

Although there is some variance in school climate between classrooms within the school, the within school differences are not so great as to rule out the existence of a characteristic climate for the school. The knowledge of the school in which a classroom is located alone accounts for 43 percent of the between classroom variance in Student Sense of Academic Futility and somewhat less but still significant proportions, 16-35 percent, of the between classroom variance in other student and teacher climate variables.

These data indicate that school climates, as measured by the variables we have identified, differ from school to school and the climates of the classrooms within a school are somewhat more like each other than they are like the climates of classrooms in other schools in the state random sample. Thus, the school is an appropriate and meaningful social unit for the analysis of the effect of social climate on achievement.

DEPENDENT VARIABLES

As indicated in Figure 1, we have examined three outcome variables in this

TABLE 2

**Mean and Standard Deviation of Mean School Variables
in Three Samples of Michigan Elementary Schools**

Variable	State Sample		Black Sample		White Sample	
	M	SD	M	SD	M	SD
Mean SES	3.03	1.01	1.86	1.29	3.19	.93
Percent White	85.44	27.37	8.20	14.23	93.98	9.30
STUDENT CLIMATE						
1. Sense of Academic Futility	45,97	2.11	42.21	1.94	46.46	1.59
2. Future Eval. and Expect.	42.68	3.60	42.70	3.29	42.68	3.67
3. Perceived Present Eval. &						
Expectations	23.11	.81	24.50	.66	22.95	.67
4. Perception of Teacher						
Push and Norms	16.63	.59	16.52	.70	16.61	.58
5. Academic Norms	22.81	.62	22.72	.83	22.80	.62
TEACHER CLIMATE						
1. Ability, Eval., Expect.						
and Qual. of Educ./Coll.	31.60	6.19	33.65	6.29	32.48	6.38
2. Present Eval. and Expect.						
for H.S. Completion	35.24	3.05	31.91	3.58	35.84	2.47
3. Teacher-Student Commit.						
to Improve	31.52	3.86	34.52	4.20	31.25	3.88
4. Perception of Princ.						
Expectations	16.01	3.77	16.54	3.35	16.04	3.89
5. Academic Futility	21.86	2.34	20.85	2.04	21.93	2.32
PRINCIPAL CLIMATE						
1. Parent Concern and Expec.						
for Qual. Education	22.54	2.30	21.83	2.68	22.66	2.24
2. Efforts to Improve	7.75	1.56	8.63	1.40	7.69	1.54
3. Principal and Parent Eval.						
of Present School Quality	15.35	2.40	13.53	2.11	15.59	2.39
4. Present Eval. and Expect.						
of Students	29.22	4.53	27.52	5.05	29.68	4.45

research: the mean achievement of students in the fourth grade in each of the schools, the mean self-concept of academic ability of the students, and the mean self-reliance of the students. Although there are, of course, numerous other outcomes that could be identified, these are indicative of major areas of interest in American education.

Mean School Achievement

The measure of academic achievement is the average of the percentage of students mastering each of the 49 objectives in the Michigan School Assessment Test (Michigan Department of Education, no date) administered in the fall of the 1974-1975 academic school year. These tests are administered to the fourth grade of each school and are designed to measure the objectives identified by committees of teachers and other educators for early fourth-grade students. Nineteen such objectives have been identified for reading and 30 objectives for arithmetic. Five test items are used to measure the mastery of each objective. Correct answers on four of the five items is identified as mastery of each particular objective. The percentage of the fourth-grade students who answer correctly at least four of the five questions measuring each objective is the basis for the calculation of the mean school percentage mastering the 49 objectives. The school mean percentage mastering the objectives may be conceived as either the average of the percent of pupils attaining each objective or the average of the percents of objectives mastered by each pupil; the two are algebraically identical.

Analysis of the intercorrelations among the school mean percentage mastering all objectives, the school mean percentage mastering the reading and mathematic objectives separately, an average weighting reading and mathematics equally, reading total scores and arithemtic total scores, and weighted and unweighted averages of reading and mathematics total scores revealed minimum correlations above .97. These intercorrelations indicate that any of these measures of school mean achievement would provide about the same results in our analysis. We have used the mean percentage of all reading and mathematic objectives mastered because it reflected achievement on the total range of objectives and all 245 questions on the objective referenced examination. As will be noted in Table 3, the mean of the school percentages of students who attained the 49 objectives in the statewide random sample of schools is 74.88. The percentages in the representative state sample range from 46 to 88. The mean of the augmented black sample is 56 percent and the 30 schools included in this sample range from 42 percent to 74 percent. The mean of the white schools is 77 percent, and they range from 62 percent to 88 percent. Although the standard deviations are reported in Table 3, it should be recognized that the distributions are not bell-shaped in any of the samples. The school mean achievement scores in the statewide representative sample of schools is heavily skewed to the higher end of the distribution. Since the State Assessment instruments are based upon the objective referenced principle, there is little basis for determining the degree to which the distribution of mean school achievement scores are typical. Throughout this research we are analyzing the between-school variance in achievement based upon the mean percentage of the 49 objectives that students in each particular school mastered. The variance within each of the sub-samples of schools which we have analyzed is somewhat less than in the statewide random sample, but the smallest standard deviation, in the high SES school sample, is over 5 percent.

TABLE 3

Unweighted Mean and Standard Deviations of Dependent Variables in Samples of Michigan Public Elementary Schools

| | State Representative Sample | | Majority White Schools | | | | | | Majority Black Schools | |
| | | | Total White | | High SES | | Low SES | | | |
	M	SD	M	SD	M	SD	M	SD	M	SD
Achievement	74.88	9.53	77.36	6.11	80.13	5.08	75.50	5.83	56.83	7.77
Self-Concept	28.77	1.08	28.51	.77	28.75	.39	28.27	.79	30.81	.84
Self-Reliance	17.08	.56	17.06	.57	17.24	.54	16.86	.54	16.99	.49

Self-Concept of Academic Ability

The self-concept of academic ability scale developed at Michigan State University has been widely used in research throughout the United States. The original version of this scale was developed for junior-high-school and high-school-age students (Brookover and others, 1962, 1965, and 1967). The latter reference provides validity and reliability data for that version. In the research on elementary schools a comparable instrument adapted slightly to a lower age/grade level of students has been used. This version was originally developed by Joiner (1966). This instrument has been used in various projects including the preliminary study of elementary schools in Michigan (Brookover, Gigliotti, Schneider, Henderson, 1973, and Brookover and Schneider, 1975) as well as in numerous other research projects.

It should be emphasized that the self-concept of academic ability focuses specifically on the student's perception of himself as a student. It makes no attempt to measure a wide range of self-concepts. As will be noted (see Appendix B), all items refer to the student's conception of himself as a student and in comparison with other classmates and students whom he knows. Extensive research has demonstrated that individual student scores on the self-concept of academic ability scale are significantly and highly correlated with individual school achievement. As will be noted subsequently, however, the school mean self-concept of ability scores are not consistently positively correlated with mean achievement scores. This will be discussed in a subsequent section.

Student Self-Reliance

The third dependent variable which we have examined in this research is a measure of students' self-reliance. This instrument is a modification of one developed at the Center for Study of School Organization at Johns Hopkins University (Epstein and McPartland, 1975). Examination of the items in this instrument (Appendix B) reveals that the scale is designed to determine the extent to which students are able to and desire to carry on activities by themselves and to solve problems on their own rather than have others assist them. Although such instruments have not been widely used as measures of the outcomes of education, many people have identified such behavior as a desirable outcome of school experience. This particular version of a self-reliance scale has not been previously used. Its validity is dependent on an analysis of the content of the items. It is used simply as an exploratory measure of school outcomes.

INTERRELATION OF VARIABLES

One of the complications of research on the functioning of educational systems is the interrelationship of many of the variables which may affect the outcomes. This research is no exception. With few exceptions, the independent and intervening variables which we have identified in three clusters, (1) inputs, (2) structure, and (3) climate, are significantly correlated with each other. These correlations are shown in Appendix C. Several observations about them are worthy of further examination here.

Input Variables

The two composition criteria which we have used, the mean socio-economic status of the student body and the percentage of whites in the student body, are sometimes examined separately and in other analyses combined in a standardized measure of social composition. As would be expected, these two measures of social composition are related to each other. In the representative state sample of 68 schools, the simple correlation between mean SES and the percentage of whites is .58. The percentage of non-white students is, of course, associated with the lower socio-economic status of the families of these students. This correlation is affected by the fact that the variance in the percentage of whites in the random sample is very great. Sixty percent of the schools have 96 percent or more white students while 7 percent of the schools have 3 percent or less white students. There are no schools with 3 percent to 33 percent white and only four schools with 33 to 67 percent white.

If 20 to 80 percent white is defined an an integrated school, only 7 of the 68 schools in this representative sample of Michigan public elementary schools are integrated. As indicated in the previous discussion of the samples, 7 of the 68 schools have more than 50 percent black students.

In the augmented black sample of 30 schools and the white sample composed of those schools with more than 50 percent white students the correlation between SES and the percentage of whites is greatly reduced. In the 30 majority black schools the percentage of whites and the mean SES are correlated at .29. The comparable correlation for the 61 white schools is .44. Contrary to popular assumption, the range of socio-economic status in the black sample is considerably greater than in the white sample. The standard deviation of the mean SES in the black sample is 1.29 compared to .93 in the white school sample. This is in part the result of the fact that one majority black school has a very high socio-economic status compared to other schools in the black sample. Since some variance in the percentage of whites remains in both the majority white and majority black samples, these two measures of composition, mean SES and percentage of whites, are combined in a standard social composition score for some analyses in all of the samples.

The index of other school personnel inputs including measures of school size, average daily attendance, professional personnel per thousand students, experience and education of teachers, and the mean teacher salary, is related to the combined index of social composition of the school at a significant level. The standardized score of other personnel inputs correlates with the standardized composition scores at .53 in the representative state sample. The correlation is lower when the variance in percentage of whites is controlled in the majority-white and augmented majority black school samples. In the majority white school the correlation between the standardized score of composition and other personnel inputs is .39; in the augmented majority black sample the comparable correlation is .40. These interrelated measures of student body social composition and other characteristics of the membership in the school social system are sometimes combined by standard scores into a single measure of inputs for the analysis of relationships between the three sets of school social system variables and school outcomes. The extent of the interrelation among the several input variables varies with the sample of schools. The intercorrelation in each instance is greater for the representative state sample than in either of the other samples.

The School Structure Variables

Four of the five variables that are used to identify various aspects of the school social structure are positively and significantly correlated with social composition and other input variables and are intercorrelated with each other. These four variables are the staffs' satisfaction with the social relationships within the school, the degree of parent involvement in the school social system, the estimated time devoted to instructional activities, and the degree of open versus closed classroom organization. The fifth measure of social structure we have identified as the degree of differentiation of programs for varying types of students. It is not highly correlated with either the input variables or the other structural variables. The correlation between the other four structural variables and the combined composition measure varied from .29 to .62 (see Appendix C). The lowest correlation, .29, is between composition and the measure of open-closed classroom organization; the other three structure variables correlate with composition at about .60. In contrast, the correlation between the degree of differentiation and the combined composition is .01. The correlation between the index of differentiated programs and other personnel inputs as well as correlations with the other measures of structure are all low negative or positive correlations. The four other structural variables—staff satisfaction with patterns of social relations, parents' involvement, time allocated to instruction, and open and closed organization—are all less highly correlated with other personnel inputs than they are with composition. In all instances, however, they are positive and significant correlations. The intercorrelations of these four variables are also all positive and range from about .20 to .60. Thus, although these variables are interrelated with each other and with composition measures, they are not entirely dependent on composition nor are they different measures of the same variable. The degree of differentiation of programs for different students is quite independent of both the input variables and the other structural variables.

Climate Variables

As will be noted in the correlation matrix, Appendix C, Table 1, the 14 climate variables are correlated with each other in varying degrees and with both the input and structural variables. We will not elaborate on all of the intercorrelations at this time, but it is important to recognize that some measures of school climate are highly correlated with the composition of the student body. A later section of this report is devoted to an analysis of the effects of climate on the variance in mean school achievement as compared to the effect of school composition specifically. This intercorrelation, of course, makes the separation of the effects particularly difficult. The most important of these intercorrelations is the relationship of the students' sense of academic futility with the composition of the school. This correlation is .87 when the combined student body composition index is related to the student sense of academic futility. This climate variable is also highly correlated with the separate measures of mean SES and percentage of whites, .79 and .76, respectively, in the representative state sample of schools.

The mean students' sense of futility is also significantly correlated with the other personnel input variables and three of the five structural variables. The latter are parents' involvement, estimated time allocated to instruction, and the staffs' satisfaction with their relationships with members of the organization. These range from .40 to .51 in the sample. The relationships between students' mean sense of academic futility and the degree of differentiation is an insignificant -.01 in that sample. The open-closed classroom organization variable also has a low association with futility, .20. In this case, the degree of openness is associated with a lower mean sense of student futility.

The other climate variables are associated with the composition, input and structural variables in widely varying degrees. Teachers' present evaluations and expectations of students are generally more highly correlated with student body composition, other personnel inputs, and organizational variables than are the other climate variables. In no case, however, is the emphasis upon differentiated programs for different students highly correlated with any of the climate variables.

In general, it is safe to say that except for the emphasis upon differentiated programs, all of the input, structure, and climate variables are interrelated to some degree. The burden of part of our analysis, therefore, will be to try to partition or examine the relative impact of the various independent variables on the variance in achievement and other outcomes.

The Interrelation of Dependent or Outcome Variables
The three dependent or outcome variables examined in this research, mean school achievement, mean student self-concept of academic ability, and mean student self-reliance, are variously interrelated in the representative state sample of schools and the sub-samples. The most important of the interrelationships of which the reader should be aware is that between

mean school achievement and mean self-concept of academic ability. In the representative state sample this relationship is negative and significantly high at -.549 (see Table 4 and Appendix C). This negative relationship exists between mean scores in spite of the fact that individual self-concept of academic ability is consistently correlated in a positive manner with individual achievement measures (Brookover, and others, 1962, 1965, 1967). This reversal of direction in correlation between the mean school scores and individual scores reflects the difference between the mean self-concept of academic ability of students in majority black schools and those in majority white schools. Students in majority black schools have significantly higher mean self-concepts of academic ability than students in white schools, even though their achievement is lower. In the majority black school sample of 30 schools, there is essentially no correlation between mean achievement and mean self-concept of academic ability, $r =$ .0038. In the majority white schools, the correlation is only a little higher than in the black school sample, .039. There is a negative relationship, $-.233$, among the lower socio-economic-status white schools. We do not have a firm explanation for the fact that students in majority white schools have lower self-concepts of academic ability than students in majority-black schools. We hypothesize, however, that the phenomenon is a function of the reference group to which the students compare themselves when assessing their own academic ability. (A further analysis of this phenomenon will be found in Passalacqua, 1979).

The relationship between mean school achievement and mean student self-reliance scores is low, but in a generally positive direction. In the representative state sample, the correlation is only .058. In the black and lower SES white schools, the correlation is .20. Self-reliance as measured by the scale used here is not highly related with achievement. We do not at the present time have data on the relationship between individual achievement and individual self-reliance scores.

The relationship between the two non-cognitive outcome measures, self-concept of academic ability and student self-reliance at the mean school level, is positive and significant. In the representative state sample, the correlation is .29. In the black sample, it is slightly higher, at .34. Most of the correlation between these two variables in majority white schools is accounted for by the correlation in the lower SES white schools, where it is .50. Although the mean school outcome variables are interrelated to some extent, it is quite clear that the achievement of high self-concept of academic ability or self-reliance is not an automatic indicator of high cognitive achievement among these elementary school students. Neither is high mean cognitive achievement a good indicator of high mean self-concept or high mean self-reliance. In fact, the indications are that high achievement outcomes on the average may be associated with lower aggregate self-concepts of ability. The relationship of each of these outcome variables and the various independent variables will be the subject of our analysis in the subsequent sections of this report.

TABLE 4

Correlation Between Dependent Variables
Mean Achievement, Mean Self-Concept, and Mean Self-Reliance
in Samples of Michigan Public Elementary Schools

	State Representative Sample		Total White		High SES		Low SES		Majority Black Schools	
	S-C	S-R	S-C	S-R	S-C	S-R	S-C	S-R	S-C	S-R
Self-Concept	1.00		1.00		1.00		1.00		1.00	
Self-Reliance	.291		.396		.080		.498		.340	
Achievement	−.549	.058	.039	.213	.012	−.067	−.233	.205	.004	.203

3

The School Social System
and School Achievement

This chapter of the report presents the findings concerning the contributions of various aspects of the school social system to an explanation of the between-school differences in reading and mathematics achievement. Although there is much variance in the individual achievement of children within the school, our focus is on the mean difference in mastery of minmum levels of arithmetic and reading skills during the first few years of elementary school. Since some have concluded that there is not a lot of difference in outcomes between schools and since we are measuring outcomes at the fourth grade level, at which time less difference may exist than later, we emphasize that there are major differences in achievement. As we noted earlier (see Table 3) the variance between schools in the mastery of arithmetic and reading objectives is extensive. Among the schools in our sample there is a difference of 46 percent between the school with the highest mean percentage and the school with the lowest mean percentage of objectives mastered. Although racial and socio-economic composition of the student bodies are related to these cognitive outcomes, we hypothesize that the patterns of interaction among members of the school social system contribute to the differences in outcomes as well as the composition. We, therefore, examine three clusters of variables—inputs, structure, and climate—to estimate their relative contribution to cognitive achievement in the school and to identify the contribution of various specific variables in the clusters.

We recognize that experimental or longitudinal data would provide more definitive answers to the questions we raise concerning the impact of the school social system on these cognitive outcomes of the system. We do not have such data, but we believe that a series of multiple regression analyses including a partitioning of the variance contributed to achievement by each of the three sets of variables will illuminate the questions which we raise.

Prior to the multiple regression analyses, we calculated the simple correlations between each of the independent variables and mean school achievement. These are shown in Appendix C. It will be noted that there is significant correlation between many of the variables and mean student achievement. The correlation matrices in Appendix C also reveal significant intercorrelation between some of the independent variables examined in this research. This is particularly true of some of the school climate variables and the socio-economic and racial composition of the student bodies. The Student Climate Variable 1, the Students' Sense of Academic Futility, which, incidentally, is the climate variable most highly correlated with mean school achievement, is also very highly correlated with the combined index of socio-economic and racial composition of the student body. In fact this correlation is so high in the representative state sample, .86, that one may question the attempt to explain achievement by the students' sense of futility when one knows the social composition of the student body. We hypothesize that, if it were possible to separate the contribution of composition and the contribution of sense of futility, the latter would be more directly relevant as an explanation of the differences in achievement. As we noted in our general model, Figure 1 (p. 7), we hypothesize that the norms, expectations, and feelings that characterize the school and which we identify as climate are in part a function of the composition of the student body, which represents their family backgrounds. The teachers, principals, and others interacting in the social systems of the school come to define the norms, expectations, and beliefs in a particular fashion partly as a result of their perceptions of the characteristics of the students' family backgrounds. If these norms and expectations could be isolated from the students' background, we would hypothesize that the nature of the school climate would explain more of the variance than the family background factors. In the absence of this isolation of these two sets of variables, we have examined the impact of both the composition variables and the climate variables before we introduce the other personnel inputs and the social structure variables into the multiple regression analyses.

REGRESSION ANALYSIS OF THE EFFECT
OF SCHOOL COMPOSITION AND SCHOOL
CLIMATE ON MEAN SCHOOL ACHIEVEMENT

Prior to performing multiple regression anaylses, we computed simple correlations between each of the 14 climate variables, and mean school achievement. These correlations for the state sample and the white and black school samples are shown in Table 5. These correlations indicate some variation between groups in the relationship of the several climate variables to achievement. In general, climate as measured by teacher and student variables seems to be slightly more highly correlated with mean achievement in the black school sample than in the white sample. These differences are not consistent, however. For example, both students' perception of future evaluations and expectations and the teachers' evaluations and expectations for college are more highly related to achievement in the majority black schools while the present evaluations and expectations as reported by both the students and teachers are more highly related to achievement in majority white schools. The teachers' reports of their own and the students' commitment to improve, the teachers' perception of the principal's expectations and the principal's evaluations and expectations are somewhat more related to achievement in the black school sample than in the white one. The only climate variable that consistently has a low correlation with mean school achievement is the teachers' feelings that there is little demand or chance for high achievement which we identified as Teacher Climate 5, Teacher Academic Futility. Some other climate variables have low correlations with achievement in some samples but are significantly correlated with mean achievement in other samples.

The rather high negative correlation between Student Climate 3, perceived present evaluations and expectations, calls for some explanation. Examination of the items that compose this variable reveals that the student is asked to compare him or herself to other students, e.g.: "Would your teacher say that you can do your school work better, the same or poorer than other people your age?" When the students respond to these questions they are generally referring or comparing themselves to their fellow students in their schools. The academic performance of the reference

TABLE 5

Simple Correlation Between the School Means*
of 14 Climate Variables and 1974 Mean School Achievement
in Three Random Samples of Michigan Elementary Schools

Climate Variables	State Sample (68)	Black Sample (30)	White Sample (61)
STUDENT			
1. Student Sense of Academic Futility	.769	.694	.514
2. Future Eval. and Expect.	.218	.397	.381
3. Perceived Present Eval. and Expectations	−.568	.022	−.174
4. Perception of Teacher Push and Norms	−.090	.203	.013
5. Student Academic Norms	−.080	.350	−.083
TEACHER			
1. Ability, Eval., Expect., & Qual. of Ed. for Coll.	.228	.521	.279
2. Present Eval. & Expect. for H.S. Completion	.664	.267	.419
3. Teacher-Students' Commit. to Improve	−.105	.392	.090
4. Perception of Prin. Expectations	.198	.547	.340
5. Teacher's Academic Futility	−.128	−.065	−089
PRINCIPAL			
1. Parent Concern & Expect. for Qual. Education	.320	.186	.315
2. Efforts to Improve	−.237	−.229	−.225
3. Evaluations of Present School Quality	.365	.248	.232
4. Present Eval. and Expec. of Students	.377	.407	.216

*Climate variables expressed by principals for each school were based on only one respondent in each school.

groups in high-achieving schools is somewhat higher than comparable reference groups in low-achieving schools. The respondents in the latter, therefore, may tend to rate themselves higher in comparison to their peers than respondents in high-achieving schools. The absence of this negative relation in the black school sample suggests that black students' perception of others' evaluation and expectation may develop differently than among students in white schools.

The other significant and consistent negative correlation is between mean achievement and Principal Climate 2, efforts to improve. Here it is apparent that principals in high-achieving schools are less likely and probably feel less need to try to improve their schools than principals in low-achieving schools.

Since our primary focus here is on the relative contribution of composition variables and climate variables to differences in mean school achievement, a series of multiple regression analyses was carried out on each sample of schools.

Since the composition and climate variables are intercorrelated, we carried out two multiple regression analyses on each sample to assess the *unique* contributions of both composition variables and climate variables to the prediction of school mean achievement. In the first regression analysis, we entered mean socio-economic composition and the percentage of whites in the school in that order prior to the 14 school climate variables.

TABLE 6

**Summary of Multiple Regression Analysis Showing Comparative
Contribution of Composition Variables, Mean Socio-Economic Status
and Percentage of Whites, and Mean School Climate Variables
to Variance in Mean School Achievement
in Samples of Michigan Elementary Schools**

Variance in Mean School Achievement Attributed to:	State Sample (68)		Black Sample (30)		White Sample (61)	
	R^2	R^2 add	R^2	R^2 add	R^2	R^2 add
SES entered first	.456		.361		.309	
Percentage of whites	.785	.329	.416	.056	.433	.124
Climate variables	.826**	.041	.778	.362	.553*	.120
Climate entered first	.725		.728		.445	
SES	.746	.021	.777	.049	.494	.049
Percentage of whites	.827	.081	.778	.001	.553	.059

*One climate variable, Teacher Climate 2, was omitted because the F-level was insufficient for computation.
**One climate variable, Principal Climate 1, was omitted because the F-level was insufficient for computation

In the second analysis, the climate variables were entered as a set into the multiple regression analysis followed by mean socio-economic composition and the percentage of whites. The results of these two sets of multiple regression analyses are shown in Table 6.

More than one-half of the variance in mean achievement between schools in each sample is explained by the combination of SES, racial composition, and the climate variables. About four-fifths of the variance in achievement between schools in the representative state sample and majority black schools is explained by this combination of variables. The composition variables account for more of the explained variance in achievement, when entered prior to the climate variables, in the state sample than in the black or white school samples. In both the latter samples the variance in the composition measures is less than in the state sample. When the percentage of whites is added as the second variable, it adds 33 percent to the explained variance in mean achievement in the state sample, but only 6 and 12 percent respectively in the black and white samples. Although a major portion of the variance in the percentage of whites is controlled in the latter two samples, some majority black schools have a minority proportion of white students and some majority white schools have a small proportion of black students.

Variance in Mean School Achievement
Explained by Climate After Composition

In each of the samples the addition of the climate variables to the multiple regression analysis following the inclusion of the two school composition variables yields a significant increase in the R^2. In the state sample the increase in the R^2 is only four percent, but climate variables add 36 percent in the black sample and 12 percent in the white sample. The climate variables, therefore, make some contribution toward the prediction of mean school achievement over and above that made by the two school composition variables. In the majority black school sample, the climate variables explain a much larger share of the variance in mean achievement over and above that explained by socio-economic and racial composition than in the white or state sample.

Variance Explained by Climate When
Entered Prior to Composition

The second portion of Table 6 presents the results of the multiple regression analysis when the 14 climate variables are entered prior to mean socio-economic status and the percentage of whites. In all samples, most of the explained variance in mean achievement between schools is attributable to the climate variables. Approximately 10 percent or less of the total variance in mean school achievement is explained by the composition variables, SES, and percentage of whites, after controlling for the climate variables. In the statewide random sample of 68 schools in which 82 percent of the variance in mean school achievement was explained, more than 72 percent is explained by the climate variables. Although there are some differences in the relative contribution of the composition variables in explaining variance in mean achievement over and above the contribution of the climate variables in the samples, the fact remains that 80 percent or more of the explained variance in mean achievement that may be attributed to composition variables may actually be the result of differences in climate associated with composition. The very high correlation between the percentage of whites and several of the climate variables indicated that climate in elementary schools is highly associated with the racial composition of the student body. When the climate variables were entered in the regression equation first, the inclusion of racial composition added little.

Analysis Using Mean SES as a Single Composition Variable

Since Coleman (1966) has indicated that socio-economic composition contributed more than racial composition, and racial composition was partially controlled in our majority white and majority black school samples, a similar multiple regression analysis was made with socio-economic status as a single measure of composition. The results of this analysis are shown in Table 7. The total variance in mean school achievement explained by the combination of SES and climate variables is slightly less than that explained with the percentage of whites included. The greatest difference is in the state sample of 68 schools where the climate variables had contributed only four percent to the explanation of the mean school achievement variance over and above both composition variables; they explained 29 percent over and above SES. The general pattern of results, however, is similar to those in the previous table. Climate variables explain a very significant additional amount of the variance after the effect of SES has been removed in each of the samples. Approximately one-fifth or more of the total variance is explained by mean climate variables.

When the reverse process is used in the multiple regression analysis, the mean SES composition adds little to the explained variance after the effect of climate variables has been controlled. In none of the samples does SES add more than 5 percent to the variance explained after the effect of climate variables is removed. This analysis reaffirms the previous analysis in that the school climate variables which we have identified explain a significant proportion of the difference in achievement between schools beyond that explained by socio-economic composition and that much of the variance explained by socio-economic composition is also explained by differences in climate variables. When entered in the regression first, the differences in school social climate explain more of the between school differences in achievement than mean socio-economic composition.

TABLE 7

Summary of Multiple Regression Analysis Comparing the Effect of Mean Socio-Economic Status and Climate Variables on Variance in Mean School Achievement in Random Samples of Michigan Elementary Schools.

Variance in Mean School Achievement Attributed to:	State Sample (68)		Black Sample (30)		White Sample (61)	
	R^2	R^2 add	R^2	R^2 add	R^2	R^2 add
SES	.456		.360		.309	
Climate Variables	.746*	.290	.777	.417	.496	.186
Climate Variables	.725		.728		.445	
SES	.746	.021	.777	.049	.494	.049

*One climate variable, Student Climate 4, was omitted because the F-level was insufficient for computation.

Relative Contribution of Several Climate Variables to Variance in Mean Achievement

Since it is clear that the combination of school climate variables identified in this study contribute significantly to the explanation of the variance in mean school achievement, we examined the individual contribution of each of several climate variables to mean achievement. The results of forward step-wise multiple regression analyses of mean school achievement on mean school climate variables in each of the three random samples are presented in the Appendix D. The variables are entered in the order of their partial correlation with mean achievement after partialling out previously entered variables. A summary of the variables contributing to the variance in achievement with significance less than .01 is in Table 8. In all three samples, the students' sense of academic futility clearly contributes more than any of the other climate variables. This variable is more important in the prediction of achievement in black schools than in majority white schools. Student and teacher variables concerned with the present evaluations and expectations which teachers hold for the students, and the students' perception of present evaluations also contribute

TABLE 8

**Multiple Regression of Mean School Climate Variables
That Contribute Significantly (P.<.01) to Variance in
Mean School Achievement in a Representative Random Sample
of 68 Michigan Elementary Schools, the 61 Majority
White Schools in that Sample and a Random Sample
of 30 Majority Black Schools**

Variable	Simple R	Multiple R	R^2	R^2 Change	Problty.
REPRESENTATIVE STATE SAMPLE					
Student Climate 1					
Student Sense of					
Academic Futility	.769	.769	.591		.000
Student Climate 2					
Perceived Present					
Evaluations and Expec.	.569	.801	.641	.050	.004
Teacher Climate 2					
Present Evaluations					
and Expec. for H.S.					
Completion	.664	.826	.682	.041	.006
MAJORITY BLACK SCHOOLS					
Student Climate 1					
Student Sense of					
Academic Futility	.694	.694	.481		.000
Teacher Climate 3					
Teacher-Student					
Commit. to Improve	.392	.779	.606	.125	.00
MAJORITY WHITE SCHOOLS					
Student Climate 1					
Student Sense of					
Academic Futility	.514	.514	.264		.000

significantly in the statewide sample. These three variables explain more
than 68 percent of the between-school variance in mean achievement. In
the majority black school sample two variables, student sense of futility
and teacher-student commitment to improve, explain 60 percent of the
total variance in mean school achievement between schools. In the

majority white school sample, student sense of futility explains 26 percent of the variance in achievement between schools. Although this is the only single contribution significant at the .01 level, other climate variables accounted for an additional 18 percent of the variance in mean achievement.

It will be noted that a somewhat different set of variables contributes more highly to mean school achievement in majority black schools as compared to majority white schools. In the black schools, the teachers' commitment to improve enters the regression analysis immediately following the students' sense of academic futility and contributes an additional 13 percent to the explained variance in mean achievement. The teachers' commitment to doing a good job and their perception of similar student commitment makes more difference in achievement in the majority black elementary schools than in the white ones. Four climate variables account for an additional 2 percent or more of the variance in mean school achievement in the majority white sample after that explained by student sense of academic futility. These are student academic norms, the teachers' present evaluations and expectations, principal's perception of parent concerns and expectations and the principal's efforts to improve. The 14 climate variables explain over 44 percent of the variance in mean school achievement in the white sample while they explain over 72 percent in both the state and black school samples. It appears, therefore, that other unidentified variables are contributing more to the variance in mean school achievement in representative white elementary schools than in the majority black ones.

Summary of Composition and Climate
Contribution to Variance in Achievement
The two student body composition variables, mean SES, and percentage of whites, and the 14 climate variables explain 83 percent of the between-school variance in achievement in the representative state sample of schools, 78 percent in the black sample and 55 percent in the white sample. The multicollinearity among the composition and climate variables makes it difficult to attribute specific amounts of the between-school variance in achievement to either set of single variables in the two sets. The above analysis demonstrates, however, that the racial and SES background of the students composing the school is not the only explanation of the achievement variance between schools. Clearly the school climate, as measured by our variables, explains almost as much between-school achievement difference in the state sample as the SES and racial composition. When racial composition is partially controlled in the black

school sample, the climate variables explain as much as SES after the effect of composition has been removed, and nearly all the explained variance when their effect is removed first. Although the contribution of climate variables to differences in achievement between white schools is not as dramatic as in the black sample, they explain slightly more of the variance in mean achievement than the composition variables when the effect of each is removed first.

Although we have not separated the effects of the two sets of variables, school social-psychological climate explains about as much of the between-school variance in elementary school achievement as mean SES and racial composition. Further, we believe that climate along with other school environment variables is more directly relevant to achievement. In the following section we examine the contribution of these two sets of variables in conjunction with other school characterisitics.

SCHOOL INPUTS, SOCIAL STRUCTURE, AND CLIMATE VARIABLES AS CONTRIBUTORS TO MEAN SCHOOL ACHIEVEMENT

In the previous section we have established that the school climate variables identified in this research offer a viable alternate explanation of the differences in achievement between Michigan elementary schools. Although climate varies substantially with the socio-economic and racial composition of the school student bodies and it is difficult to separate the effects of this from school climate, the latter explains the differences in achievement as well as the differences in composition do.

In this section we add additional variables to the package used to explain differences in mean school achievement. In addition to the two measures of student body composition, mean socio-economic status and percentage of whites and the school social climate, we examine here an additional set of personnel input variables and a set of school social structure variables. These other personnel input variables as described earlier include mean teacher salary, number of professional personnel per thousand students, size of the student body, average daily attendance in the school, mean years of teacher tenure in this school, and percentage of teachers with graduate degrees. The items in this set of variables are shown in Appendix B.

Also shown in Appendix B are the items in the set of variables identified as school social structure. This set is composed of five clusters of variables identified as (1) the staff satisfaction with the school social

TABLE 9

Test of Significance of the Difference
of Means of Several Independent Variables in Sub-Samples
of Michigan Elementary Schools

Variables	61 White & 30 Black Schools	31 High SES & 30 Low SES White Schools	30 Black & 30 Low SES White Schools
	Prob. Dir.*	Prob. Dir.*	Prob. Dir.*
INPUTS VARIABLES			
Combined Composition	.000 W	.000 H	.000 W
Other Personnel Inputs	.009 W	.005 H	.304 NS
SOCIAL STRUCTURE VARIABLES			
Personnel Satisfaction	.000 W	.610 NS	.000 W
Parent Involvement	.000 W	.000 H	.001 W
Grouping and Differentiation	.760 NS	.989 NS	.768 NS
Time Allocation	.000 W	.009 H	.048 W
Open-Closed Classrooms	.000 W	.435 NS	.002 W
CLIMATE VARIABLES			
Student Climate 1	.000 W	.000 H	.000 W
Student Climate 2	.981 NS	.000 H	.003 B
Student Climate 3	.000 B	.433 NS	.000 B
Student Climate 4	.320 NS	.081 NS	.800 NS
Student Climate 5	.585 NS	.370 NS	.454 NS
Teacher Climate 1	.410 NS	.000 H	.011 B
Teacher Climate 2	.000 W	.000 H	.002 W
Teacher Climate 3	.000 B	.962 NS	.005 B
Teacher Climate 4	.340 NS	.008 H	.039 B
Teacher Climate 5	.032 B	.822 NS	.035 B
Principal Climate 1	.127 NS	.023 H	.804 NS
Principal Climate 2	.006 B	.663 NS	.006 B
Principal Climate 3	.000 W	.025 H	.029 W
Principal Climate 4	.040 W	.001 H	.795 NS

*Sample with the higher value is identified by W—white, B—black, H—high SES, L—low SES, NS—not significant.

system, (2) parent involvement in the school social system, (3) grouping and differentiation of student programs, (4) staff time allocated to instruction and (5) open and closed characteristics of the classrooms. These five variables are examined separately and in combination as a single set of school social structure variables.

The third set of variables used in this analysis are the 14 climate variables which were examined in the previous section of this chapter.

In this analysis we have subdivided the white majority school sample into high and low SES sub-samples in order to compare the interrelationships in these two sub-samples and to compare the low SES white schools with black schools in the sample. As shown in Table 9, there are numerous significant differences in the various samples. For example, the combination of other personnel input variables is significantly different in the white and black school samples. The same is true of all the structural variables except the grouping and differentiating variable. There are significant differences between black and white samples on 8 of the 14 climate variables. Similarly, on 7 of the 14 climate variables, there are significant differences between high and low SES white schools. The other personnel inputs, the degree of parent involvement and time allocation to instruction are also significantly different between the high and low SES schools. The low SES white and the black schools are significantly different on several of the climate variables and three of the social structure variables: teacher satisfaction, parent involvement and open and closed classrooms.

The differences in the personnel inputs, social structure and climate of the black and white schools as well as the high and low SES majority white schools led us to analyze the sub-samples in order that we might better understand the way the three sets of social system variables affect the outcomes of the school.

In the process of identifying the variables that are included in the cluster of other personnel inputs, we calculated the simple correlation between each of several variables and mean school achievement. These correlations for the variables used are shown in Table 10 for each of several samples of schools. It will be noted that school size is negatively associated with mean school achievement in both the representative state sample and the majority black school sample. In the majority white school sample, however, size has a low positive correlation with mean school achievement. The fact that the black schools are nearly all in the larger cities and have sizable student bodies explains the negative correlation in the representative sample. It also indicates that those black schools with higher mean achievement tend to be somewhat smaller than the less effective black schools. Average daily attendance as reported by the principal is positively associated although not highly so in all samples except the higher SES white schools. In the latter, average daily attendance is slightly negatively associated with achievement.

TABLE 10

Simple Correlation of Input (Student Body Composition and Other Personnel Inputs) Variables with Mean School Achievement in Several Samples of Michigan Elementary Schools

| Input Variables | State Sample | Majority White Schools | | | Majority Black Schools |
		Total White	High SES	Low SES	
Mean Student SES	.675	.556	.396	.328	.600
Percent White	.868	.563	.274	.576	.398
Combined Student Body Composition	.863	.630	.433	.544	.646
School Size	−.425	.107	.188	.175	−.451
Average Daily Attendance	.391	.280	−.108	.323	.173
Professional Personnel per 1,000 Students	.091	.061	−.366	.284	.273
Mean Teacher Salary	.279	.142	−.047	.069	.507
Mean Years of Teaching Experience	.310	.201	.181	.061	.434
Mean Years Teacher in School	.289	.318	.426	.297	.173
Percent of Teachers Graduate Degree	.180	.385	.166	.364	.294
Combined Other Personnel Inputs	.532	.394	.132	.396	.673
Number of Schools in Sample	68	61	31	30	30

Interestingly enough, it is in the high SES white schools that the higher number of professional personnel per thousand students is also negatively associated at .366 with school mean achievement. In all the other samples there is a relatively low positive relationship between professional personnel per 1,000 students and mean achievement. In the lower SES and black school samples, the correlation is .28 and .27 respectively.

Similarly, mean teacher salary is positively correlated with mean school achievement in all of the samples except the high SES white school sample, where a very slight negative relationship is found. It should be noted that only in the black school sample is the relationship of mean salary with achievement high enough to justify any confidence. The .507 correlation suggests that majority black schools with higher paid teachers are more likely to be high achieving schools than those with lower salaries.

It will be noted that mean years of teaching experience shows a consistently low positive association with mean school achievement in all the samples, but is most highly associated with mean school achievement among black schools. The mean number of years in which the teacher has served in a particular school is also positively associated with mean school achievement with the higher association found in the white school samples.

Our data indicate that the proportion of teachers in the school system with advanced degrees is positively but not highly related to mean school achievement. This variable, of course, is associated with mean teacher salary.

The combination of these other personnel inputs in a combined standard score results in a clearly significant positive correlation—.532 in the representative state sample and .673 in the black school sample—with mean school achievement. The relationship of these personnel inputs to mean school achievement is somewhat lower in the majority white schools with the lowest correlation in the higher SES white schools.

It will be noted that the simple correlations of the combined student body composition, mean student SES and percentage of white students, with mean achievement are slightly different from the comparable correlation between either of the component measures and achievement in the various samples. In all cases the combined student body composition variable is highly correlated with mean school achievement. As the percentage of whites and the mean SES are controlled in the several sub-samples, the correlation is significantly lower than in the representative state sample, where it is .863.

In the development of the combined personnel inputs index for this analysis, several other variables were examined but not included. A couple of these are worthy of mention because of the widespread assumptions concerning their contribution to school achievement. Large public resources have been provided by both state and federal governments for the programs designed to improve the achievement particularly of minority and low SES white schools. One of the common programs intended to achieve greater learning in such schools has been the addition of teacher aides to the school personnel. We had two reports on the use of teacher aides, one by the fourth- and fifth-grade teachers and the other by the principal of the school. In the former, the teachers in these grades simply indicated whether or not they had a teacher aide. The presence of teacher aides in these classrooms is negatively associated with mean school achievement in all samples, except the higher SES white schools, where the correlation is a low positive one. A more representative measure of the impact of the presence of teacher aides in the schools is the principals' report of the percentage of teachers who had teacher aides in the school. These data indicate that there was essentially no relationship between the proportion of classrooms with teacher aides and mean school achievement. In the representative state sample the relationship is a low –.15, but in the various sub-samples this correlation was .05 or below. It does not, therefore, seem likely that the use of teacher aides is contributing very greatly to mean school achievement in Michigan elementary schools. Our decision not to include this in the cluster of personnel inputs was based upon the fact that it contributed little to the prediction of the achievement.

Another interesting characteristic of personnel inputs in schools which was not included in the combined input measure was the number of years teaching experience the principal had prior to becoming principal. Our data indicate that the longer the principal had taught in school the lower the mean school achievement of the students in his school. The correlation was –.22 in the statewide sample, and –.25 in the high SES white sample, but not significantly different from zero in the other sub-samples. The correlation, however, is consistently in the negative direction. This simply says that extensive experience as a classroom teacher does not produce principals who are associated with higher achieving schools.

School Structure Variables and Achievement
As indicated earlier, we have used five variables to measure various aspects of the school social structure. Although we think these are important characteristics of the school social system, they certainly do not exhaust the possible characteristics of school social structure. For example, we have no measures of the various types of relationships between members of the social system. The particular patterns of interaction between teachers and administrators, other teachers, parents and other personnel are not identified or measured in any way. As a proxy for such patterns of interaction, however, we have used the teachers' response to questions concerning their satisfaction with the school social system, particularly the degree of satisfaction in their relationships with the principal, parents, other teachers, and the students, as well as measures of their general satisfaction with the school.

We also did not measure the nature of parental interaction with the other members of the school social system. We do, however, have a measure of the extent of parent involvement as reported by the teachers and the principal.

The simple correlations between the five structural variables which we have used and mean school achievement are shown in Table 11. It will be noted that the degree of teacher satisfaction with school social structure is positively correlated with the mean school achievement in the representative state sample at .548. Since teacher satisfaction is quite highly related to combined student body composition, .62, the correlation between teacher satisfaction and mean school achievement is much lower in the sub-samples of white and black schools. In the high SES white schools there is actually a slightly negative, −.056, correlation between mean teacher satisfaction and achievement.

Parent involvement in the school social system correlates .447 with mean school achievement in the state sample. However, high parent involvement is associated with lower achievement in the high SES white schools. This suggests that parents of students in middle class white schools are not likely to be involved with the school unless the level of achievement is unsatisfactory. The positive relationship in the black schools suggests that black parents may have some impact on the way the school affects achievement.

The third variable designed to measure differences in the school social structure is one identifying the degree to which instructional programs are differentiated for various students. This involves homogeneous grouping, and other patterns of relationship designed to provide different instructional programs for students with presumably different needs. As we have noted earlier, this pattern of relationship among teachers and students is not highly correlated with other measures of the social structure or with student body composition. In other words, it cuts across the other measures to a considerable degree. The pattern of simple correlation between the degree of differentiation in student instructional programs and mean school achievement is quite different from the other measures of the social structure. In fact, except in the majority black school sample, the relationship between degree of differentiation and mean school achievement is negative. Correlations are not high in any instance, but in all of the majority white school samples and in the state sample the direction is negative. This indicates that the more differentiation, the lower the mean school achievement. In the majority black schools, the direction is reversed but it is a low .129. There is no evidence here that differentiated programs contribute greatly to the variance in mean school achievement but are more likely to be associated with lower mean achievement in the white schools than with higher achievement. The highest correlation is –.313 among the high SES white schools. These findings do not lend any support to the widely held assumption that highly differentiated or individualized instructional programs contribute significantly to improved school learning.

The fourth social structure variable is the principals' report of the amount of time teachers devote to activities of an instructional nature and of his time devoted to supervision and relationships with parents. In the representative state sample there is a significantly high positive correlation of .445 with mean school achievement. This reflects some correlation between the variables and socio-economic and racial composition. In all the sub-samples of white and black schools the correlation is decidedly lower. We should reiterate at this point that our examination of the teachers' report of time devoted to instruction has not been used because our observation of a small number of schools indicated that the teachers' reports were not valid. We do not know the extent to which the principal's report is a valid measure of the actual time devoted to instruction, but the significant sample correlation suggests that this may be a contributing factor in the explanation of the variance in school achievement.

The last of the structural variables is one designed to measure the degree of open or closed type of interaction in the classrooms. This reflects the teachers', students' and principal's perception of the degree to which students are able to move about on their own volition and sit in places which they choose. It also reflects the extent to which teachers are relating to the classroom group as a whole in contrast to specific individuals at a given time. In the representative state sample, the correlation between openness and mean school achievement is a low positive one, .156. Among the majority white schools, both the total sample and two sub-samples of high and low SES schools, the relationships between openness and mean school achievement are low negative ones. The pattern of relationship between openness and mean achievement is apparently different in the majority black schools, where there is significant positive correlation of .332. It should be recognized, however, that the extent of openness in the black schools is decidedly less than in some of the white schools. None of the majority black schools could be characterized as having a high degree of open classroom organization.*

When these five structural variables are combined by standard scores into a single variable reflecting these aspects of school social systems, the relationship with mean school achievement in the representative state

*A more definitive analysis of the relation of openness to several variables will be found in McGhan, 1977.

TABLE 11

**Simple Correlation of Five School Social Structure Variables
with Mean School Achievement in Several Samples
of Michigan Elementary Schools**

Structure Variables	State Sample	Majority White Schools			Majority Black Schools
		Total White	High SES	Low SES	
Teacher Satisfaction/School Social Structure	.548	.071	−.056	.136	.127
Parent Involvement in School Social System	.447	.208	−.280	.154	.587
Differentiation in Student Instructional Programs	−.138	−.169	−.313	−.061	.129
Principal's Report of % Time Devoted to Instruction and Parents	.445	.267	.184	.102	.163
Student and Staff Report of Open-Closed Classrooms	.156	−.134	−.197	−.215	.332
Combined Structure (Standard Score of Five Variables)	.477	.068	−.244	.037	.447
Number of Schools in Sample	68	61	31	30	30

sample is .477 and in the black school sample is .447. In the majority white schools, however, the relationship between the combined social structural variables and the mean school achievement is either very low positive or negative. The latter is found in the high SES white schools.

The observation of the pattern of simple correlations in Table 11 reveals an interesting contrast between the majority black schools and the majority white schools, particularly the higher SES white schools. All the social structure variables are positively associated with mean school achievement in the majority black schools. In the majority white schools the correlations are quite different, with the direction being reversed in two instances for the total white sample of 61 schools and in four out of five of the variables among the high SES white schools. The contrast is most notable in the measures of differentiated programs and open and closed schools. The correlations of these two measures with mean achievement are consistently negative with mean achievement in the white school sub-samples and positive in the black sample. One must, therefore, be very cautious in maintaining that differentiated or individualized programs of instruction or open classroom organization will contribute significantly to the improvement of school achievement. This caution is certainly most relevant to the white schools, where both are more highly practiced.

Climate Variables and Achievement

For convenience we have included simple correlations of the 14 climate variables and mean school achievement in the various school samples at this point as well as earlier. Table 12 showing these correlations includes data for the high and low SES white sub-samples in addition to the ones provided in the previous section. In addition to the comments on these relationships in the previous section, it should be noted that there are few differences in the correlations in high SES and low SES schools. There are, however, several significant differences between the correlations in black and low SES white samples. It will be noted again that the students' sense of academic futility, Student Climate 1, is more highly correlated with mean school achievement than any other climate variable in the representative state sample, the total white sample, and in the black school sample. When SES composition is further controlled in the high and low SES school sample, this correlation is reduced, reflecting the fact that students' sense of futility is correlated with socio-economic as well as racial composition. The correlations between composition variables and some climate variables explain other variations in the correlations between climate and achievement in the sub-samples. In the following analysis we have sought to determine how each of the three sets of variables—inputs, social structure, and social climate—contributes to differences in mean school achievement.

MULTIPLE REGRESSION ANAYLSIS OF MEAN SCHOOL ACHIEVEMENT ON THREE SETS OF SOCIAL SYSTEM VARIABLES

In this section we examine the contribution of three sets of social system variables, inputs, social structure, and school climate, to the explanation of variance in mean school achievement between schools in the various samples. The several variables included in each of the three sets have been described in earlier sections of this report. A comment, however, about the relative contribution of the two subsets of inputs is helpful at this time. As we have noted, the input set is made up of the two measures of student body composition, mean SES and percentage of whites, and several other personnel inputs including school size, average daily attendance, professional personnel per 1,000 students mean teacher experience, mean years of teacher tenure in the particular school, and the percentage of

TABLE 12*

**Simple Correlation Between Mean School Scores
on 14 School Climate Variables and Mean School Achievement
in Several Samples of Michigan Elementay Schools**

Climate Variables	State Sample	Majority White Schools			Majority Black Schools
		Total White	High SES	Low SES	
Student Climate					
1. Student Sense of Academic Futility	.769	.514	.300	.329	.694
2. Future Eval. & Expec.	.218	.381	.405	−.147	.397
3. Perceived Present Eval. & Expect.	−.568	−.174	−.140	−.337	.022
4. Percept. of Teach. Push & Norms	−.090	.013	−.120	−.095	.203
5. Student Academic Norms	−.080	−.083	.027	−.276	.350
Teacher Climate					
1. Ability, Eval., Expect. & Qual. of Ed. for Coll.	.228	.279	.157	.016	.521
2. Present Eval. & Expect. for H.S. Completion	.664	.419	.219	.225	.267
3. Teacher-Student Commit. to Improve	−.105	.090	−.076	.234	.392
4. Percept. of Prin. Expectations.	.198	.340	.137	.280	.547
5. Teacher's Academic Futility	−.128	.089	−.030	−.213	−.065

*Table 12 is continued on the next page.

TABLE 12 (continued)

Climate Variables	State Sample	Majority White Schools			Majority Black Schools
		Total White	High SES	Low SES	
Principal Climate					
1. Parent Concern & Expect. for Qual. Ed.	.320	.315	.153	.253	.186
2. Efforts to Improve	−.237	−.255	−.386	−.254	−.229
3. Eval. of Present School Quality	.365	.232	.189	.067	.248
4. Present Eval. & Expect. of Students	.377	.216	.067	.009	.407
Standard Score of all 14 Climate Variables	.292	.068	.103	.015	.538
Number of Schools in Sample	68	61	31	30	30

teachers with graduate degrees. It should be recognized that the latter set of personnel inputs contributes relatively little additional explanation of variance in mean school achievement after the combined composition of the student body effects have been removed. There is, however, a significant difference between the majority black schools and the other samples in this regard. As will be noted in Table 13, the other personnel inputs add only .007 to the R^2 in the state sample after the combined student body composition effects are removed. These combined personnel inputs also do not contribute much in the majority white schools, but they add 20 percent in the majority black schools. When other personnel input variables are entered into the multiple regression first, these combined personnel input variables explain 45 percent of the variance in mean school achievement in the predominantly black schools and less than 30 percent in all the other samples. The combined student body composition variable adds significantly to the explained variance in mean school achievement after the other personnel inputs are taken out in all the samples, but decidedly less in the majority white and majority black sub-samples than in the representative sample. The limited contributions of the other personnel variables to the effect of total input variables must be kept in mind as we examine the relationship of inputs, structure, and climate to mean school achievement.

Our primary concern at this point is to determine the extent to which the three sets of variables measuring various aspects of the school system

TABLE 13

**Contribution of Other Personnel Input and
Summary of Multiple Regression Analysis Showing the
Student Body Composition to Mean School Achievement
in Several Samples of Elementary Schools**

| | State Sample | | Majority White Schools | | | | | | Majority Black Schools | |
| | | | Total White | | High SES | | Low SES | | | |
	R^2	R^2 add	R^2	R^2 add	R^2	R^2 add	R^2	R^2 add	R^2	R^2 add
Combined Student Body Composition	.744		.397		.187		.296		.415	
Other Personnel Inputs	.752	.007	.424	.027	.191	.004	.376	.079	.620	.204
Other Personnel Inputs	.283		.155		.017		.157		.453	
Combined Student Body Composition	.752	.469	.424	.269	.191	.174	.376	.219	.620	.167

explain the difference in mean school achievement between elementary schools in Michigan and, in so far as possible, to examine the relative contribution of each of the sets to the explanation of differences between schools in mean school achievement. To examine the latter of the two questions we carried out two different analyses. First, we placed the three sets into multiple regression analysis in different sequences in order to determine the amount of variance in mean school achievement removed by each and the amount of additional variance explained by each of the sets in second and third positions. The results of the analysis are presented in Table 14. Second, we have partitioned the variance attributable to each of the three sets of variables and common to the combination of variables in each of the samples of elementary schools. These data are summarized in Table 15.

The total amount of the variance explained by the three sets of variables characterizing the school social system varies from one sample to another, but in all samples this amount is well above 60 percent of the total variance in achievement between schools. In the representative state sample, 85.8 percent of the total variance in achievement between schools is explained by the combination of inputs, social structure, and climate. The proportion of the variance in mean school achievement in the majority black schools explained by these three sets of variables is slightly higher, 89.5 percent. In the total white sample the three sets of variables explain 66.3 percent of the total variance in achievement between schools. When the white sample is divided into high SES and low SES schools, in which, of course, the variance in achievement is reduced, the three variables explain a somewhat larger proportion of the total variance in achievement between schools, 86.9 percent in the high SES white schools and 73.7 percent in the low SES schools. These data clearly indicate that a major portion of the variance in mean achievement between public elementary schools in Michigan can be explained by characteristics of the school social system identified by these three sets of variables.

As we noted in an earlier section, the inputs, particularly mean socioeconomic status and percentage of whites, are highly correlated with some of the climate variables. It is difficult to separate the effect of these two sets of variables on mean school achievement. Although it is clear the social structure set explains considerably less of the variance in mean school achievement than either of the other two sets of variables, it is correlated with them in such a way that removal of the effect of social structure first in the multiple regression analysis reduces the contribution of the other sets of variables to the variances in mean school achievement drastically.

In order to understand the relative contribution of the three sets of variables we have entered each into the multiple regression formula in all possible sequences. When entered into the multiple regression first, the combined input set explains about 75 percent of the variance in mean school achievement, the social structures set explains 41 percent and the climate variables explain 72 percent in the representative state sample. In this sample, the set of school social structure variables adds only about 5 percent or less to the explained variance in achievement between schools when added either second or third with climate or school input entered previously. Both climate and inputs add materially to the explained variance in the representative state sample, 36 and 38 percent after the effect of social structure has been removed. Thus, although the structural variables contribute significantly to the explained variance in school achievement, this set of variables does not add greatly to the total variance explained by inputs and school climate.

In the sample of majority black schools, the pattern of contributions to the variance between schools in achievement is somewhat different than in the representative sample. The set of input variables including SES and the remaining variance in percentage of whites contribute considerably

TABLE 14

**Summary of Multiple Regression Analysis Showing the Contribution
of Three Clusters of Independent Variables, Inputs,
Structure, and Climate* in Various Sequences to the Variance
in Mean School Achievement in a Statewide Sample
of Michigan Public Elementary Schools
and Four Sub-Samples of Such Schools**

Independent Variables in Order Entered In Regression	State Repres. Sample		Majority White Schools						Majority Black Schools	
			Total White		High SES		Low SES			
	R^2	R^2 add	R^2	R^2 add	R^2	R^2 add	R^2	R^2 add	R^2	R^2 add
Inputs	.752		.424		.191		.376		.620	
Structure	.795	.042	.504	.080	.547	.356	.466	.090	.647	.027
Climate	.858	.063	.663	.159	.869	.322	.737	.271	.895	.248
Inputs	.752		.424		.191		.376		.620	
Climate	.814	.062	.553	.129	.543**	.352	.670**	.294	.802	.182
Structure	.858	.044	.663	.110	.868	.325	.737	.067	.895	.093
Structure	.413		.172		.199		.113		.433	
Inputs	.795	.382	.504	.332	.547	.348	.466	.353	.647	.214
Climate	.858	.063	.663	.159	.869	.322	.737	.271	.895	.248
Structure	.413		.172		.199		.113		.433	
Climate	.776	.363	.562	.391	.662	.463	.662	.549	.860	.427
Inputs	.858	.082	.663	.101	.869	.202	.737	.075	.895	.035
Climate	.720		.447		.420		.464		.728	
Inputs	.814	.094	.553	.106	.543**	.123	.670(+)	.206	.802	.074
Structure	.858	.044	.663	.110	.868	.325	.737	.067	.895	.057
Climate	.720		.447		.420		.464		.728	
Structure	.776	.056	.562	.115	.662	.243	.662	.198	.860	.132
Inputs	.858	.082	.663	.101	.868	.206	.737	.075	.895	.053

*The variables included in each cluster are listed in Appendix B.
**The open-closed school variable was omitted because the F-level was insufficient to include in computation.
+The differential variable was omitted for the same reason.

less, 62 percent, than in the state sample. This, of course, is in part explained by the fact that the variance in the percentage of whites is greatly reduced in this sample of black schools. The range of variation in mean SES, however, is greater than in the representative sample. Although the contribution of the inputs to the variance in mean school achievement is less, the total variance explained by the three sets of variables is slightly greater in the majority black schools than in the representative state sample. Both climate and structure variables contribute more to the variance in achievement in the black sample than in the state sample.

It will be noted that the contribution of the input variables is less in the total white sample than in either the state sample or the majority black sample. This, of course, is partially explained by the smaller variance in percentage of whites, but the addition of the structure variables and the climate variables to the regression analysis in the white school sample does not make up for the reduced contribution of inputs. The total proportion of the variance in mean school achievement explained in the white sample is only 66 percent as compared to 85 percent and 89 percent in the representative state sample and the majority black sample. It appears, therefore, that the three sets of variables explain decidedly less of the total variance in achievement between schools in the white schools than in samples of majority black or the representative state sample, which includes some black schools. When the majority white school sample is divided between the high and low SES schools, thereby controlling for more of the variance in mean SES, the contribution of inputs, of course, is further reduced. In these two sub-samples, however, this reduction is more than made up by the greater contribution of the climate variables and some increase in the contribution of social structure. It will be noted that both input and climate contribute somewhat more to the explained variance after structure has been removed than they contribute when entered first into the regression formula in the high and low SES sub-samples of majority white schools. We have not analyzed the precise nature of the apparent moderating effects that explain this phenomenon.

Partitioning the Variance
In order to further delineate the contribution of three sets of variables, we have partitioned the variance using the Mood (1971) technique. The results of this analysis are shown in Table 15. It will be noted that in the representative state sample only a small percentage of the variance is uniquely attributable to each of the three sets of independent variables: 8 percent to input, 4 percent to structure, and 6 percent to climate. The largest portions of the variance in the mean school achievement are attributable to input and climate in common, 30 percent and to all three sets of variables in common, 36 percent. In the majority black school sample, somewhat less of the variance in mean school achievement is uniquely attributable to the input set of variables and slightly more to the

structure set and decidedly more, approximately 25 percent is uniquely attributable to climate. Another 18 percent is common to the input and climate variables, while 37 percent is common to all three sets of variables. Although somewhat more of the variance in mean achievement is uniquely attributable to climate variables in the black schools than in the state sample, or in the white schools, it is clear from this analysis that in the state sample most of the variance accounted for by these three sets of independent variables is variance common to input and climate and a combination of the three. In the total majority white schools, the proportion uniquely attributable to the three sets of variables is somewhat greater than in the random sample, 10 percent to input, 11 percent to structure, and 16 percent to climate. Thus more than half of the explained variance in mean school achievement in white schools is uniquely attributed to each of the three sets of variables. Another 23 percent is common to climate and input. This tendency to have the three sets of variables functioning independently in their contribution to the variance in mean school achievement is most evident in the high SES white schools. As will be noted, 21 percent is uniquely attributable to input, nearly 33 percent to structure, and 32 percent to climate. This leaves only a small proportion to be common to pairs or all of the variables. It is apparent from this that the moderating or suppressing effects of one set of variables on the other is reduced in the high SES white schools, where both the range of SES composition and percentage of whites are controlled.

In the low SES white schools and the majority black schools, the amount of variance in mean school achievement uniquely attributable to school climate is considerably greater than the amount uniquely attributed to either of the other variables. This suggests again that the school climate variables are somewhat more powerful explanations of the between-school variance in achievement in the less affluent white and minority group schools. Perhaps the family background effects involved in the composition variables are more likely to be modified by the school climate among children from lower SES and minority families.

It is important to recognize that except in the majority white, particularly the high SES white schools, less than half of the between-school variance in achievement is uniquely attributable to each of these sets of variables independently. In all of the sub-samples, as well as the representative state sample, two-thirds to nine-tenths of the total between-school variance in achievement is explained by this complex of social system variables. The way in which they interact in the explanation of this variance with as yet unidentified suppressant or moderating effects in some instances varies significantly from one sample to another, but the total

TABLE 15

**Percent of Variance in Mean School Achievement Removed
by Three Clusters of Variables and Combinations of
These Clusters, the Partitions of the Variance Uniquely
Attributable to Each and Common to Combinations
in Several Samples of Elementary Schools in Michigan**

Variance	State Random	White Schools	High SES White	Low SES White	Black
Removed by:					
Input	.752	.424	.191	.376	.620
Structure	.413	.172	.199	.113	.433
Climate	.720	.447	.420	.464	.728
Input & Structure	.795	.504	.547	.466	.647
Input & Climate	.814	.553	.543	.670	.802
Structure & Climate	.776	.562	.662	.662	.860
Input & Structure & Climate	.858	.663	.869	.737	.895
Partitioned Variance:					
Unique to Input	.082	.101	.207	.075	.035
Unique to Structure	.044	.110	.326	.067	.094
Unique to Climate	.063	.159	.322	.271	.248
Common to Input & Structure	.021	.003	−.083	.131	.039
Common to Input & Climate	.300	.231	.141	.278	.179
Common to Structure & Climate	−.001	−.031	.030	.023	−.066
Common to All Three	.358	.089	−.074	−.108	.366

picture is quite clear and the analyses clearly support the contention that a complex of characteristics of a school social system explain most of the variance in achievement between schools.

This analysis does not clearly indicate which variable or set of variables in the social system has the major impact in all school situations. It is clear from the earlier analysis that the students' sense of academic futility is a major contributor to the variance in achievement in all school sub-samples as well as the representative state sample. The interactions between this and other climate variables with the several social structure variables as well as the input ones moderate the effects in different school samples. The small proportion of the variance uniquely attributable to the set of input variables which is predominated by the student body composition does not give credence to the contention that only the family background of the student makes any difference in the achievement outcomes. Certainly that portion of the variance in achievement that occurs between schools is attributable, in part at least, to other characteristics of the school social system which we have here identified as social climate and social structure. The former apparently is a larger contributor to this between-school variance in achievement than the latter.

4

Students' Self-Concept of Academic Ability and Self-Reliance Within the School Social System

In the past score of years there has been an extensive amount of research dealing with self-concept and its relationship to the performance of students in schools (Brookover, et al., 1962, 1965, & 1967). This research has demonstrated that the individual student's self-evaluation of his academic ability is highly related to his perception of others' evaluation of him. The research has also demonstrated that the individual self-concept of academic ability is highly correlated with individual school achievement. There are, however, little data on the relationship of the school social system in which the acadamic self-concept is, at least in part, developed and the level of students' self-concept of academic ability. We have, therefore, investigated the relationship of the composition, other personnel inputs, school social structure variables, and school climate variables to mean self-concept of academic ability in the Michigan elementary schools.

We should emphasize again that the measure of self-concept used in this study is limited to the student role and specifically to the student's perception of his academic ability in comparison to others in the school social system. There is no effort to measure student's self-concept in other roles or a general self-concept that might characterize the student's perception of himself in a variety of social situations.

RELATIONSHIP OF SCHOOL SOCIAL SYSTEMS
TO MEAN STUDENT SELF-CONCEPT

We also reiterate that we are examining the relationship of school social characteristics to mean self-concept of academic ability of the fourth and fifth graders within the school. We have not and cannot in this study relate individual self-concept of academic ability to individual levels of achievement because we do not have individual student achievement data for the same population of students of which we have self-concept of academic ability data. Several versions of the self-concept of academic ability scale used in this research have been extensively used in a wide range of studies of individual self-concept of academic ability. This body of research has demonstrated that individual self-concept of academic ability is highly correlated, generally in the range of .50 to .70, with individual measures of academic achievement. This high positive correlation between individual self-concept of academic ability and individual achievement is not, however, reflected in the relationship between the mean self-concept and mean achievement of the school. As already noted in Table 4, there is a rather high negative relationship in the state representative sample of schools, -.549. This negative relationship between the means is not, however, reflected in the sub-samples. In the separate samples of white and black schools, there is essentially no relationship between mean self-concept of academic ability and mean school achievement. The specific figures are .039 for the 61 white schools and .004 for the 30 black schools. This fact complicates the meaning of self-concept when comparisons are made across reference groups and across, in this instance, school social systems.

Student Body Composition in
Relation to Self-Concept
Contrary to much popular assumption, the academic self-concepts of black students are not lower than those of white students. As noted in Table 16, the mean of the school mean self-concepts in the 30 black schools is significantly higher than the mean of the school means in the white schools. This finding supports that of other recent research which indicates that black students generally have higher self-concepts of academic ability than white students (Hara, 1969; Henderson, 1974). This probably results from the fact that black students of this age group in majority black schools do

TABLE 16*

Mean and Standard Deviations of Dependent Variables
in Samples of Michigan Public Elementary Schools
(Means of Schools Means Unweighted)

| | State Representative Sample | | Majority White Schools | | | | | | Majority Black Schools | |
| | | | Total White | | High SES | | Low SES | | | |
	M	SD	M	SD	M	SD	M	SD	M	SD
Achievement	74.88	9.53	77.36	6.11	80.13	5.08	75.50	5.83	56.83	7.77
Self-Concept	28.77	1.08	28.51	.77	28.75	.39	28.27	.79	30.81	.84
Self-Reliance	17.08	.56	17.06	.57	17.24	.54	16.86	.54	16.99	.49

*This duplicate of Table 3 is shown here for convenience of the reader.

not evaluate their own ability on the same basis as middle-class white educators evaluate their ability, but rather base their conceptions of their own ability on their perception of the evaluations made by family members, fellow students, and others in the school and neighborhood social systems who are predominantly black. The difference in mean self-concept between students in predominantly black schools and those in predominantly white schools is, of course, reflected in the negative correlation between mean self-concept and the percentage of white students in the student body. This figure is shown in Table 17.

The pattern of relationship between racial composition and self-concept does not hold in the case of the socio-economic status composition of the schools. The higher SES schools have a slightly higher mean school self-concept than do the lower SES schools, and as noted in Table 17, mean self-concept has a low positive association with mean socio-economic status in each of the white and black school samples. The predominantly lower SES of the black schools, however, produces a negative correlation between mean self-concept and mean socio-economic status in the representative state sample. In view of the higher self-concepts of students in majority black schools, one might anticipate that students in the lower SES white schools would have similarly higher self-concepts of ability than students in high SES white schools, but this is not the case. We are continuing our study of the differences in mean student self-concept to further explain them.*

Other Personnel Inputs and Mean Self-Concept
The higher mean self-concept in black schools is reflected in a low positive
*See Passalacqua, 1979.

TABLE 17

**Simple Correlation of Mean School Input
Variables with Mean Self-Concept of
Academic Ability in Several Samples of
Michigan Public Elementary Schools**

| Input Variable | State Sample | Majority White Schools | | | Majority Black Schools |
		Total White	High SES	Low SES	
Mean Student SES	−.177	.273	.013	.105	.336
Percent White Students	−.697	−.080	.136	−.381	−.246
Combined Student Comp.	−.491	.203	.043	−.181	.201
School Size	.442	.118	.104	.189	.061
Average Daily Attend.	.149	−.112	−.252	.068	-.256
Professional Personnel/1,000 Students	−.033	.004	.078	−.102	.089
Mean Teacher Salary	−.073	.185	−.123	.343	−.096
Mean Teacher Exper.	−.065	.186	−.252	.480	−.091
Mean Years Tenure	−.149	−.068	−.310	.145	−.342
Percent Teachers w/Grad. Degrees	−.130	−.089	.098	−.048	−.060
Combined Other Personnel Inputs	−.211	.134	−.173	.191	−.044
Number Schools in Sample	68	61	31	30	30

association between school size and mean self-concept of academic ability. The black schools in the state representative sample are on the average somewhat larger than the white schools. Size is also significantly related to mean self-concept in both the white and black schools, but not at a high level. The other personnel inputs which we have identified in these discussions involving staff-pupil ratio, teacher salary, teacher experience, teacher tenure, and teacher advanced degrees generally have low correlations with mean self-concept. The correlations are more often negative than positive, but only one or two are significant.

In general, neither the composition or other personnel input variables are highly correlated with mean student self-concept of academic ability except the higher level of self-concept in the majority black schools as compared to the white schools.

Social Structure Variables and Mean
Self-Concept of Academic Ability

Two of the variables which we have identified as social structure measures are significantly negatively related to mean self-concept of academic ability in the representative state sample of schools (see Table 18). The level of teacher satisfaction with the social relations in the school and degree of parent involvement are both significantly related to student mean self-concept of academic ability, with higher satisfaction and higher parent involvement associated with lower self-concept of academic ability. The degree of openness in the classrooms is only slightly related in a negative direction in the representative state sample

TABLE 18

**Simple Correlation of Five School Social Structure
Variables with Mean Student Self-Concept
in Several Samples of Michigan Public Elementary Schools**

Structure Variable	State Sample	Majority White Schools			Majority Black Schools
		Total White	High SES	Low SES	
Teacher Satisfaction with Social Structure	−.396	.105	.273	−.073	−.100
Parent Involvement in School Social System	−.253	.055	−.134	−.083	.124
Differentiation in Student Programs	.033	.047	.087	.006	.118
Principal's Report of % Time Devoted to Instruction & Parents	−.160	.272	.264	.139	−.119
Student & Staff Report of Open-Closed Classroom	−.172	.077	.091	.007	.071
Combined Structure (Standard Score of Five Variables)	−.310	.191	.181	.006	−.004
Number of Schools in Sample	68	61	31	30	30

The relationship between the amount of time devoted to instruction and parent concerns varies with the sample. The relationship is negative in the statewide sample, positive in the white sample, but negative among the black schools. None of these relationships are high and, as we will note, when entered into the multiple regression analysis, they do not contribute significantly to the explanation of the differences in mean self-concept of academic ability.

The extent of differentiated programs for different groups of children, which we have noted is significantly related to mean achievement, is not correlated significantly with mean self-concept of ability.

Relation of Climate Variables to Mean
Self-Concept of Academic Ability
The simple correlations between the 14 climate variables and mean self-concept of academic ability, as shown in Table 19, reveal several significant findings. First of all, the relationship between mean student sense of academic futility and mean self-concept of academic ability is worthy of some examination.

Some have assumed that sense of control, which, as we have noted previously, is a portion of the sense of futility variable, is similar to the student self-concept. Examination of the simple correlation between mean sense of futility and mean self-concept causes one to question this asumption.* The correlation between the mean sense of futility variable, coded so that high futility is a low score, and mean self-concept indicates that state sample schools with high mean student self-concepts tend to have a high mean student sense of futility. This may be due in part to the fact that students in majority black schools tend to have a high sense of futility (or low sense of control of the school social system) while they have high self-concepts of academic ability. The correlation indicates that students in predominantly black schools believe that they have high ability to achieve in school, but the school system functions in such a way that they cannot succeed there. Students in higher SES white schools, particularly, have lower feelings of futility, which indicates that they feel they can master the school social system, but evaluate their own abilities somewhat lower than students in black schools. There is essentially no correlation between the means of these variables among the high SES white schools. The students in low SES white schools reflect a relationship in which high mean self-concept is associated with a high sense of futility. The relationship is reversed in the sample of black schools. Here mean self-concept of academic ability is positively related to feelings of control or mastery of the

---

*Grace Henderson (1974) found a negative relation between individual sense of control and self-concept among similar students.

school social system. These feelings of mastery or control are, of course, not as high as they are in higher SES white schools.

TABLE 19

Simple Correlation Between Mean School Scores on 14 School Climate Variables and Mean Student Self-Concept of Ability in Several Samples of Michigan Public Elementary Schools

Climate Variables	State Sample	Majority White Schools			Majority Black Schools
		Total White	High SES	Low SES	
STUDENT CLIMATE					
1. Sense of Academic Futility	−.430	.104	.008	−.285	.280
2. Future Eval. & Expec.	.376	.531	.375	.536	.696
3. Percv'd. Pres. Eval. & Expectations	.879	.794	.834	.784	.861
4. Percep. of Teacher Push and Norms	.353	.365	.396	.252	.242
5. Academic Norms	.280	.329	.371	.273	.343
TEACHER CLIMATE					
1. Ability, Eval., Expec. & Qual. of Ed. for Coll.	.211	.388	.320	.263	.222
2. Pres. Eval. & Expec. for H.S. Completion	−.252	.288	.314	.048	.370
3. Teacher-Stud. Commit. to Improve	.335	.257	.234	.301	−.061
4. Percep. of Prin. Expec.	.083	.132	.156	−.060	.035
5. Academic Futility	.246	.210	.072	.370	.240
PRINCIPAL CLIMATE					
1. Parent Concern & Expec. for Qual. Education	−.100	.074	−.194	.095	−.010
2. Efforts to Improve	.197	.188	.030	.346	−.181
3. Eval. of Pres. School Quality	−.135	.118	.110	−.021	.125
4. Pres. Eval. & Expec. of Students	−.111	.161	.163	−.047	.190
Standard Score of All 14 Climate Variables	.275	.545	.532	.432	.422
Number of Schools in Sample	68	61	31	30	30

Student Climate 3, the perceived evaluations and expectations which others hold for the students, and Student Climate 2, their perception of the future evaluations and expectations held for them, explain most of the variance in mean self-concept of academic ability. The present evaluation and expectation variable is correlated at about .8 in the various samples with mean self-concept of academic ability. The climate variables based upon teacher and principal data are generally less highly correlated with mean student self-concept of academic ability than are the student variables, but Teacher Climate 3, the teachers' commitment and their perception of student commitment, is significantly correlated at .33 in the representative state sample.

Combined Input, Social Structure and Climate
Contribution to Mean Self-Concept of Ability
As will be noted in Table 20, when the three sets of variables identified as Inputs, School Social Structure and School Social Climate are used as independent variables in the multiple regression analysis, they explain about 90 percent of the variance in school mean self-concept of academic ability. The set of 14 climate variables when entered into the multiple regression analysis first explains 86 percent of the variance and when these 14 variables are placed in the regression analysis after the other two sets, input and structure, the climate variables add from 57 percent to 84 percent to the explanation of the variance in mean self-concept of academic ability.

When each of the 14 climate variables, combined composition, other personnel inputs, and five social structure variables are entered into multiple regression analysis in a step-wise fashion, letting each enter the regression on the basis of the partial correlation after the most highly correlated variable enters first, the mean school score on the students' perceived present evaluations and expectations, Student Climate 3, contributes most to the variance in mean self-concept in the statewide sample and in all of the sub-samples. This one climate variable accounts for 63 percent of the variance in mean self-concept of academic ability in the representative state sample of schools and 70 percent more in both the majority black and majority white schools. The mean students' perception of future evaluations and expectations, Student Climate 2, contributes the next highest amount to the variance in mean self-concept in the representative state sample and in all the sub-samples. The amount of variance added by Student Climate 2 ranges from 4 percent to 13 percent. None of the other climate variables, social structure variables, personnel input, or student body composition contribute significantly after the effects of the two student climate variables reflecting their perceptions of others evaluations and expectations have been removed. The combined social class and racial composition of the student body does not contribute significantly to mean self-concept in any of the samples after these two climate variables. When entered into regression analysis first, the combined composition variable explains 24 percent of the variance in mean

TABLE 20

Summary of Multiple Regression Analysis Showing the Contribution of Three Clusters of Independent Variables, Input, Structure and Climate, in Various Sequences to the Variance in Mean Student Self-Concept of Ability in a Statewide Sample of Michigan Public Elementary Schools and Four Sub-Samples of Such Schools

Independent Variables in Order Entered in Regression	State Represen. Sample		Majority White Schools						Majority Black Schools	
			Total White		High SES		Low SES			
	R^2	R^2 add	R^2	R^2 add	R^2	R^2 add	R^2	R^2 add	R^2	R^2 add
Inputs	.244		.045		.035		.089		.059	
Structure	.302	.058	.102	.057	.231	.196	.173	.084	.096	.037
Climate	.888	.576	.814	.712	.913	.682	.854	.681	.938	.842
Inputs	.244		.045		.035		.089		.059	
Climate	.864	.620	.791	.746	.871	.836	.786	.697	.865	.807
Structure	.888	.024	.814	.023	.913	.042	.854*	.068	.938	.073
Structure	.160		.082		.229		.028		.055	
Inputs	.302	.142	.102	.020	.231	.002	.173	.145	.096	.041
Climate	.888	.576	.814	.712	.913	.682	.854	.681	.938**	.842
Structure	.160		.082		.229		.028		.055	
Climate	.887	.727	.803	.712	.899	.670	.850	.822	.933	.878
Inputs	.888	.001	.814	.011	.913	.014	.854	.004	.938	.005
Climate	.860		.769		.864		.779		.861	
Inputs	.864	.004	.791	.022	.871	.007	.786	.007	.865	.004
Structure	.888	.024	.814	.023	.913	.042	.854*	.068	.938	.073
Climate	.860		.769		.864		.779		.861	
Structure	.886	.026	.803	.034	.898	.034	.850	.071	.933	.072
Inputs	.888	.002	.814	.011	.913	.015	.854	.004	.938	.005

*Parent involvement not included.
**Principal Climate 1 not included.

self-concept in the representative state sample, but only a very small amount in the sub-samples where part of the variance in composition is controlled. The combined personnel inputs other than school student body composition contribute very little to the variance in mean self-concept of academic ability even when placed in the regression analysis first.

The five social structure variables explain about 16 percent of the variance in mean school achievement in the representative state sample when placed in the multiple regression analysis first, but very little after the effects of school climate variables have been removed. The total inputs, student body composition, and other personnel inputs, contribute even less after climate has been removed. The partitioning of the variance in mean self-concept attributable to the three sets of variables shown in Table 21 confirms that most of the explained variance in mean self-concept between schools is uniquely attributable to the school climate variables. This ranges from 59 percent in the state sample to 84 percent in the black school sample. Very little variance is uniquely explained by either of the other sets, inputs or social structure.

Summary of School System Relationship to Student Mean Self-Concept

Perhaps the most significant finding of the examination of students' self-concept of academic ability is the confirmation of previous findings that the mean self-concepts of students in predominantly black schools are significantly higher than the mean of students in white schools (Henderson, 1974, and Hara, 1969). It is also important to recognize that the differences in mean self-concept between schools can be largely explained by differences in the social climate of the school, primarily by the students' perceptions of others' expectations and evaluations of them. There is, of course, much variance in individual self-concept of academic ability within each school. The variance in individual self-concepts within a school has been shown to be positively related to individual student's achievement within a school. The examination of school mean self-concept as a school outcome may, therefore, help to understand achievement as well.

The recent emphasis upon importance of producing favorable self-concepts in a school suggests the desirability of understanding how the social system functions in relation to differences in mean self-concept between schools. The foregoing analysis of data from the sample of Michigan public elementary schools casts some doubt on popularly held notions concerning self-concept and throws some light on other aspects of relationship of the school social environment to self-concepts of academic ability. Certainly the evaluations and expectations held for students as

TABLE 21

**Percent of Variance in Mean Student Self-Concept
Removed by Three Clusters of Variables and Combinations
of These Clusters, the Partition of the Variance
Uniquely Attributable to Each and Common to Combinations of Clusters
in Several Samples of Elementary Schools in Michigan**

Removed by	State Sample	White Schools	High SES White	Low SES White	Black Schools
Input	.244	.045	.035	.089	.059
Structure	.160	.082	.229	.028	.055
Climate	.860	.769	.864	.779	.861
Input & Structure	.302	.102	.231	.173	.096
Input & Climate	.864	.791	.871	.786	.865
Structure & Climate	.887	.803	.899	.850	.933
Input & Structure & Climate	.888	.814	.913	.854	.938
Partitioned by					
Unique to Input	.001	.011	.014	.004	.005
Unique to Structure	.024	.023	.042	.068	.073
Unique to Climate	.586	.712	.682	.681	.842
Common to Input & Structure	−.003	−.011	−.007	.003	−.001
Common to Input & Climate	.141	−.009	−.012	.141	.036
Common to Structure & Climate	.034	.034	.154	.016	−.036
Common to All Three	.105	.014	.040	−.059	.019

perceived by them are major contributors to the differences in self-concepts between schools. High mean self-concepts in a school may not, however, be associated with high mean achievement. The racial characteristics of the student body may affect the general level of self-concept which exists in the school.

RELATION OF SCHOOL SOCIAL SYSTEMS
TO MEAN STUDENT SELF-RELIANCE

Following the lead of scholars at the Johns Hopkins Center for Social

Organization of Schools, we identified student self-reliance as a possible outcome of schools (Joyce L. Epstein and James M. McPartland, 1975). Although many have been concerned about noncognitive outcomes of schooling, there has been little effort to validate measures of such outcomes. It must be recognized that the measure of student self-reliance which we have used here may not measure what others consider an important outcome. We therefore present the findings of this research as tentative suggestions concerning the impact of school social systems on student self-reliance. The five items in the student questionnaire used to measure self-reliance are shown in Appendix B. Three of the five items are definitely oriented toward the school social situation in an attempt to determine the extent to which students prefer to work alone and figure out the assignments on their own or prefer to have significant help from teachers or friends. The other two items are less directly oriented to the school situation, but focus on the students' desire to solve problems and make decisions by themselves as compared to asking for help from other people in solving their problems.

Input Variables and Self-Reliance
As was noted in Table 4, the mean self-reliance scores in the state representative sample as well as in the sub-samples, are positively correlated with mean self-concept of ability but the correlation is not high, .291 in the representative sample. The highest correlation (.498) is found in the 30 low SES white schools and lowest in the high SES white school, where it is .080.

The correlation between mean self-reliance and mean achievement is quite low and in the sub-samples in which SES is controlled, the direction varies. As noted earlier in Table 4, the correlation between mean achievement and mean self-reliance in the representative state sample is .058, the correlation in the white sample is .213, and in the black sample, .203. In the high SES white schools the correlation becomes an insignificant -.067. The mean self-reliance scores for the various sub-samples are not greatly different (see Table 16). In contrast with the other dependent variables, achievement and self-concept, there is not a major difference in mean self-reliance between the majority black schools and the majority white schools. The white school mean self-reliance is slightly higher than in the black schools, but not sufficient to make any conclusions concerning the differences. The high SES white schools have slightly higher mean self-reliance than the low SES white schools, but not of sufficient magnitude to indicate a significant difference.

There is a low positive correlation between mean socio-economic status and mean student self-reliance, .329 in the representative state sample, .449 in the white sample, and .131 in the majority black schools (see Table 22). The correlations between the percentage of whites and mean self-reliance is lower and inconsistent, -.012 in the representative sample, .224 in the white schools, and .334 in the majority black schools. When the combined student composition variable is correlated with mean self-reliance, there are low but significantly positive relationships between composition and mean self-reliance.

In contrast with cognitive achievement outcomes, these data suggest that we should have little confidence in the conclusion that students in

TABLE 22

Simple Correlation of Inputs
(Student Body Composition and Other Personnel Inputs)
with Mean Student Self-Reliance
in Samples of Michigan Public Elementary Schools

| Input Variables | State Sample | Majority White Schools | | | Majority Black Schools |
		Total White	High SES	Low SES	
Mean SES	.329	.449	.377	.300	.131
Percent White Students	−.012	.224	.069	.146	.334
Combined Student Composition	.180	.440	.369	.258	.225
School Size	−.051	−.222	−.340	−.137	−.063
Average Daily Attendance	.134	.210	.283	.078	.147
Professional Personnel/ 1,000 Students	.120	.061	−.032	.082	.145
Mean Teacher Salary	.136	.183	.001	.215	−.047
Mean Teacher Experience	.149	.166	.073	.141	.099
Mean Years Teacher in School	−.009	.007	.074	−.064	−.145
Percent Teachers/ Graduate Degrees	.042	.083	−.055	−.007	−.145
Combined Other Personnel Inputs	.143	.256	.152	.168	.045
Number of Schools in Sample	68	61	31	30	30

higher SES white schools have higher self-reliance scores. It seems likely, however, that mean SES has a positive correlation with mean self-reliance.

Further observation of the data in Table 22 indicates that none of the other personnel input variables is highly correlated with the mean self-reliance of the students. There is a small positive correlation between the combined standard score of other personnel inputs and mean self-reliance in each of the sub-samples as well as the representative state sample, but all correlations are lower than that required for confidence at the 2 percent level.

Social Structure and Self-Reliance

Examination of the simple correlations between the five school social structure variables and mean student self-reliance indicates that there is little significant relationship in any of the samples (Table 23). The degree of parent involvement in the school social system has a low positive relationship with mean self-reliance that approaches significance in the

TABLE 23

**Simple Correlation of Five School Social Structure Variables
with Mean Student Self-Reliance in Sample of
Michigan Public Elementary Schools**

Social Structure	State Sample	Majority White Schools			Majority Black Schools
		Total White	High SES	Low SES	
Teacher Satisfaction with School Social Structure	−.065	.123	−.045	.263	−.142
Parent Involvement in School Social Sys.	.221	.328	.202	.233	.066
Differentiation in Student Programs	.073	.050	.059	.044	.106
Prin. Report of % Time Devoted to Instruction	.017	.057	−.120	−.066	−.099
Student and Staff Report of Open-Closed Classrooms	−.134	−.142	−.335	.023	.296
Combined Structure (Standard Score on Five Variables)	.037	.137	−.100	.195	.007
Number of Schools	68	61	31	30	30

representative state sample and the white school sample, but is very low in the black schools. The extent to which student programs are differentiated for different types of students is not significantly correlated in any of the sub-samples or the representative state sample. Neither is the reported percentage of time devoted to instructional activities. The only other simple correlations that approach significance are between the index of open classrooms and mean student self-reliance in the high SES white schools and the black schools. It will be noted that the relationship, -.335, is negative in the high SES white schools and positive .296 in the majority black schools. Elsewhere we have noted that the majority black schools have significantly lower degrees of openness than the white schools. The range of openness and the extent of openness in the black schools is therefore very low, and the low positive correlation between openness and mean self-reliance is probably not indicative of any significant relationship. The greater variance in openness of white schools and the negative correlation causes one to question the commonly assumed positive relationship between openness and self-reliance and the Epstein and McPartland finding (1975). None of the negative correlations in the representative sample or the white samples are significant at the one percent probability level, but the -.335 correlation in the high SES white schools suggests the need for further examination of the relationship between classroom openness and student self-reliance.

School Climate and Self-Reliance
Although the combination of school climate variables contributes more to the explanation of variance in mean school self-reliance than either the input variables or social structure variables, there is no one or combination of two or three variables within the set of climate variables that is consistently correlated with mean self-reliance. It will be noted from Table 24 that students' perceived future evaluations and expectations, Student Climate 2, is consistently positively associated with mean student self-reliance and that the correlations, .343, in the representative state sample and .410 in the majority white schools are high enough to have some confidence in the relationship. Similarly, the Teacher Climate 1 variable, which reflects the teacher's evaluations and expectations of the student for later education, is correlated with self-reliance in the state sample and majority white schools samples. Principal Climate 4, the principal's present evaluations and expectations of students, is similarly related to mean school student self-reliance. The pattern of relationship between these climate variables and mean self-reliance is not clear in the majority black schools. Student Climate 4 and 5, the student's perception of teacher push

and teacher norms, and the student academic norms, are the only variables in which the simple correlation between climate variables and mean self-reliance approaches significance in the majority black sample. In general, these findings suggest that climate variables concerned with evaluations and expectations of students as perceived by the students and expressed by the teachers and the principal are more likely to be positively associated with mean self-reliance in the white schools but the pattern of relationship between climate variables and self-reliance is quite different in the majority black schools.

TABLE 24*

Simple Correlations Between Mean School Scores
on 14 Climate Variables and Mean Student Self-Reliance
in Samples of Michigan Public Elementary Schools

Climate Variables	State Sample	Majority White Schools			Majority Black Schools
		Total White	High SES	Low SES	
STUDENT CLIMATE					
1. Sense of Academic Futility	.159	.341	.359	−.018	.089
2. Future Eval. & Expectations	.343	.410	.245	.316	.220
3. Perceived Pres. Eval. & Exp.	.123	.124	−.132	.298	.234
4. Perception of Teacher Push and Teacher Norms	.079	.093	−.082	.127	.395
5. Academic Norms	.042	.048	−.087	.083	.399
TEACHER CLIMATE					
1. Ability, Eval., Expectations & Qual. of Ed. for College	.274	.328	.130	.290	.078
2. Pres. Eval. and Exp. for H.S. Completion	.198	.378	.240	.270	.184
3. Teacher-Stud. Commit. to Improve	.144	.144	−.096	.362	.162
4. Perception of Prin. Expec.	.262	.297	.022	.369	.011
5. Teacher's Academic Futility	.174	.218	.118	.352	−.046

*Table 24 continued on next page.

TABLE 24 (continued)

Climate Variables	State Sample	Majority White Schools			Majority Black Schools
		Total White	High SES	Low SES	
PRINCIPAL CLIMATE					
1. Parent Concern & Expectations for Qual. Education	.306	.318	.054	.398	.027
2. Efforts to Improve	−.206	−.035	−.012	−.113	−.135
3. Eval. of Present School Quality	.185	.227	.011	.259	−.167
4. Pres. Eval. & Expectations of Students	.232	.287	.288	.093	.140
Standard Score of All 14 Climate Variables	.368	.446	.157	.484	.231
Number of Schools in Sample	68	61	31	30	30

Multiple Regression of School Social
System Variables and Mean Student Self-Reliance

The multiple regression analyses of the mean self-reliance on the three sets of independent variables, input, structure and climate, are summarized in Table 25. It is apparent from these analyses, in which the three sets of variables are inserted into the anaylsis in different sequences, that combined inputs, student body composition and other personnel inputs, contribute very little to the variance in mean student self-reliance. Only in the majority white school sample do the inputs contribute significantly to the variance in mean self-reliance. In this white school sample, however, most of the contribution of inputs is explained by variance in climate when climate is placed in the regression anaylsis first.

Social structure variables explain slightly more of the variance in mean self-reliance than do the input variables in all but the majority white school sample. This contribution of the structure variables is also more independent of the climate variables than are the input contributions. It will be noted in Table 25 that the structure variables consistently contribute more to the variance in mean self-reliance after the effects of climate are removed than do the input variables.

The combination of the three sets of variables explain only 38.7 percent of the variance in the representative state sample of schools. This percentage increases to 44.9 in the white schools and 75.2 in the majority

TABLE 25

Summary of Multiple Regression Analysis Showing the Contribution of Three Clusters of Independent Variables, Input, Structure and Climate, to the Variance in Mean Student Self-Reliance in Samples of Michigan Public Elementary Schools

Independent Variables Order Entered in Regression	State Represent. Sample		Majority White Schools						Majority Black Schools	
			Total White		High SES		Low SES			
	R^2	R^2 add	R^2	R^2 add	R^2	R^2 add	R^2	R^2 add	R^2	R^2 add
Inputs	.036		.202		.145		.079		.053	
Structure	.173	.137	.267	.065	.380	.235	.136	.057	.191	.138
Climate	.387	.214	.449	.182	.649	.269	.829	.693	.752	.561
Inputs	.036		.202		.145		.079		.053	
Climate	.250	.214	.337	.135	.294	.149	.736	.657	.625	.572
Structure	.387	.137	.449*	.112	.694*	.355	.829	.093	.752	.127
Structure	.144		.160		.275		.096		.155	
Inputs	.173	.029	.267	.107	.380	.105	.136	.050	.191	.038
Climate	.387	.124	.449	.182	.649	.269	829	.693	.752	.561
Structure	.11		.160		.275		.096		.155	
Climate	3.48	.204	.410	.250	.612	.337	.807	.711	.738	.583
Inputs	.387	.039	.449	.039	.649	.037	.829	.022	.752	.014
Climate	.240		.305		.259		.709		.528	
Inputs	.250	.010	.337	.032	.294	.035	.736	.027	.625	.097
Structure	.387	.137	.449*	.112	.659*	.355	.829	.093	.752	.127
Climate	.240		.305		.259		.709		.528	
Structure	.348	.108	.401	.096	.612	.353	.807	.098	.738	.210
Inputs	.387	.039	.449	.048	.649	.037	.829	.022	.752	.014
No. of Schools in Sample	68		61		31		30		30	

*Teacher satisfaction with social structure not included because F-level insufficient.

black schools. The increase in the proportion of the variance explained in these sub-samples suggests that some of the effects of climate variables on self-reliance are being suppressed by the composition variables in the representative state sample.

The partitioning of the variance, shown in Table 26, confirms that the school climate variables contribute more to the explained variance in mean student self-reliance than either of the other sets of variables. Very little variance is uniquely attributable to the inputs in any of the samples and very little is attributable to any combination of the three sets. It should also be noted that the unique contribution of school climate to mean self-reliance is much greater in the low SES and black school samples, while the structure variables contribute more in the high SES sample.

TABLE 26

**Percent of Variance in Mean Student Self-Reliance
Removed by Three Clusters of Variables and Combinations
of These Clusters; The Partitions of the Variance
Attributable to Each and Common to Combinations of the Three Clusters
in a State Random Sample and Sub-Sample
of Elementary Schools in Michigan**

Variance Removed by	State Sample	White Schools	High SES White	Low SES White	Black
Input	.036	.202	.145	.079	.053
Structure	.144	.160	.275	.096	.155
Climate	.240	.305	.259	.709	.528
Input & Structure	.173	.267	.380	.136	.191
Input & Climate	.250	.337	.294	.736	.625
Structure & Climate	.348	.410	.612	.807	.738
Input & Structure & Climate	.387	.449	.649	.829	.752
Partitioned Variance					
Unique to Input	.039	.039	.037	.022	.014
Unique to Structure	.137	.112	.355	.093	.127
Unique to Climate	.214	.182	.269	.693	.561
Common to Input & Structure	−.029	−.007	−.002	.005	.083
Common to Input & Climate	−.007	.068	.068	.018	.022
Common to Structure & Climate	.002	−.047	−.120	−.036	.011
Common to All Three	.031	.097	.042	.034	−.066

Summary of Social System Relationship to Student Mean Self-Reliance

Although we urge caution in the interpretation of this analysis of the relation of student self-reliance to school social system variables, the findings suggest tentative observations. Unlike achievement in reading and mathematics, little of the variance in mean student self-reliance is explained by school input variables alone. The characteristics of the school social structure and climate may contribute to variance in self-reliance somewhat differently in the different sub-samples with structure more important in high SES schools and climate uniquely explaining more of the variance in low SES and black schools.

5

Case Studies
of Four Low SES Schools
by Participant Observers

The findings of the research presented in Chapter 3 clearly demonstrate that SES and racial composition alone do not adequately explain differences in achievement among elementary schools. Some low SES white and black schools have school climates that are conducive to higher achievement. It is, therefore, clear that school composition (i.e., SES and racial composition) does not necessarily determine school climate, and that changes in school composition variables without concomitant changes in school climate may not bring about desired changes in school level achievement. Favorable climate is, we believe, a necessary condition for high achievement.

The findings of this research show that school climate may have a mediating effect upon school level achievement. However, the way in which a given climate is developed and the way in which students, teachers and principals become socialized in it are questions which cannot be answered through our statistical analysis. To address these and other questions, four of the schools from the random samples were selected for

*This chapter was prepared by Charles Beady and Patricia Flood, who conducted the observations.

more intensive study using the participant observation method. Two staff members who had been involved with the research project from the outset conducted the case studies. The primary source of data was information obtained through participant observations in the classrooms although meaningful additional data were obtained through formal and informal interviews with teachers, principals, and students. The time spent in each of the schools ranged from three weeks to three months. The purpose of this chapter is to present and discuss the findings and conclusions from the case studies as well as resulting implications.

SCHOOL SELECTION

The criteria used in the selection of the schools to be studied were mean school achievement, mean SES level, racial composition and community type. It was the consensus of our research staff that the pairs of schools to be observed should have similar racial composition and SES levels, be located in similar communities, and have differing levels of achievement. The two options open for school selection were then (1) to select a low SES-high achieving school and pair it with a low SES-low achieving school, or (2) to select a high SES-low achieving school and pair it with a high SES-high achieving school. Since students in lower SES schools commonly fail to achieve at relatively high academic levels, it was felt that selecting lower class schools which had managed to break the SES-achievement pattern would provide more insight into the question of what can be done to break the SES-achievement patterns in other schools and at least provide some possible solutions to the "problem." Consequently, lower SES schools were selected for observation.

The measure of achievement used in selecting the four schools was the mean school score on the Michigan Assessement Test for 1974. The measure of SES used was the school mean score derived from the survey data. The criteria used in selecting the four schools were (a) similar racial composition, (b) similar SES levels that were significantly lower than the mean SES level for the sample, (c) achievement scores above the sample mean in one school and below the sample mean in the other within each pair, and (d) urban area location. Table 27 provides a summary of each of the four schools selected with respect to the above mentioned criteria.

As is apparent from the table, both the SES levels and achievement levels are significantly different between the black school and the white school samples. Within each pair the SES level, community type, and racial composition are very similar, but have significantly different levels of

TABLE 27

**Percentage of Whites, Mean SES, Mean Achievement,
Community Type of Schools Observed Compared to
White and Black Sample Means**

	Percent White	Mean SES	Mean Achievement	Community Type
White B School	98.1	2.03	71.59	50,000+
White A School	99.2	2.21	80.38	50,000+
Mean White School Sample		3.17	77.37	
Black B School	3.8	1.48	47.18	50,000+
Black A School	7.1	1.42	63.10	50,000+
Mean Black School Sample		1.86	53.84	

achievement.

In order to control for the effects of these demographic variables on achievement, the schools within each pair were matched as closely as possible with respect to these variables. With the effect of these variables minimized, differences in school achievement attributable to school social system variables could be more easily identified.

Several similarities and differences between the schools within each pair not included in the table warrant some mention. Both of the predominantly white schools selected are located in the "urban fringe" of a large city. Both communities are nearly all white and have a substantial number of first and second-generation Appalachian area migrants. Both communities depend primarily upon the automobile industry for employment. Both schools are kindergarten through sixth grade; however, White A is a good deal larger (approximately 600 students) than White B (approximately 300 students).

The two predominantly black schools that were selected for observation are similar in that they both contain grades K-6 and have approximately 300 students each. Both schools also contain large numbers of students from single-parent families, many of whom receive some form of public assistance. The two communities are almost exclusively dependent upon the automotive industy for employment. Black A is located on the urban fringe of a fairly large metropolitan area while Black B is located within the city limits of a slightly larger metropolitan area.

We shall first describe each school in terms of the school-community setting and several aspects of the school environment and teaching activities. The latter include the time devoted to instruction, reinforcement practice, team teaching, games, grouping and classification of students. In addition we will examine the role of the principal and the level of expectation which characterizes the school social system. Following the description of each school we make some comparative observations which identify factors that may explain the different levels of achievement in the schools observed.

CASE STUDY, WHITE A

School-Community Characteristics

The White A school is a relatively high achieving low SES school located in an all white lower class community in a large southeastern Michigan metropolitan area. The majority of residents in the community are first- and second-generation southern migrants from Kentucky and Tennessee. While some proportion of the population is transient, the makeup of the community has been and continues to be very stable. When people move out of the community they tend to be replaced by people having very similar backgrounds. The community is then fairly homogeneous with respect to social class and background and entirely homogeneous with respect to race. The community's "ability" to remain all white and largely southern is interesting in light of its location in a large metropolitan area including a large minority population. The housing available in the community is such that it would be easily affordable for many white and non-white city residents seeking to leave the city for the suburbs. However, migration into the community almost entirely consists of white southern migrants with few, if any, families moving in from the city.

The neighborhood seems to possess the same general characteristics as the school. The houses, while not in need of extensive repair, seem to reflect the slightly "run-down" appearance of the school. The majority of the houses are small wood-frame single-family dwellings. The community is almost entirely residential with virtually no industry and very few business establishments. For the most part, the employed residents work outside the community in the automobile industry.

The White A school is very much a "neighborhood school." The students all come from the neighborhood immediately surrounding the school. The children walk or are driven to school by their parents — in fact, all but a very few go home each day for lunch. The school is also used by the community for non-academic activities. Scouting, sports, and other community activities are regularly held in the school building in the evenings and on weekends

The building itself is fairly old and not particularly well kept. Several windows in the building were broken and not repaired during the three-month observation period. While the grounds surrounding the school are substantial in area, there are few recreational facilities. In fact, the grounds were littered with broken glass and other debris which made the playground area relatively unsafe for students' play.

The inside of the building is kept in a somewhat better state of repair than the outside and playground area. The first floor contains all of the K through 3 classrooms, the principal's office, the library, gym, teachers' lounge, and skills rooms. The upper-grade classrooms are on the second floor as is the learning disability room. Most of the rooms are located on one very long corridor. Students coming to the school in the morning line up at one of five different doorways, depending on what grade and classroom they are in.

While, during the observation time, the children were rough and disorderly before school, during lunch and recess periods, and after school, they were all well behaved when in the school building. There is a great deal of structure regarding student behavior in the building. Students are "led" into and out of the building and to and from their classrooms by their teachers every time movement is necesssary. Children in the lower grades are also "led" to the restrooms several times during the day. Boy-girl lines are used for these "movement" activities. Students are not allowed to talk when moving in these lines through the building. If students are talking, the teacher will stop the line and wait for "quiet" before moving on. While some disturbances were observed, particularly in one of the fourth-grade classrooms, the students were, as already noted, generally well behaved when in the school building. The classrooms are very traditionally structured with desks in relatively neat rows facing the front of the room. Two exceptions to this are the rooms used for the skills program and for helping students who had various learning disabilities. These rooms are very open, carpeted, and filled with various learning aides, games, and so forth.

When we made our observations, the staff at White A school was relatively large, with 18 classroom teachers, a reading specialist, six reading aides, and a learning disability specialist and aide. In addition to these full-time staff members, there were three gym teachers, a librarian, a music teacher, and an art teacher who came to the school several days a week. The staff was relatively stable. Most of the teachers had been in the school for more than a few years, several for more than 10 years. The staff was predominantly female with only two male regular classroom teachers. Several of the teachers were over 50 but the majority were in their late 20's or in their 30's. Because of an increase in the kindergarten and pre-K student population, two new teachers had recently joined the staff. One of the new teachers worked full-time as a pre-school and special education teacher; the other worked half-time as a kindergarten teacher.

This school contains grades K-6. There are no remedial programs at any grade level outside of the "learning disability" program which serves approximately 20-30 students. The overwhelming majority of the 600 plus student population participate, then, in regular curricula programs. There is a basic skills reading program in which all students must participate. This program is designed to ensure that reading skills up to the third-grade level are mastered by all of the students. The reading skills program is performance-based with mastery of different level skills serving as the objective for all students participating. Every student must participate so there is no "stigma" or label associated with students in the program.

The school day begins at 8:00 A.M. for teachers and 8:45 A.M. for the students. The 45-minute period before the students arrive is used by the teachers for classroom preparation, union meetings, and other school business. Most of the time seems to be spent in grading papers or preparing new assignments. The teachers' lounge is used by almost all the teachers every morning for these activities and for conversation. A striking fact is that by far the greatest proportion of time spent in the lounge is student-oriented. While non-school topics are discussed, they are in the minority. When we were there, teachers talked about behavior problems, students' personal problems, and a great deal about student achievement. There is a sharing of experience that is at once both potentially helpful and potentially harmful to the students. Because the staff at White A is quite stable, the opportunity for sharing "notes" and experiences with different children, siblings, and so on, exists, and is frequently done by the teachers. Observations of the school indicate that for the most part this "sharing" has a positive effect on school performance.

Time Spent in Instruction

During our observations, the teachers at the White A school seemed to expect the same attitude toward "working" from their students as they exhibit themselves. As earlier mentioned, much of the non-teaching activities which must be done by teachers such as grading papers and drawing up lesson plans are done on the teachers' own time in the lounge. The time spent in the classroom was for the most part, left free for instruction.

With only one exception in the observed classrooms, nearly all of the time spent in the classroom was devoted to instruction. One teacher in the school seemed to have a good deal of difficulty controlling the students. This classroom was the only one observed where the time spent on instruction did not approach 80-90 percent of the time available.

While somewhat less time was spent on instruction in the first grade and kindergarten rooms, the observer was impressed with the amount of teaching that did go on at this level. While there was perhaps a tendency for the kindergarten and first-grade teachers to be more concerned than the other teachers with their students "having fun," it did not seem to be at the expense of teaching. That is, even at the kindergarten and first-grade levels a good deal of time was spent on reading and learning numbers. Further, it was apparent that the students' age was not used as an excuse for non-teaching, nor did it lead to much non-academic play.

All but one of the teachers at this school, then, were apparently dedicated to spending their class time teaching. This attitude was apparently accepted by the students — at least for the most part. Interviews with students as well as the survey data on this school indicated that the students did not think the teachers made them work too hard. Our observations support these data in that the students seemed prepared to work when they came into the classroom.

Write-Offs

Many people believe, and much research suggests, that students from poor families cannot learn very much; that those who "make it" are the exceptions, not the rule; and that family background (when race is not a factor) is the primary determinant of achievement. Fortunately for the students at White A, most of the teachers apparently have not read the research on the subject and have not been informed of poor students' predestined failures. When we speak of write-offs, we are referring to those students who are perceived by the teachers as destined to fail — academic "hopeless cases." The notion of writing off students leads to what Rosenthal (1968) has termed the self-fulfilling prophecy. The teachers do not expect these students to learn and in fact may think them incapable of learning. Consequently, they do not "waste" their time trying to teach them much and instead devote their teaching energies to those whom they feel are more likely to succeed. Not suprisingly, students who are "written off" tend not to learn a great deal, thus justifying and perhaps reinforcing their teachers' perception of them.

The teachers in White A, with very few exceptions, did not "write off" their students. They were certainly aware that many students did not get much academic support or encouragement outside of the classroom. The general attitude of the teachers regarding this, however, seemed to be that it is the teacher who is primarily responsible for teaching — not parents or others outside school. They did indicate to the observer that some students were more difficult to "reach" than others but in the context that they had the same obligation to "see to it" that these students learned as they did for the more reachable students. Another indicator that a very small number of students are written off is the fact that there are no remedial programs at this school. This will be discussed in some detail later. At this point it is sufficient to note that the underlying assumption of remedial programs is that quite a number of students may not "make it," at least not the first time around. White A apparently does not operate on this assumption.

Teacher Expectations
To some extent the teachers' expectations of their students have already been discussed in the preceding section. Writing off students, however, involves establishing expectation *ceilings*, while the general term "teacher expectations" here refers to establishing expectation *floors*. To establish an expectation "ceiling" is to estimate how much a student can learn and then make no attempt to teach any more than that. Establishing an expectation floor, on the other hand, refers to the minimum level of student learning acceptable to the teacher. Our observations indicate that there is a substantial difference in teaching expectations between higher and lower achieving schools.

Expectations are often considered in the research literature as being future oriented, i.e., referring to expectations regarding high school achievement or college attendance. This future orientation did not seem to be a salient dimension of the teachers' expectations in this school. The teachers didn't talk much about their students going to college and, in fact, when asked they more often than not indicated they expected relatively few of their students to go beyond high school. While these comments may be said to constitute low expectations, it is the writers' opinion that this is not in conflict with earlier comments concerning write-offs or even with high achievement. The teachers in White A expect their students to read, write, and do arithmetic *at grade level*. This then is the "floor"—the minimum requirement set for the students. Conversations with the teachers as well as classroom observations indicated that the teachers perceive achieving this level of learning to be their primary responsibility to the students. The teachers feel that whether or not students do well in high school or go on to college, for the most part, is not subject to their control. They seem determined, however, to provide their students with the basic skills necessary to make these alternatives possible.

In summary, teachers in this school expect the students who complete the sixth grade to be capable of doing seventh-grade work. Observations in the classrooms indicate that the teachers generally have been successful.

Reinforcement Practices

The writers accept the basic assumption of reinforcement theory which posits that behaviors that are positively rewarded tend to be repeated and, conversely, those that are negatively rewarded tend in time, to be extinguished. In classrooms, students exhibit a wide range of behaviors, of which some are conducive to high achievement—and some not. Students are rewarded both positively and negatively and in a variety of ways by both their teachers and their peers. If it is assumed that behaviors conducive to high achievement should not be rewarded, two possibilities exist for reward "messages" sent to the student. Very simply, students may be either appropriately or inappropriately rewarded. Reward messages are not always clear and straightforward. A teacher may, for example, respond "Good try" to a student who has incorrectly answered a question simply because he or she answered at all. Such confusing messages are considered by the writers to fall in the "inappropriate" category. Teachers in White A school for the most part reward students clearly and appropriately. While some confusing reinforcement messages were observed they were not common.

Two examples of reinforcement messages observed in two different classrooms will prove illustrative of the differences between what the writers perceive to be appropriate and confusing rewards. The first example is typical of the reinforcement pattern that was by far the most often observed in this school. The following instance of an appropriate reward pattern was recorded by the observer while sitting in a third-grade classroom. The teacher had given a handwriting assignment to the students and was walking up and down the rows of students observing each one's efforts. At one point she leaned over a student seated in the back of the room near the observer and said something like, "I told you to start at the edge of the page. You're never going to fit it all on one line if you start in the middle . . . and Wednesday begins with a capital letter, not a small one." She then erased the student's work and said, "Now do it over." Apparently he did not get the "W" right, because she learned over, erased his paper again and said something like, "A capital, I said, don't you know what a capital 'W' looks like? Here watch me." She took the student's pencil, wrote on his paper, then gave the pencil back and told the student to try it again. The student did, and the teacher said something like, "Well, see, I knew you could do it, that's very good, keep it up." The teacher clearly had a performance standard which she expected the student to meet and withheld any praise until that standard was met.

While there were not many, most of the confusing reinforcement messages which were observed occurred in the first-grade rooms. This may be due to the teacher's reluctance to make learning "unpleasant" for the younger students. The observer recorded this example while sitting in a first-grade reading group. The teacher was using flash cards with color words—holding up one card at a time and then calling on a member of the group to read the word. When the teacher held up the flash card with "black" written on it, the student she called on didn't answer. She pointed to the "b" and said something like, "What sound does this make?" and then made "b" noises. The student repeated the sound but still did not read the word. The teacher then pointed to the "l" and as with "b" said, "What sound does this make?" and then made "l" noises. Again the student enunciating them as though they were syllables instead of letters. The student at this point reminded the observer of the cartoon characters who get light bulbs in their eyes after getting an idea or experiencing a kind of "I got it now" feeling. At any rate, the student blurted out "blue" and seemed eminently pleased with himself and sure of his answer. The teacher said something like, "Almost, it looks a lot like blue, doesn't it?" She then asked if anyone could "help" the student and one raised her hand and answered correctly. After this, the teacher said something like, "Reading is tricky, isn't it—that was a good try," to the student who had answered incorrectly. The message "blue is almost black" seemed to the observer to be a confusing one at least when contrasted with the clear message present in the first example.

Again, and in sum, the teachers generally gave appropriate reward messages.

Grouping Procedures

The only grouping in White A is within classrooms for reading. Most of the grouping is done in grades 1-3. Of particular interest is the number of reading groups in the first-grade classroom. In the two observed first-grade rooms, the teacher had divided the students into five groups rather than the more usual two or three. Both teachers reported that their reason for having so many groups was that many of the students who came in knowing nothing at all about reading would catch on quickly and would be penalized if there were only two or three groups. Having five groups kept the differential among them relatively small and facilitated movement from one group to another. All three first-grade teachers reported that all of their students were expected to reach grade level though some of them would go well beyond it. After the third grade there is no grouping—not even for reading. Observations in the upper grades support the teachers' assessment of their students' reading achievement. The vast majority of students seem to be reading at grade level, although there do seem to be some differences in both fluency and comprehension levels.

For the most part, students are assigned to classrooms randomly, though there are several exceptions to this. Parents may request that their child be assigned to a certain teacher and some students who create behavior problems when together may be purposely separated. There is one split 2/3 section in the school—the students in this class are selected from the "higher achieving" students. Beyond these exceptions, there is no homogeneous grouping in this school. The teachers tend to set class objectives and then work toward bringing all of their students at least to that level.

Teaching Games

Teachers of the early grades, 1-3, tend to spend a good deal of time playing various learning games with their classes. These games most often are used in conjunction with math lessons though some reading and "telling time" games were observed. The game-playing served the dual purpose of being an effective teaching tool and heightening the students' interest in the material being presented.

It is difficult to discuss teaching games without referring to already discussed factors such as reinforcement practices, expectations, and time spent on instruction. It is difficult to separate the use of teaching games from other characteristics of the learning environment when teaching games reflect high expectations of the teacher, incorporate appropriate reinforcement patterns, and utilize time which might otherwise be spent on non-instructional activities, yet they may serve as an aid to higher achievement. The teaching games observed in the White A school seemed to reflect all of these. While games were used in nearly all of the classrooms, they were most frequently observed in the lower grades. The following examples taken from a third-grade classroom are illustrative of the kind of games used by most of the lower-grade teachers.

The games used in this classroom combine group and individual competition. The class was divided into girl-boy teams without regard to individual student competencies. For the math games the teams would line up in single file on opposite sides of the room. The students at the head of each line were in competition with each other. The teachers would state a problem, i.e., 8 + 7, and whoever answered correctly first (of the two people competing) would go to the back of his or her line. The "loser" would have to sit down. This process was repeated until only one student remained standing. The "team" was treated as the winner rather than the individual student. The game would be played three times with the team winning twice being the "winner." The daily scores were kept on the board throughout the week with the team winning the most games being the weekly "champions."

The emphasis on "team" rather than individual performance may have been at least in part, responsible for the enthusiasm and supportive behavior exhibited by the students. An important feature of the game is that different students "win" for their team (see DeVries and Slavin, 1976, for evidence of the effectiveness of team games). Certainly some students are more competent in math than others, but these students do not consistently remain unbeaten. In fact, the teacher exhibited some ingenuity in making the competition more "equal." The following example is instructive as to how competitive games can lead to increased enthusiasm and positive reinforcement of even the "slowest" students.

One girl student in this class was behind her classmates in mastery of the math problems used in the game. When adding or subtracting she would either count aloud or use her fingers. Both of these techniques are very slow in producing answers even though they may be right. Consequently, in the game situation this student would be almost certain to "lose" on her first problem if the teacher did not somehow "equalize" the competition. The teacher's solution was one which we feel to be indicative of the teacher's concern over creating a positive learning climate for all of her students. Every day the teacher would assign this particular student two problems, i.e., 7 + 8, 9 + 5 and their reverse, 8 + 7, 5 + 9. The student knew that the teacher would give one of those four problems whenever it was her turn. The other students, on both teams, also knew that one of those four problem statements would be given. Before the game the student was generally coached by one of her teammates in memorizing the problems and answers. Although the boys' team had the same advantage of knowing which problems to expect, this girl very often "beat" her opponent. On one observed occasion this "poor" student was the "winner," having "beat" the best boy math student in the class. While the boy seemed somewhat embarrassed, nearly every student cheered, and clapped their hands for the "unlikely" winner. It did not take a person trained in psychology or observation methods to recognize the feelings of pride and happiness felt by this little girl who made her team the winner. It was "written all over her face."

This example suggests several ways that games can be used effectively as learning aides and as motivations. The necessity for speed requires the students to memorize the problems and answers if they are to win. The reinforcement received by the students is immediate and straightforward. If a student is wrong, he or she must sit down and is made aware of the "right" answer. The encouragement and support of teammates also seems to have a positive effect on the students. Finally, the emphasis on the team rather than the individual, coupled with the teacher's attempt to "equalize" the competition, makes the game more exciting and less threatening to potential "losers." The point repeatedly made to the students by the teacher is that anyone can make their team the winner.

Principal's Role

The principal in the school serves both as administrator and educational leader of the school. His primary concern, as expressed by him and as evidenced by his behavior, is student achievement. The principal's secretary and administrative assistant performs much of the routine administrative work, leaving him more time for involvement with instructional concerns.

The principal's perception of his role as instructional leader and of his responsibilities to the students and teachers was made evident in the first staff meeting. This meeting took place on the day before classes started and was attended by the observer. Several of the comments made by the principal at this meeting are illustrative of his concern and involvement with the teaching function of the school. At one point during the meeting, the principal told his staff that he intended to "visit", unannounced, each of the classrooms at least 30 times as he had done the year before. He told them the purpose of the visits was not to "take notes" or in other ways evaluate the teacher's performance but, rather, to make the students aware of his interest in their progress. The teachers' reaction to the statement suggested to the observer that they did not fully share the principal's perception of the "visits". There was some laughter and several comments were made to the effect that the teachers "knew" the real purpose of the visits was to "check up" on them. They did not seem to object to the visits, however, or at least did not indicate any objections in the observable ways. Whatever the "real" purpose of the visits, it seems to the writers that they are indicative of the principal's ongoing concern with instructional function of the school.

At another point in the meeting the principal asked the teachers if they were again willing to devote some in-service time and personal time to meetings with him to discuss ways of improving the school. He wanted the teachers to get involved with a Teacher Effectiveness Training program which would require a considerable investment of personal time. He also wanted to continue discussion meetings which had been started the year before involving problem solving at the teacher-principal, teacher-teacher and teacher-student levels. He urged teachers who had not already done so to read *Schools Without Failure* (Glasser, 1969), since the book and its underlying assumptions would be discussed at some of these meetings.

It seems clear to the observer that the principal not only is concerned with the educational function of the school but assumes some measure of responsibility for the school's performance in that aspect. He stressed his availability for meetings with teachers individually or in groups and in fact urged the teachers to "use" him as often as they felt warranted. He seemed very concerned that the teachers not define him solely as an administrator. He told them that he regarded his administrative duties as "necessary evils" and stressed that his primary concern was with the quality of instruction in the school.

The teachers did not all react to the principal in the same way. During the observation period many of the teachers talked with the observer about their perceptions of the principal and his role in the school. Several of the teachers, particularly the older ones, seemed to feel that the principal should primarily be a disciplinarian and not quite so concerned with classroom activities. Others expressed a belief that the principal should assume some responsibility for the quality of instruction and were pleased that their principal had. Almost without exception teachers in this school, through their behavior and comments, indicated that they respected their principal. Even those who would have preferred the principal to play more of a disciplinarian role and less of an educational-leader role seemed to recognize and appreciate the principal's concern with students' academic achievement.

Commitment

In the White A school the teacher and principal were "committed" to providing their students with an education on a par with that normally reserved for middle class youngsters. This commitment to high achievement has already been illustrated in the preceding sections of this example. A point which deserves restating and special attention is the teachers' belief that the students are capable of high achievement. Stating this belief aloud to each other, to the parents and the students themselves, in some sense makes the teachers vulnerable—more "open" to failure. That is, by making public declarations of the students' ability to learn, the teachers have assumed a good deal of responsibility for the students' success or failure.

This acceptance of responsibility for student achievement is, in the opinion of the writers, perhaps the single most important factor underlying the "success" of this school. Neither the teachers nor the principal excused student failure on the basis of the child's family background or academic ability. Classroom behaviors and discussions in the lounge clearly demonstrated the staff's concern with and commitment to insuring high levels of achievement by their students. Commitment in this school is the sum total of those variables already discussed—expectations, time spent in instruction, innovativeness, and so forth.

CASE STUDY, BLACK A

School-Community Characteristics
The Black A school is a relatively high achieving, low SES, predominantly black school. It is located on the urban fringe of a fairly large metropolitan area in a predominantly black community. A number of Chicano families also live in the community along with a smaller number of white families.

The neighborhood was originally all white. It gradually became predominantly black as white families moved out. A socio-economically defined migration pattern presently exists in the community. That is, as black families become more affluent they tend to move out of the attendance area for the Black A school.

For the most part, the homes in the community reflect the low socio-economic status of the residents. With only a few exceptions, the homes are modest wood-frame single-family dwellings, usually in need of repair.

The school itself consists physically of two combined structures: the initial building which is old but kept in good repair and the added wing which is relatively new and also kept in good repair. Most classes are conducted in the new wing. This wing also houses the principal's office and a multipurpose room which serves as a gymnasium, lunchroom, assembly hall, and as a center for various community activities. The old structure houses additional office space, a storage area for curriculum materials, and the teachers' lounge. The last is a small room which is used primarily by teachers and other staff members during lunch time and during breaks. Throughout the entire observation period the principal never came into this room.

At the time of our observation, the educational staff consisted of the principal, a black male; 11 teachers, seven white and four black; 9 teachers' aides, six black, two white, and one Chicano; and a black female librarian. The academic staff was all female with the exception of the principal and one teacher aide, who were both male. For the most part, the teaching staff was experienced, with the majority of them having taught at this school for several years. There was no observable relationship between the racial identification of teachers and student performance.

The staff was required to be at the Black A school at 8:30. Classes began at 9:05. The time in between was designated and used for preparation. Our initial impressions of the school are reflected in the principal's own words at the initial staff meeting of the year. Here, he stated to his teachers that it was essential that, when the students were allowed to enter the building in the mornings, the teachers establish an atmosphere of discipline and order. He indicated that this type of entry should set the tone for behavior for the remainder of the day.

On a walk through the halls of the school, it immediately became apparent that order and discipline was a goal that all staff members attempted to achieve and maintain. All movement in the halls was orderly and quiet.

Discipline, and the behavior of specific students, were almost exclusively the topics of conversation whenever the teachers were in the lounge talking among themselves. Given the fact that this was a relatively high achieving school, it was expected that achievement would be a regular topic of conversation. This was not the case, however, among the teachers and the principal.

There were eleven classrooms at the Black A school, pre-kindergarten through sixth grade. Again, the purpose of our observations was to gain insight as to the nature of the climate that existed in this relatively high achieving, predominantly black school. The following are what we perceive to be the most salient findings resulting from our observations.

Time Spent on Instruction
One of the first salient findings resulting from the observations conducted in this school had to do with the kind, and amount, of time spent by teachers and students on academic activities. It quickly became apparent that, for the most part, the teachers at this school did a great deal of teaching. That is, the majority of classroom time was either devoted to instruction, or given over to students working on classroom assignments.

A great deal of this time centered on teacher-student interaction. Each classroom had a similar format. Students were usually divided into three groups, according to academic achievement. The teacher would spend time with each group instructing and discussing assignments. After instruction and discussion, an assignment was made, and another group worked on their assignment as instruction and discussion took place for the next group. After instructions were given and discussed and assignments were made, both the teacher and her aide (where aides were available) worked with individual students where individual attention seemed warranted. Not all lessons were given in groups. When the same assignment was given to the class as a whole, the same format of instruction, discussion, assignment, and working with individual students was followed.

While students were working, the teachers were working also. They did not use this time to attend to administrative classroom duties; rather, they were almost always engaged with students, giving further instruction, monitoring progress and giving re-instruction when necessary.

Write-Offs

A second finding based on our observations of the Black A school, which appears to be characteristic of the academic climate prevailing in the school, has to do with the extent to which teachers do or do not give up academically on large numbers of their students. Conversations with the teachers in this school revealed that they generally felt the vast majority of their students were capable of mastering the material presented to them. The teachers generally indicated that while the social backgrounds of their students did appear to have some impact upon their classroom performance, they did not feel that their backgrounds should be permitted as an excuse for low achievement. In this regard, there was no general tendency for the teachers to "give up" on large numbers of their students. On only a few occasions did a teacher suggest that she had little hope that a particular student would "make it" academically. One teacher pointed out that one of her Chicano students would feign not being able to understand English well whenever he had difficulty with a problem or an assignment. She stated that she refused to be fooled by this behavior and simply worked a little harder with that particular student. This attitude appeared to characterize the approach that teachers at this school took with regard to the socially related "deficiencies" that the students brought to school with them.

The innovativeness that the teachers generally demonstrated in their approach to educating their students stands as a further example of their tendency not to write off their students. Where traditional methods of instruction did not appear to work, other strategies were used. A second-grade teacher, for instance, pointed out that she was having great difficulty getting a particular student to grasp a concept. After several attempts which resulted in failure, she asked a student who had mastered the concept to help her. With the aid of that student, the first student finally managed to grasp the point that the teacher was trying to get across.

Teacher Expectations

The relatively high expectations for academic success that the teachers held for the majority of their students emerged as another significant aspect of the academic climate that prevailed in the Black A school. The teachers in this school generally reported that they expected at least 75 percent of their students to master the material presented in the classroom, and that this same percentage would probably complete high school.

Teachers rarely voiced to their students either the immediate or the long-range academic expectations that they held for them. On one occasion, a teacher indicated to her class that she expected them all to do well on a test because of the amount of work that had been invested preparing for the test. On another occasion a teacher pointed out to her students that she expected them all to do well in junior high school. For the most part, teachers communicated their relatively high expectations to their students and were frequently observed criticizing students for poor performance on assignments. It was not at all uncommon to hear a teacher telling a student, "I know you can do better than that." Thus, our observations suggest that the behaviors that teachers demonstrated, with regard to the achievement that their students maintained, played a major role in conveying the message that poor academic performance would not be tolerated.

Reinforcement Practices
Another factor that presented itself as a significant characteristic of the climate in this school was the appropriate use of reinforcement that the teachers here exhibited. The teachers in this school tended to use reinforcement patterns that were likely to encourage higher achievement. Appropriate academic behaviors were rewarded and inappropriate academic behaviors were not rewarded. This observation is more significant in light of the findings of Fernandez, Espinosa, and Dornbusch (1975). They report that the teachers they studied tended to reward minority students for substandard achievement. That is, where a student had been performing at a very low level of achievement and showed some improvement, the tendency was for the teacher to tell the student that he or she had done a good job. If the increased achievement was still below that of the student's classmates then, in effect, the teacher had rewarded substandard achievement. While the teachers at this school did reward increased achievement, they were quick to point out any need for improvement.

This appropriate use of reinforcement was observed on a number of occasions. In a first-grade classroom, for instance, a teacher was observed instructing a student in the drawing of a figure which would later be used for coloring. The teacher indicated to the student that she felt that his drawing was inadequate. The student replied that he couldn't do any better. The teacher insisted that he could. She provided additional instruction, then watched the student as he redrew the figure. After the student redrew a figure that she felt was acceptable, she praised his performance. This example, we feel, illustrates a reinforcement pattern that was often observed in the Black A school.

Teaching Games

The use of teaching games appears to have been another significant aspect of the academic climate that prevailed in this relatively higher achieving, predominantly black school. For the most part, the games that were used did not pit individual students against one another. They were usually team games. This use of team games, it appears, made it possible for all students to participate with equal enthusiasm. Rather than competing against one another, a climate of cooperativeness among groups was established as the games were played. One fourth-grade teacher, for instance, frequently held spelling bees. This was a split fourth-fifth-grade classroom and the spelling bees were arranged with the two grades competing against one another. While the individual champions from each grade were rewarded, it was significant to notice the spirit of cooperation that existed among the teams. Each student, whether he was the "brightest" or "slowest" student in the class, received the total support of his group when his turn came. This use of games and the reinforcement that all of the participants received, we feel, served to facilitate an attitude of "Try a little harder" among the students. Conversations with students supported this position.

Grouping

The manner in which students were grouped and the attitudes toward grouping held by teachers also emerged as a significant aspect of the academic climate at this school.

Students were grouped primarily on the basis of performance on math and reading pre-tests. Students could advance from a lower group to a higher group depending upon mastery of classroom materials presented. Mastery was determined by performance on the post-tests that came with the classroom material.

For the most part, the teachers at this school perceived grouping as an opportunity to provide for the unique needs of faster and slower students. The groups were taught different levels of the same materials. We did not consider this to be a favorable practice because teachers implied that the "slower" groups were not capable of handling the same material studied by the "brighter" groups. This practice was considered unfavorable also because it became increasingly obvious that the teachers here taught in accordance with the expectations that they held for their students. Several teachers did point out, however, that the goal of a full year's academic growth for all students was an achievement floor and not a ceiling, and that because a student initially scored as a slower achiever did not necessarily mean that he would remain a slower achiever. They further pointed out that they taught with the purpose of advancing students from "slower" to "brighter" groups rather than for the purpose of maintaining groups.

Also central to the issue of grouping at this school was the use of the reading and math "labs" for the upper grades. Initially, the labs had been set up for remedial instruction for the school's slowest students. It was the principal's decision that all of the upper-grade students should receive what he perceived to be the benefits of the math and reading labs. Consequently, all upper-grade students were required to spend one hour per day in the math lab and one hour per day in the reading lab. While the grouping format in the labs was the same as in the regular classrooms, the labs were not identified by either teachers or students as remedial rooms. Thus the math and reading labs were not used to bring the school's "slow" students together as an identifiable group. Such procedure is often used in other schools to conveniently "write-off" students.

Commitment

The commitment exhibited by the teachers toward insuring higher achievement for their students appears to have been another significant aspect of the academic climate at this school. Certainly those factors that have already been discussed are related to and reflect teacher commitment. However, the teachers also demonstrated their commitment in a number of other ways. Almost all of the teachers indicated that their school was a good place to work because of the positive working relationships that prevailed among the teachers and because the parents in the community were generally supportive. They indicated that such factors made them want to do a good job. Our observations suggest that this attitude was reflected in the behaviors that the teachers exhibited in the total school environment.

The positive climate that was generally evident in the classrooms stands as an example of the teachers' commitment to higher achievement and to the general welfare of their students. The teachers often touched students, hugged them, and demonstrated patience in attending to the individual needs of their students, both personal and academic. It was not unusual to see one of the teachers who taught in the upper grades sitting with one of her students on the back steps of the school discussing the student's personal problems. Another teacher indicated that she had to stay conscious of her weight so that she could stay physically active with her students. She was rarely behind her desk. She was always among the students, either sitting at their desks, or on the floor with them. In two of the lower grades, during the middle of a long lesson or at the end of one, the teachers would have their students sing a song, or teach them a new one, then resume work.

While most teacher-student interaction was confined to the classroom, several teachers and other staff members divided time supervising after-school student activities. While attendance was generally required at staff meetings, seminars, and workshops, the extent to which the teachers actively participated in such activities deserves mention. At a district-wide workshop for instance, the teachers from the Black A school appeared to participate with more enthusiasm than teachers from other schools in the district. They asked questions, responded to questions, and voluntarily participated in small work groups.

In sum, the attitude that teachers expressed toward insuring quality education for their students appeared to be reflected in the behaviors they exhibited both in and out of the classroom with regard to school-related activities.

Principal's Role

At the time of observation, the principal was beginning his fourth year as the school's chief administrator. Conversations with teachers who had been at the school before his arrival indicated that the fact that the Black A school was a relatively higher achieving school could be attributed to the innovativeness of the previous principal. The previous principal was described as being an educational leader as well as an administrator. They indicated that he devoted as much, if not more, time to the educational aspects of the school as he did to his administrative duties.

The present principal was almost exclusively an administrator, and apparently a good one. He kept records in order, supervised his staff, and tended to the daily administrative aspects of running the school. The primary difference between the present principal and the previous principal was said to have been the manner in which they defined their roles as principal. Where the present principal was supportive of his teachers attending seminars and workshops, the previous principal was not only supportive, but was more likely to run his own workshops and in-service for his teachers.

The present principal's role at this school can best be summarized as administrative, although he periodically observed and critiqued his teachers' classroom skills. He indicated that he felt that the primary responsibility for the quality of education in the school rested with the individual teachers. He implied that his primary responsibility with regard to the quality of education in his school was supervision of his teachers, and encouraging and supporting their attendance and participation in seminars, workshops, and in-service programs designed to increase their effectiveness in the classroom. He expressed the view that his teachers should rely upon their own skills and resourcefulness to resolve classroom crises, including academic, personal and behavioral problems, and that he should be used only as a last resort.

Our observations of the Black A school indicate that in general the academic staff was strict, behaviorally and academically, but not mean. They appeared to be sensitive to the personal and academic problems their students faced, but did not appear to let these problems lower the standards they had set. Above all, they appeared to be concerned about the academic and general welfare of their students. This concern was reflected in the attitudes they expressed and the behaviors they exhibited.

CASE STUDY, WHITE B

School-Community Characteristics

The White B school is located in an all-white lower class community in an urban fringe area in southeastern Michigan. The homes in the community are predominantly small single-family dwellings kept in relatively good repair. Many of the residents are first- and second-generation southern migrants. There is also a substantial number of residents of Italian descent. The community borders other communities having large numbers of black residents but has not yet experienced an in-migration of this minority population.

The population in the community is quite stable. A large number of residents have been in the community for many years. Apparently there is little attraction for "young marrieds," as was noted by the school's principal. According to him, there are no employment opportunities that attract white collar and professional workers. Consequently, what "new" families do settle in the area are often the children of "old families" who have not elected to pursue a professional or skilled occupation requiring post-secondary education. A substantial number of the residents are employed by one of the several nearby auto plants.

The community has experienced a decline in school-age population in recent years. This may be due to the low numbers of "young marrieds" moving into the community and (or) the economic conditions of the "new" families remaining in the community. At any rate, several elementary schools in the area have closed in the past several years. The White B school presently serves youngsters from one of these closed schools as well as its "own" student population. The number of kindergarten children increased significantly during the year in which the school was observed. The principal attributes the increase to the fact that the parochial schools in the area have increased their tuition fees substantially. The principal reported that, if more families could afford to send their children to parochial schools, the public schools would experience a further decline in their enrollment.

The White B school is a relatively small school serving approximately 250 students in grades K-6. The building itself is well kept as is the large playground area surrounding it. There are 11 classrooms, a small library and a standard-sized gymnasium. There are few items of equipment—in fact, none were observed in use other than a movie projector and mimeograph machine.

During the period of observation it was noted that only a few teachers arrived in the mornings more than a few minutes before classes were to begin. The teachers' lounge was used by most of the teachers during the noon hour but seldom before classes. When teachers were in the lounge they were seldom engaged in academically related behavior. When conversations about students did occur they generally took the form of discussions about particular students' family circumstances, or about the frustrations and even impossibilities associated with teaching at this school. In terms of preparing for classes, the only activity observed in the lounge was the use of the ditto machine.

There seemed to be a very strained relationship between the teaching staff and school administrators. This "discontent" was often the topic of discussion in the lounge. The teachers seemed to be very insecure in their positions, partially due to the "bumping" system used by administrators. Because of declining enrollments and the closing of several schools, many teachers in the district had lost their jobs. The bumping system was designed to keep those teachers having seniority employed, generally at the expense of other, less experienced teachers. One result of this system is that high school teachers who had been "bumped" could in turn "bump" elementary school teachers. There was one instance of this in the White B school.

One consequence of this "insecurity" was a distrust of both the administrators and the observer. Due primarily to the poor communication between the principal and his staff, the teachers were not fully aware of this study's intent or design. The early perception of the observer by the teachers was that she was a "spy" for the administration. The situation was further complicated by the fact that the teachers had not yet successfully negotiated a contract for that school year although the observation began in January. A great deal of verbal persuasion and written assurance of the intent of the study and the observer's non-alliance with any administrative body were required to enlist the cooperation of the teaching staff. Some of the information and analysis presented below are based on "recall" data recorded after the observer left the school building as several teachers were uncomfortable with "note-taking" in their classrooms.

Time Spent on Instruction

In the White B school the amount of time spent on actual instruction varied a great deal between classrooms. In several classrooms instruction accounted for, at best, 10 percent of the available time. In one fourth-grade room, on the other hand, 75-80 percent of classroom time was devoted to instructional activities. While the teachers' ability to maintain discipline seemed to be related to the amount of time spent on instruction, the exceptions indicated that the relationship is not a causal one.

Several teachers in the school seemed to have great difficulty maintaining sufficient order in the classrooms to allow for instruction. In one second-grade classroom, the observer noticed that the teacher spent the entire afternoon session trying to establish order in the room. During this time, the teacher tried to teach math and science but failed in both endeavors. Almost no instruction took place in this classroom during any of the observation periods.

In contrast, several teachers maintained quiet, orderly rooms but failed to utilize their classroom time for teaching. In one of the first-grade rooms, the students were very well behaved yet spent only about 20 percent of the classroom time engaged in interaction with the teacher. A substantial amount of time was spent doing "seatwork" with little instruction, direction, or help given from the teacher. An equally substantial amount of time was spent in such activities as coloring, working puzzles, and working with modeling clay.

In general then, a relatively small proportion of class time was devoted to instruction. In some cases it seemed to be due to the lack of discipline. In others it seemed to be a result of the teacher's prerogative of spending classroom time for such activities as grading papers or carrying out other routine duties.

Write-Offs

There was a substantial number of students who were, in effect, written off by their teachers as academic failures at every grade level. A comment made to the observer by a first-grade teacher is instructive in this regard. The observer asked this teacher to fill out a questionnaire that had been designed for teachers at the fourth, fifth, and sixth grade levels. A number of items asked the teacher to evaluate their students' potential for academic success at the high school and college levels. The observer told the first-grade teacher that these items were probably inappropriate because her students were so young. The teacher emphatically stated that she could tell *at the kindergarten level* who could "make it" and who could not.

Unfortunately many of the teachers in this school had firm beliefs in their ability to identify future academic failures at a very early age. Even more unfortunate was the tendency for teachers to spend far less time teaching these academic "hopeless cases" than students who were perceived as having greater abilities. During observation periods in several classrooms a number of these "slow" students were observed to be totally left out of the instructional activities. On several occasions these students were engaged in such activities as cleaning out desks and pencil boxes, coloring, and simply staring out a window for the duration of the observation period which usually lasted three hours. These students were clearly written off by their teachers—they did little more than take up space.

Not all of the "slow" students were completely written off by the teachers. Usually only two or three per classroom remained pretty much outside the learning process. However, nearly all of the "slower" students were observed to be less frequently engaged in academic activities and in teacher-student academic interaction than were the other students.

Expectations

The teachers in the school without exception expressed to the observer that the students' academic capabilities were limited by their family background. Most of them allowed for the possibility of academic success for a few of their "brightest" students but did not perceive success to be an attainable goal for most of the students.

Expectations for student achievement were low in general but especially low for those students in the "slow" reading tracks. These students were not expected to "catch up" to the faster students and consequently move from the slower group to the faster. A fifth-grade teacher reported to the observer that many of the "slow" students were reading more than two years below grade level by the time they reached the fifth grade. When asked whether these students could make up any of that deficit, the teacher indicated that in all probability they would fall further behind.

Grade level achievement was not considered to be a realistic goal for many of the students. When asked about their expectations for student achievement, teachers' comments usually reflected a "We do the best we can given what we have to work with" mentality. It was difficult to determine whether there were any expectation floors for these students at all. It seemed to the observer that having a substantial number of fifth- and sixth-grade students achieving two or three years below grade level in reading was in some sense considered to be a natural or expected consequence of the students' abilities and backgrounds.

There were no special programs, no special classroom activities designed to raise the achievement levels of either the "faster" or "slower" students. In fact, we observed no activity indicating that the teachers expected or hoped for any improvement in student performance. The teachers seemed more surprised at student success than student failure. In sum, student performance was consistent with teachers' expectations— both were very low.

Reinforcement

Teachers in this school varied considerably with respect to their use of reinforcement patterns in the classrooms. Several teachers seemed to consistently use appropriate reinforcement practices when engaged in teacher-student interaction. These teachers were predominantly in the upper grades. On the other hand, several teachers were observed to use confusing and (or) totally inappropriate reinforcement practices most of the time.

One teacher repeatedly gave positive reinforcement for poor performance and negative reinforcement for good performance when interacting with her "slow" students. During one classroom visitation the teacher was observed making very negative and even derogatory comments to a student who had successfully completed an assignment with the observers' guidance. The teacher compared the student's efforts with those of her "best" students and told the observer *in front of the student* that the student wasn't capable of doing the assignment properly. Not only did the teacher exhibit a lack of sensitivity, she actually punished, through her comments, the positive attempts at achievement made by this particular student.

Several instances were observed when teachers positively rewarded poor performance, particularly in the case of the lower achieving students' assignments which were partially completed and (or) partially correct and were treated as though they were complete and (or) all correct. Students handing in written assignments which were done neatly but wrongly were praised for their neatness with no comments made as to the content of the assignment.

Some confusing reinforcement messages were given in nearly all of the classrooms although there was a great deal of variance in their frequency. Teachers at all grade levels were frequently observed making responses such as "good try" or "that's close" to students giving wrong answers. Several teachers reported to the observer that they felt a wrong answer was better than no answer at all and that they tried to reward students' efforts. They failed to clearly communicate to the students, however, that while their effort was appreciated, their answers were wrong. Such reinforcement messages were seldom accompanied by reinstruction to assist the students in correcting mistakes.

Grouping-Individualization

Students in this school were grouped for reading from the first-grade level through the sixth grade. There were only two reading groups in each of the early grade level classrooms. Teachers in each of the first three grade levels reported that there was very little movement between groups and virtually no upward movement at all. Students were assigned to different reading tracks at the first-grade level and usually stayed in that track for their remaining years in the school.

The academic grouping procedures seemed, in some classrooms, to create a social grouping as well. In some instances this appeared unintentional but in others it was encouraged if not created by classroom organization. Separation by reading ability was extreme in one first-grade classroom. In this room the "fast" students were given seats along one wall of the classroom and the "slow" students seats along the opposite wall. Two banquet-like tables were in the center of the room adding an additional physical barrier separating the two groups. Almost no interaction between students from different groups occurred during the more than eight hours of observation in this classroom. The very limited interaction consisted of one of the "faster" students helping one of the "slower" students at the teacher's request. During these interactions, the "faster" students appeared to play more of the teacher role than a peer or friend role. Groups were not as rigidly separated in the other classrooms, but there was a tendency for students to associate only with classmates in their own ability group in all classrooms.

Having only two reading groups—"fast" and "slow"—seemed to the observer to insure that the "gap" between groups would be substantial. Mobility between groups, especially from slow to fast, would be difficult to achieve on the one hand, and probably detrimental to the student on the other. When teachers were asked about the two-group system, they reported that there was simply not enough time to teach more than two reading groups. When asked about the "gap" between groups, the teachers indicated that indeed the gap widened with time and that students in slow groups had little, if any, chance to "catch up" to the faster students.

In the observer's judgment, grouping procedures in this school were detrimental to the students' achievement possibilities. For the most part, grouping procedures were designed to meet the needs of the teachers rather than the needs of the students. Students were placed in the two groups on the basis of their teachers' perceptions of their abilities and competencies. The students identified as "slow" tended to perform at a low level and fall further below a normal level of achievement. In the "fast" group there was little recognition of differences in performance or effort to enhance the comprehension of those who didn't succeed.

Principal's Role

The principal in this school can best be characterized as a part-time administrator and part-time disciplinarian. Because he served as the principal of two schools, he was in this building only on alternating mornings and afternoons. He could not be characterized as an educational or instructional leader. Perhaps because of his dual responsibilities as principal, there was little interaction between him and the teaching staff.

The principal reported to the observer that his main responsibilities lay in the administration of the school and handling "problem" kids. He reported that he kept a file on all those children, mostly boys, who were behavior problems. He maintained contact with them and their parents throughout the year with the purpose of reducing or eliminating "acting out" behavior in the classrooms. He reported that he had been successful in this regard.

The principal was only observed in an educational leader-type activity once during the observation period. This occurred during a teachers' meeting which was called for the purpose of selecting a new series of reading books for the next school year. During this meeting it became clear that the principal was not likely to serve as an impetus for change in the area of increasing achievement. Several times during the meeting he stressed the "fact" that their students were not "Birmingham kids" (Birmingham and Grosse Pointe are wealthy communities with presumably high achieving students) and therefore shouldn't be expected to read the same books as those students. In fact, one reading series was rejected because Birmingham and Grosse Pointe school districts used that series.

The principal made clear to the teachers and the observer that the students, because of their social class background, could not be expected to achieve at high levels. In response to a question put to him by the observer, the principal expressed the belief that expecting the students to learn even 80 percent of that learned by "rich" kids was being unrealistic.

His low expectations for student achievement were further confirmed in a conversation with the observer regarding career education. He noted that career education was long overdue in schools of the type he served because stressing college education in these schools was totally inappropriate. He expressed his intention of bringing in people to speak to the students about their various occupations. For the girls, he expressed the intent to bring in beauticians, stewardesses, and secretaries; for the boys, plumbers, policemen, and sanitation workers. He stressed the dignity of all honest work and added that these occupations were in line with the students' background and abilities. His perception of the students clearly defined them as unable, unwilling, and uninterested in becoming professionals.

The principal did not seem to have much interaction with either the teachers or the students. He did not "visit" classrooms or spend much time in the halls or on the playground. The teachers seemed to identify the principal as part of administration along with the school board, the superintendent, and the State Department of Education. There was no indication that teachers sought out the principal for help on any problems other than disciplinary ones and there was no indication that the principal offered unsolicited advice. In fact, there seemed to be a good deal of tension between the principal and the teachers.

In sum, the principal in this school did not seem to serve as a catalyst for improving student achievement. He indicated that this school's scores on achievement tests were in line with other schools in the district and therefore were not cause for concern. He repeatedly stressed that his students came from family backgrounds which severely limited their chances for doing well academically. Finally, he perceived himself as an administrator, not an educational leader. The teaching of the students and their academic achievement did not seem to be primary concerns for this principal.

CASE STUDY, BLACK B

School-Community Characteristics
The Black B school is a low achieving, low SES black school. It is located in

an all black lower class community, within a relatively large city. The community has been predominantly black for a number of years and has become all-black over the past few years. The major source of employment in the community is the automobile industry.

For the most part, the homes are fairly well kept but in need of some repair. The school itself consists of three combined structures. The initial structure is old but is in good repair. A wing was added in the mid-1960's to provide additional classroom space and administrative offices; a new gymnasium was added later. The school playground facilities are very adequate.

The Black B school is in actuality two schools housed in the same building—a traditional school whose student body is all black and an experimental open school with a student body population approximately 50 percent black and 50 percent white. Only the traditional school was observed.

During the observation, the teaching staff at this school consisted of 20 teachers, nine white and eleven black. The administrative staff consisted of the principal, a black female; the community director, a black male; the assistant principal, a white male; the home school counselor, a black female; and a school social worker, a black female. The staff also contained four teacher aides, all of whom were black females. The educational staff at this school appeared to be well mixed in terms of ages and experience. There did not appear to be any significant differences in teacher attitudes or behaviors related to differences in race.

Teachers were required to be at school at 8:00 a.m. Classes began at 8:55. The time in between was set aside for preparation. The teachers did this either in their rooms or in the teachers' lounge. The teachers' lounge was a gathering place for the entire staff, including the principal. Here they prepared lessons, ate lunch, and held staff meetings. When the teachers were in the lounge, there was rarely any conversation regarding either achievement or discipline.

Time Spent on Instruction
The majority of classroom time at this school was allotted for academic activity. In general, however, it did not appear that this time was used economically. The teachers here did not spend a great deal of time engaged in academic interaction with their students. The following description of a morning's observation in a classroom in the Black B school generally reflects the kind of instruction and amount of time spent on instruction at this school. Class began at 8:55. Students entered the room and took out a large sheet of paper and began copying an assignment from the board

without the teacher telling them to do so. The teacher was busy working at the desk for 25 minutes as the students worked. At 9:20 she began giving directions for a class assignment. While the students were working on the assignment, the teacher worked at the desk. A reading group was called to the back of the room at 9:45. They were assigned a story to read to themselves; they read quietly for 15 minutes. The class went to the library at 10:00. The class returned to the room at 10:35 following a lavatory break. They resumed working on their board assignment. At 10:40 another group was called to the back of the room. The teacher interacted with them verbally, identifying shapes and colors. They were given a coloring assignment in their workbooks. They returned to their seats at 10:50 and another group was called back. This group responded to various questions asked by the teacher, and read sentences aloud.

For the most part, the morning appears to have been well planned by the teacher. The students were engaged all morning in academic activity; however, there was relatively little teacher-student interaction. The teacher answered questions that were raised by individual students, but most of the teacher's time was spent at the desk and as long as the students were quiet there was little interaction between the teacher and the students, whether they had finished their assignments or not.

A similar format was observed in several different classrooms, with the primary difference in teacher-student interaction being determined by how noisy the students were. It appeared that while the teachers here attempted to keep their students busy, not a great deal of time was spent on group or individual instruction. In several classrooms, it was noticed that where attempts at keeping students busy failed, the teacher spent a large amount of time attempting to maintain discipline. The time spent attempting to maintain discipline varied considerably among teachers.

Write-Offs

Our observations suggest that the teachers at this school did tend to write off large numbers of their students. Conversations with teachers generally indicated that they did not feel that the majority of their students were capable of high achievement. One teacher pointed out that this attitude should be obvious by the manner in which the teachers utilized the several remedial programs that were established in the school. In the teacher's own words, the remedial programs were nothing more than "dumping grounds" for teachers who did not want to be bothered with certain students, particularly if they presented behavior problems in the classroom. It was certainly obvious that large numbers of students were required to attend the remedial math and reading programs.

For the most part, the teachers indicated that such large numbers of students were required to receive remedial instruction because of their poor academic skills. They attributed these "poor" skills to the background and family environments of their students. One teacher pointed out that there was relatively little that she, as a teacher, could do to overcome the negative effects on achievement that were caused by social class and family environment. Several other teachers with whom we talked agreed that the lower achievement that their students maintained was due primarily to their family backgrounds and that there was relatively little that they could do to overcome the effects of these conditions on achievement. Consequently, they indicated, most of the students from this school would probably never be higher achievers. Such attitudes tended to suggest that, in general, the teachers in this school did in fact "write off" large numbers of their students as academic losses in that they felt there was little hope of overcoming the "social deficiencies" of their students.

Teaching Games
One game was observed in use in only one of the regular classrooms during the three-week observation period. It was a "map" game in which the class was divided into two teams and the members of the team were to correctly determine the name of the state which the teacher was pointing to on the United States map. The team giving the most correct answers won the game. The students appeared to enjoy playing this game and participated with enthusiasm. The enthusiasm with which the students participated, however, was overshadowed by the fact that the teacher had to constantly yell at the students in an attempt to maintain discipline.

A number of teaching games were observed in use in the remdeial math and reading classes. For the most part, these games were designed for use with individual students. Most of the games consisted of some form of number or picture puzzle. Upon correctly completing a puzzle, the student was rewarded by verbal praise and in some instances received a material reward such as a piece of candy. A number of students with whom the observer talked indicated that they enjoyed going to these classes because they liked the games, and they didn't have to do much work there.

Our observations of the Black B school showed that teaching games were not used often in the regular classroom. They were used extensively in the remedial classrooms, but were generally designed for use with individual students rather than groups. The use of these games and other teaching aids, it appears, did not do much to foster high achievement in this school.

Reinforcement Practices

A significant number of the teachers at this school did exhibit what we considered to be inappropriate reinforcement practices. These teachers tended to give verbal praise for performance that was obviously substandard. It should be pointed out that it was probably not the teachers' intention to reward substandard performance but rather to reward increased performance. No matter what the intention was, these teachers were, in effect, telling students that they had done a good job, when in fact, they had not. During an observation period in a first-grade classroom, for instance, the teacher pointed out a student that she described as a slow learner. She indicated that while his tests did not indicate that he was retarded, he was very slow. This youngster was observed at work in a reading group which was reading sentences from a story. When it was this youngster's turn to read, he exhibited a great deal of difficulty struggling through a sentence. When he finished, the teacher told him he had done a good job, without noting any need for improvement. This type of reinforcement was observed being given to students on a number of different occasions and in several different classrooms. In one room for instance, a teacher was observed telling a student that she had not done a good job in her reading of a sentence. The teacher then read the sentence as an indication of how it should be done. While the student's second reading was superior to the first, it still did not approach the example that the teacher had demonstrated. Nevertheless, the teacher told the student that she had done a good job, then moved on to another student.

Confusing reinforcement messages were not evident in all of the classrooms observed. Appropriate reinforcement patterns were consistently observed in the remedial math and reading rooms. Here, confusing reinforcement was only rarely exhibited primarily due to the design of the curriculum in these rooms. The curriculum materials in these rooms incorporated the theory and principles of behavior modification. If a student gave a correct response, he was rewarded; if he gave a wrong response, he was not rewarded.

For example, the remedial math room contained a computer that the students appeared to enjoy using. The computer was programmed for individual instruction. When a student gave a correct response to a problem, he was rewarded with a written message by the computer. When an incorrect response was given, the computer pointed out the error and told the student to try again.

The remedial math teacher indicated that the students really enjoyed working on the computer and that the vast majority of them advanced to the point where they could give 100 percent correct responses. She also pointed out, however, that while students mastered the computer problems, they generally could not do the same problems from the textbooks.

In other words, the increased performance that students showed in their remedial classes did not generalize to their regular classrooms. Why this generalization did not occur is open to speculation; however, the negative attitudes that several teachers expressed regarding the efficacy of the remedial programs coupled with the students' attitudes toward these classes as "fun times" may have some bearing on the situation.

The only other exception to the sending of confusing reinforcement messages that we observed in this school was exhibited in the vocal music room. Here the teacher gave an excellent demonstration of appropriate reinforcement practices. At the time of observation, the students were learning a new song for an upcoming play. The teacher gave the words to the song, then demonstrated how they should be sung. When the students did not sing as she had demonstrated, she reinstructed and had them try again. This was repeated until the students could sing the song exactly as she had demonstrated.

In summary, our observations of the reinforcement practices in this school indicated that they did not facilitate higher achievement. The teachers tended to give verbal praise for substandard academic performance. This behavior seems to reflect the low performance standards that the teachers accepted as being adequate.

Expectations

Conversations with teachers, as well as our observations of their classroom behavior, suggested that the expectations that the teachers held for their students' immediate and future academic performance were low. Teachers were generally reluctant to accept responsibility for the low achievement that their students maintained. They were quick to point out that the vast majority of their students came from poor families, and very frequently, from problem homes. They presented this as the primary cause of the low achievement of their students. This excuse was given almost without exception by the teachers and by the principal.

When asked what percentage of their students were capable of mastering the materials presented in class, the answers varied from one-third to 60 percent. When one teacher indicated that perhaps 50 percent were capable of mastering the curriculum material presented, we asked about the other 50 percent. The teacher replied that they would be lost academically. Another teacher pointed out that most of her students could master the material if they would do their homework, but the problem was that the students would not do what they were told.

In general, the teachers demonstrated that they did not set clear and concrete achievement goals for their students. When asked about achievement goals, they generally replied that they tried to help each student as much as they could.

It was pointed out by the teachers and the principal that because of pressure from the Board of Education a great deal of emphasis was placed on increasing achievement in reading. While the teachers said that this was their immediate goal, the attitudes that were expressed plus the classroom observations suggested that teachers did not expect this goal to be realized. While a great deal of time was spent on reading-related activities in the classrooms, the manner in which this time was spent, the teacher-student interaction (or lack of it), and the academic expectations that teachers expressed indicated to the observers that increased reading achievement probably would not be reflected at the end of the school year.

Grouping Procedures

In the lower grades, K through 3, students were grouped according to classroom performance and teachers' perceptions of their ability. The format was similar in all rooms, with each class generally being divided into three groups: high, middle, and low achievers. The different groups appeared to be very stable, with no built-in methods for advancement. Teachers indicated that if a student was placed in a "slow" group during his early school years, that student would, more likely than not, remain in a slow group for the duration of his elementary years at the Black B school. Students who were considered to be very slow were sent to the remedial math and reading classes at designated times during the day. Thus students were grouped within classrooms and the "slowest" students were brought together in the remedial classes as another identifiable group.

In the upper grades, 4 through 6, the school had adopted what was referred to as the Joplin Plan. Classes were described as nongraded. Students were grouped according to classroom performance and teachers' perception of their ability. For instance, a student who was chronologically a fourth grader but who was performing at the fifth-grade level was grouped with students at the same grade level. At the beginning of each period, students were sent to their respective homerooms where attendance was taken. From there, they were sent up to their respective "non-graded" classrooms which were also divided into three ability groups. Within these classes the slower students were sent to remedial math and reading classes at designated times during the day.

This extensive grouping appeared to be very disruptive and to contribute to the disorder that existed in many of the classrooms.

The manner in which grouping was practiced in this school did not appear to facilitate movement from lower to higher achieving groups but rather seemed to be a tool for classroom management. The number of students receiving remedial instruction in math or reading appeared to be very disproportionately large in relation to the total number of students attending the Black B school. The attitudes held by the teachers regarding the academic effectiveness of the remedial classes were negative, and as we pointed out earlier, the students generally perceived these classes as a place to go to have fun. They were also aware of the stigma attached to those who were required to receive remedial instruction.

Commitment

Our observations of the teachers, their behaviors, and their attitudes suggested that commitment to high achievement was very low. The teachers indicated that they did not expect much from their students academically and reflected this in their classroom behavior.

Perhaps the most salient example of lack of commitment to higher achievement at this school was pointed out by a staff member. He related that a flier had been sent out by another principal in the district asking that teachers in the district meet voluntarily on a regular basis to discuss methods of improving their effectiveness in the classroom. Two teachers from the Black B school had volunteered, but for the most part the teachers indicated that they would not do this unless they were paid. The staff member indicated that the teachers at this school rarely showed any interest in putting in any more time than they had to at the school or with school-related activities.

For the most part, the teachers demonstrated that they felt that there was little that they could do to increase achievement at this school. They did not set high standards for academic performance. In general, they did not spend a great deal of time in the classroom interacting with their students academically. They did not demonstrate much resourcefulness in the classroom, and they did not feel that the majority of their students were capable of high achievement. These factors, and others, lead us to conclude that commitment to higher achievement at the Black B school was low.

Principal's Role

The principal at this school served primarily as an administrator and disciplinarian. She saw to the day-to-day administrative functions of the school and was often called upon by teachers to resolve behavior problems. The principal interacted freely with the teachers. She was in the teachers' lounge frequently and often took part in the conversation that went on there.

The principal considered herself to be first and foremost interested in the education that the students in her school received; however, as was pointed out earlier, the principal indicated that only so much could be expected of the students attending that school given the social conditions from which the vast majority of them came.

The principal was generally perceived by her staff as someone who was nice to work for, and a good administrator. Our observations showed that while the principal consistently reminded the teachers that increased reading achievement was a priority goal for the present school year, these reminders did not appear to have much impact upon the attitudes and behaviors that teachers exhibited with respect to increasing achievement. The lack of "push" that existed between the teachers and their students was also noticeable in the relationship between the principal and her teachers.

While the principal had the ultimate responsibility for critiquing teacher performance, the assistant principal was primarily responsible for administering the academic functions of the school. The assistant principal kept achievement records, monitored students' progress and served as a resource person. While it appeared that the position was designed to monitor and control the quality of education in the school, this was not the observed effect. The assistant principal had a number of ideas as to what ought to be done to increase achievement at this school, but was relatively powerless in terms of his ability to implement these ideas. The teachers seemed to perceive the assistant principal as a peer rather than a supervisor. In general, it appears that there was relatively little pressure brought to bear by the principal and her assistant on teachers to improve their classroom performance.

Our observations in the Black B school lead us to conclude that the academic climate that existed in this school was not conducive to higher achievement. The teachers here generally indicated that they did not feel that their students were capable of higher achievement and this belief, we observed, was reflected in their classroom behavior. Also, there appears to have been little pressure exerted by the administrative staff to modify these attitudes and behaviors.

COMPARATIVE FINDINGS

These case studies were conducted for the purpose of providing some insight into the development and maintenance of school academic climate.

Four schools were selected and paired based on their SES, racial composition, and achievement levels. A research observer spent three weeks to three months in each of the schools obtaining data through classroom observations and formal and informal interviews with the teachers, students, and principals.

The data obtained from these schools indicate that there are many, often interrelated, characteristics of climate associated with school achievement. For discussion purposes, the several characteristics of climate we feel to be the most salient to achievement will be discussed separately. This separation is for ease in reading and should not be construed as suggesting that these factors are unrelated.

We feel that the manner in which climates appear to have been developed and maintained in the schools studied may serve to guide those teachers, administrators, and others who are concerned with improving achievement in elementary schools. This section, then, will compare and contrast those observed differences and similarities among and between the schools studied for the purpose of pointing out those characteristics which appear to encourage or discourage higher achievement.

Time Spent on Instruction

There appear to be substantial differences in the time spent on instruction and the kind of instruction between the higher achieving black and white schools and the lower achieving black and white schools. Teachers in White A, the higher achieving white school, spent almost all available class time on instruction. There were relatively few study periods, though small blocks of time were allocated for doing the classroom assignment. As much time as was necessary to convey new concepts, problems and so forth, was spent for each lesson. However, the teachers did not seem to "overteach" or spend inordinate amounts of time on lessons already grasped by the students. The teachers in White A then, used the instruction time economically, staying with a particular lesson until the students seemed to understand it, then moving on to something new.

The kind of instruction available to the students in the predominantly white higher achieving school appears to have been more conducive to higher achievement than the kind of instruction available to the students in the higher achieving predominantly black school. The amount of time spent on academic activities in these two schools was roughly equivalent, however. Kind of instruction refers most specifically to the extent to which teachers were willing to instruct and reinstruct when necessary to insure that the class as a whole had grasped a concept or understood a lesson. Our observations show that this academic interaction between teachers and students occurred with a greater degree of frequency in the White A school than in the Black A school. On the other hand, they show that academic interaction between teachers and students was more frequent in these two higher achieving white and black schools than in the lower achieving white and black schools.

In most of the classes observed in both the lower achieving black and white schools, the students were given large blocks of time to study, read, and (or) play quietly while the teachers tended to administrative duties such as grading papers. In general, more "study" time was made available to the students than was necessary to complete classroom assignments. Consequently much of the "study" time was used by the students, with teachers' permission, for such non-academic activities as talking, coloring, and playing games.

This over-allocation of study time without academic interaction between students and teachers was only rarely observed in White A and only somewhat more often observed in Black A, the higher achieving black and white schools. These characteristics were more frequently observed in the lower achieving black and white schools, with the highest degree of frequency occurring in White B, the lower achieving predominantly white school.

Commitment

Commitment refers to the verbal and behavioral manifestations of the teachers' acceptance of responsibility for student achievement. The teacher who believes that the students can achieve at a high level, and who assumes responsibility for seeing that they do, is one who is committed to "getting the job done." Verbally, commitment involves a public declaration of the students' ability to achieve at a high level. Once having expressed the belief that the students can learn, committed teachers translate this belief in observable ways to the students in the classroom setting. There were great differences in the degree of commitment exhibited by teachers in the observed schools.

Teachers in the White A school frequently expressed to each other and to the students their belief that the students were capable of high achievement. For the most part, teachers did not place responsibility for low achievement on someone other than themselves. Much time was spent discussing ways of improving achievement in general and "reaching" certain students in particular. Teachers often went to each other for suggestions on how to get a particular student to perform at a higher level. The teachers seemed more than willing to spend their own time meeting with the principal, students, or parents to discuss ways of increasing student achievement. Underlying these behaviors was the firm belief that the job could be done and that it was their responsibility to see that it was done.

The teachers exhibited their commitment to student achievement in a variety of ways in the classroom. For instance, if students did not perform well on the classroom assignment or test, the teachers for the most part did not simply accept the low performance as being "natural" or expected. More often than not, students who did not do well on an assignment were required to do the work over, often with the teacher's help and direction. This kind of reinstruction, we believe, is suggestive of the kind of responsibility for student achievement accepted by the teachers and of the assumptions teachers made about the students' ability to learn the material presented. Many of the behaviors and attitudes of the teachers which have been discussed are evidence of the high degree of commitment these teachers maintain. Innovativeness, the time spent on instruction, and the use of teaching games are several examples of these teachers' commitment to higher student achievement.

Teachers in White B, the lower achieving white school, did not exhibit the level of commitment to higher student achievement found in White A. As has already been noted, commitment is related to other variables such as expectations, and acceptance of responsibility for student achievement. Teachers in White B expressed the belief that their students were not capable of high achievement and consequently did not express commitment to insuring that the students did achieve at a high level.

Most of the teachers were committed to "getting the job done" as were teachers in White A. However, the definitions of the "job" to be done were strikingly different in the two schools. Teachers in White B established relatively low achievement ceilings for their students. The teachers' perceptions that the students were "bound" by their family background resulted in a low acceptance of responsibility for student achievement. Consequently teachers in White B did not spend a large proportion of time on instruction, did not often use reinstruction, and regularly accepted low performance from their students. In sum, the teachers did not exhibit behaviors indicative of a commitment to higher levels of student achievement, most probably because they did not believe high achievement was a real possibility for their students.

In general, the teachers in the higher achieving predominantly black school indicated that they were committed to insuring that their students met the achievement goals that had been set. This commitment was apparent in the attitudes they expressed and the behaviors they exhibited. The amount of time spent on instruction, the positive attitude that they displayed toward their students, the expectations that they held, and so forth, certainly stand in example of this commitment. For the most part, the teachers indicated that they felt a degree of responsibility for the achievement levels that their students maintained. They indicated that the attitudes and behaviors they exhibited toward their students had a significant impact upon student achievement levels.

Many teacher behaviors observed in the classrooms were indicative of their commitment to relatively high student achievement. These behaviors included innovativeness in the classroom, positive teacher-teacher interaction, positive teacher-student interaction, willingness to participate in staff meetings, seminars, and workshops, and willingness to participate in extra-curricular activities with their students.

The primary difference in commitment observed between the higher achieving predominantly black school and the lower achieving predominantly black school rests with the finding that the teachers in the lower achieving school were more willing to blame lower achievement on the family backgrounds of their students than they were to accept responsibility for the impact that their attitudes and behaviors had on achievement. These teachers were inclined to suggest that there was relatively little they could do with regard to increasing achievement, primarily because of the socio-economic backgrounds of the majority of their students. The behaviors of the teachers in this lower achieving school appeared to stem from the attitude that their students simply were not capable of higher achievement. In general, they were less innovative and less inclined to "push" their students. They did not spend as much time in instruction, and they tended to view lower achievement as a natural consequence of the racial and socio-economic composition of the student body.

Our findings indicate that there are substantial differences in the degree of commitment exhibited by the teachers in the four schools observed. We believe the primary source of these differences lies with the teachers' perception of the relationship between social class and (or) race and student achievement. In the lower achieving black and white schools teachers expressed the belief that the students' ability to learn was largely determined by their family background. Teachers in these schools attributed the "blame" for low achievement primarily on the social characteristics of the student bodies. In the higher achieving black and white schools the teachers expressed the belief that students could achieve at high levels in spite of their backgrounds. Further, these teachers, for the most part, accepted the responsibility for seeing to it that their students did perform at higher levels. The behaviors which appeared to be indicative of commitment to higher student achievement such as time spent on instruction, seems to stem from the teachers' belief that higher achievement was a reasonable and attainable goal. Teachers in the higher achieving black and white schools expressed this belief and translated this belief into observable behaviors in the classroom.

Teaching Games

Teachers in the White A school, the higher achieving white school, frequently used teaching games as an instructional tool, particularly for mathemathics. While the games seemed to be used most frequently by the lower-grade teachers, they were used in the upper grades as well. An interesting observation concerning the games was that they were group rather than individually oriented. The common game format was to divide the classroom into two groups based on sex. The consequence of this type of division was that the groups had roughly the same "mix" of students as far as mathematical competencies were concerned. The winner or loser of the game was the team, not any particular individual. Consequently there was substantial encouragement, reinforcement, and "helping" behavior directed from the group to the individual players. These games seemed to be effective in maintaining student interest as well as in aiding the students in their learning of the material. We believe that these games had a very positive impact on the learning environment in the classroom.

In the higher achieving predominantly black school, teaching games were also utilized to facilitate instruction. They were not used as extensively, however, as in the higher achieving predominantly white school. Perhaps the most salient aspect of the use of teaching games in this school has to do with the fact that the games were not used in a remedial sense. That is, the games were not used to help slower students "catch up" with the higher achievers. Usually, when games were played, the entire class participated. One group of students was pitted against another (i.e., boys against girls or randomly selected groups were chosen) and a winner was determined through play. The atmosphere that resulted was one of group cohesiveness with each participant carrying his or her own weight, and receiving the support of his or her respective group. The result was usually enthusiastic participation by all students with the stigma of remedial learning being noticeably absent.

No teaching games were observed in any of the classrooms in the lower achieving white school, but in the lower achieving predominantly black school some teaching games were observed. The differences in the manner in which these games were used as compared to those used in the higher achieving schools were readily apparent. Almost no game playing was observed in the "regular" classrooms. The games that were observed were used in the various remedial programs at this school. It was apparent that the teaching games were almost always used in remedial instruction, and were generally based on the principles of behavior modification. The games were oriented toward individuals rather than groups. A student would receive a token such as a piece of candy for giving a correct answer or proper response. While students did appear to enjoy playing the various teaching games that were observed, it is significant to report the concern voiced by the remedial math teacher. This concern had to do with the fact that while many of the students did well at playing the games, they did not seem to generalize the skills that were supposed to have been acquired to the regular classroom. That is, the student could give correct responses for immediate rewards but could not (or would not) give correct responses in their regular classes.

It is clear from the above discussion that the kind of games used and the purpose of these games varied considerably in the schools observed. Both the higher achieving black and the higher achieving white schools used team games as instructional aides, with games being used most frequently in the white school. In these schools, games were group oriented and were designed to create and maintain enthusiasm for the subject matter. The effect of the games in these two higher achieving schools seemed to be a very positive one. In the lower achieving black school, the games were used primarily as a tool for remedial teaching. The games here were individually, not group, oriented. In this school the games did not seem to have the same kind of positive effect on the classroom learning environment. Finally, in the lower achieving white school, teaching games were not used at all. This seems to fit in with the low degree of student-student and teacher-student academic interaction observed in this school.

Expectations

Students in the White A school were, with only a few exceptions, expected to achieve at or above grade level in every subject. Teachers did not indicate to the students in any observable way that lower achievement levels were satisfactory. Teachers in this school reported that students' family background for the most part had a negative influence on achievement. However, these teachers did not regard the students' background as a determinant of achievement. The attitude of the teachers seemed to be one of cautious optimism as far as student achievement was concerned. They set achievement goals for their students based on levels they felt were appropriate for the student grade—not for his or her social class or family background. Once having set achievement goals for the students, the teachers provided them with the means of obtaining them. The most notable observation in this regard was that teachers set expectation floors, not ceilings, for their students. The floor or minimal level of achievement acceptable to the teacher was almost always grade level. Our observations in the school indicate that teachers and students were largely successful in meeting these expectations.

The teachers in the higher achieving predominantly black school exhibited similar direction with respect to expectations for achievement and to setting achievement goals. The teachers generally reported that they expected a year's academic growth from all of their students. As was previously noted, the majority of these students were from lower socio-economic backgrounds. The teachers appeared to be cognizant of the problems that are associated with such backgrounds and took these problems into account as they worked with them in the classroom. It is significant to note that while teachers demonstrated sensitivity to their students' problems, they did not appear to use these problems as an excuse for not achieving at least one year's academic growth.

Students in the lower achieving white school were, for the most part, not expected to achieve at grade level. Teachers reported that the students could not be expected to achieve at high levels because of family background. Social class seemed to be considered as a determinant of achievement by most of these teachers. Grade level achievement was considered to be the "ceiling" or the most that could be hoped for, given the students' background. There seemed to be no floor or minimal achievement level acceptable to the teachers. Thus, students who were achieving well below grade level were not considered to be "teachers' failures." The achievement goals were bounded by the students' background. Within these bounds, achievement was attributed to individual students' ability and motivation. In general then, the achievement goals for the students were low and teachers did not seem to accept much responsibility for the students' attainment of these goals.

In the lower achieving predominantly black school, the teachers did not voice concrete achievement goals. When asked what their specific achievement goals were, they generally responded that they tried to do as much as they could for each of their students. The teachers here often indicated that the lower achievement that the students exhibited was expected, and due primarily to the socio-economic background of the students. They also attributed the high proportion of students assigned to remedial classes to this factor. The fact that such significant proportions of the students in this school were assigned to remedial programs serves to demonstrate the extent to which teachers had "given up" on many of these students. The feelings that lower achievement was to be expected of these students in the Black B school suggested that the teachers here were not willing to expend additional energy aimed at increasing achievement. We feel that the lower levels of expectations, commitment, teacher-student interaction and innovative teaching methods that were observed in this school were due, in part, to these feelings.

Expectations for student achievement varied considerably among the four schools observed. In the higher achieving black and white schools the teachers expected the students to attain at least a full year's academic growth. The expectations were highest in the higher achieving white school where almost every student was expected to achieve at grade level. Teachers in the lower achieving black and white schools did not expect the majority of their students to achieve at grade level. Teachers in both of these schools indicated that the students' family background made low achievement almost inevitable.

It is important to note that with regard to achievement goals set for the students, the higher achieving black and white schools were "more like" each other than they were like the other schools having the same racial composition.

The difference between the higher and lower achieving schools with respect to expectations seems to stem from the differences in the teachers' perceptions of the effects of race and (or) social class on achievement. In the higher achieving black and white schools the teachers expressed the belief that the negative effects that being "poor" have on achievement could be overcome. Teachers in the lower achieving black and white schools did not seem to share this belief.

Grouping
Grouping in the White A school was restricted to grades 1 through 3 and was for reading only. Teachers in the first grade maintained at least five groups throughout the year. Membership in these groups changed frequently with students moving to more advanced or less advanced groups as seemed warranted by their performance.

The teachers reported that maintaining this many groups served several purposes. First, students could advance from slower to faster groups fairly easily because the differences between groups was small. Secondly, if students fell behind due to absence, problems at home, and so forth, they could make up the "loss" in the lower group and then move ahead again. This type of grouping practice seems to be beneficial to the students. The large number of groups makes it less likely that the students will be labelled as "fast" or "slow." Coupled with the relatively high expectations of the teachers, this grouping procedure insures that a large gap between reading groups will be less likely to develop. Again, grouping even in reading only occurs through the third grade. The assumption made by teachers is that all, or at least nearly all, of the students will be reading at grade level when they finish the third grade. Thereafter, reading is combined with other subjects such as history and science with teachers making the seemingly valid assumption that the students will have acquired the requisite skills for success in these subjects.

The teachers in the higher achieving predominantly black school divided their classes into groups on the basis of student performance on reading and math tests. Reading and math groups were determined primarily by the pre-tests contained in the curriculum materials used. These tests were given to each student at the beginning of the year. Students were assigned their math and reading workbooks based on their performance on the test. Students could advance to a workbook with a higher level of difficulty only after they had mastered the lessons contained in their present workbook. Mastery was determined by the post-test score achieved after completing the book. A student could advance from a lower achieving group to a higher achieving group based upon the number of workbooks completed.

Perhaps the most positive aspect of the grouping procedures practiced at this school was that the groups were not determined solely on the basis of teachers' perceptions of students' academic ability but rather on the basis of measures that were built into the curriculum materials. This type of grouping structure does not inherently lend itself to having students become fixed to a lower achieving group based solely upon the teachers' perceptions of that student's ability.

Grouping procedures in the White B school were of a very different nature than in the other predominantly white school. The students here are sorted into two groups at the first grade level and have entirely different reading programs. Not only were children in the "slow" group reading at a lower level, they were reading from an entirely different set of books. Teachers in each of the first three grades reported that there was limited movement between groups and virtually no upward movement at all. The reading program in this school goes through the sixth grade. Teachers reported that with few exceptions students who were placed in the "slow" group in the first grade were still in the slow group at the sixth-grade level. For the most part, grouping was restricted to reading and reading related subjects. Due to the necessity of having some split sections such as 3/4, and 5/6 in the same room, room assignment was based on reading level for the affected grades. The 3/4 room for instance was comprised of "fast" third-grade and of fourth-grade readers. This method of grouping resulted in a reading "gap" between students which, as reported by the teachers, tended to widen as the students moved to higher grades.

In the lower achieving predominantly black school, a combination of performance testing and teacher judgment of student ability was used in grouping students. A most noticeable characteristic of the grouping procedure used in this school is the extremely large proportion of the students in the upper grades assigned to remedial math and reading programs. The curriculum design used at this school was based on the "non-graded" concept. That is, students attended classes with others who performed at the same grade levels. For instance, a student who was technically a sixth grader but whose test scores indicated that he was performing at the fourth-grade level in math and the fifth-grade level in reading attended math and reading classes with those who were performing at those grade levels. Students were then assigned to high, medium, and low achievement groups in their non-graded classes.

In addition, the lower achieving students in the non-graded classes left the room at designated times in order to attend remedial classes. The intent of these grouping procedures was to meet the individual needs of the students. The mean achievement level of the school and the large proportion of students who were not achieving at grade level suggests, however that such procedures did little to encourage higher achievement. Both teachers and students indicated that once a student had been placed in remedial programs he or she usually remained in such programs for his or her remaining years in the school. This extensive use of grouping coupled with the emphasis on remedial programs, we feel, reflected the lower expectations that teachers in this school held for their students' achievement.

Grouping procedures in the four observed schools varied considerably in design and in intent. The higher achieving black and white schools facilitated movement between groups. In the high achieving white school this was accomplished by having many groups with relatively small differences between them. In the higher achieving black school, group level was determined by the students' mastery of different level math and reading materials. Both of these schools based their grouping on objective student performance.

The lower achieving schools tended to group students according to those who would "make it" and those who could not. Assignment to groups in these schools was primarily based on teachers' perceptions of students' abilities and learning potential. In the lower achieving white school, students were identified as "fast" or "slow" at the first-grade level and for the most part, remained in that group for their duration in the school. Likewise, in the lower achieving black school, students placed in remedial programs tended to remain in those programs throughout their remaining years in the school. In both lower achieving black and white schools the grouping practices appeared to have a debilitating effect on achievement. The gap between "fast" and "slow" students widened with time in spite of the remedial and other compensatory programs in the schools.

Reinforcement Practices

Teachers in the four observed schools used a variety of reinforcement patterns when interacting with their students. We have categorized these patterns into three groups: appropriate, inappropriate, and confused. Appropriate reinforcement patterns are those which positively reward the student for correct answers and desired behavior and negatively reward students for wrong answers or "bad" behavior. The converse, positively rewarding wrong answers or negatively rewarding right answers, constitutes inappropriate reinforcement. Confused reinforcement patterns are those which are ambiguous in their interpretation. For instance, a teacher's response of "Good try" to a student who has given a wrong answer does not reward the effort made without implication that the answer given was acceptable. Consequently, the response is ambiguous. Our comments concerning reinforcement practices are based on these definitions.

In general, teachers in the higher achieving white school used reinforcement practices which appeared to be conducive to the higher achievement of their students. Students received quick and appropriate reinforcement from their teachers most of the time. Students were praised, usually within a short period of time after having successfully performed a particular task. Students were not praised for non-achievement or low levels of achievement. That is, if a student performed a task incorrectly he was informed by the teacher that his performance was not acceptable. Confusing or ambiguous reinforcement was only rarely observed. In general, if a student showed improvement in mastery of a particular assignment but had not yet reached an acceptable level of performance, the teacher tended to respond in a manner which recognized the improvement but at the same time made clear to the student that even greater improvement was expected. Teachers in this school tended to communicate clearly to the students when their behavior and performance met the teachers' expectations. Through reinstruction the students were presented with a reinforcement pattern which first pointed out their errors, then provided them with the means of correcting these errors, and finally gave them praise for successfully completing the task. These kinds of reinforcement patterns, i.e., negative rewards for inappropriate behaviors and positive rewards for appropriate behaviors, were observed in every classroom.

Our observations of the teachers in the higher achieving predominantly black school suggests that for the most part the teachers demonstrated reinforcement practices that were conducive to higher achievement. In general, the teachers did not give confusing reinforcement messages to their students. For instance, rather than telling a student that he or she had "made a good try", and letting it go at that, these teachers were quick to point out where a student had not met the standard that the teacher had set for a given lesson or assignment. As in the higher achieving predominantly white school, students were rewarded for increased performance but when increased performance still fell short of the standards that the teacher had set, the student was informed of this. Such reinforcement practices appeared to provide clear feedback to the students as to whether or not they had successfully completed a given lesson or assignment. Unambiguous reinforcement left no room for a student to assume that he had given an appropriate response when, in fact, he had not. It was further noticed in this school that in general, when a student failed to grasp a problem or an assignment, the teachers would often give immediate reinstruction and have the student try again, rather than moving on to a new problem or to another student. This combination of good reinforcement practices plus immediate reinstruction stood out clearly in our observation of the Black A school.

The reinforcement patterns used by teachers in the lower achieving white school were inconsistent. At times, students were praised for giving wrong answers and "punished" for giving right ones. At other times it was difficult to determine whether a response or behavior was being positively or negatively rewarded by the teacher. For the most part, teachers did not use reinstruction as a means of correcting student errors. Consequently, when negative rewards such as low grades were given for poor performance, they were unaccompanied by the type of feedback which could have produced better performance. On several occasions teachers were observed giving negative rewards for improved performance. The inconsistency of reinforcement patterns and the frequency of inappropriate reinforcement patterns are suggestive with respect to the students' academic performance. In some classes it seemed that a student was as likely to be praised for giving wrong answers as for giving right answers. We believe that the reinforcement patterns exhibited by the teachers were not conducive to increased student achievement.

In general, the reinforcement practices observed in the lower achieving predominantly black school were not considered as good as those demonstrated in the higher achieving predominantly black school. Here, teachers did appear to give confusing reinforcement messages to their students. It was not uncommon to observe a teacher telling a student that he or she had made a "Good try" when, in fact, the student had not mastered a given problem or lesson. Again, it is not our intention to criticize or condemn teachers for attempting to reward students for showing increased effort but rather to point out what appear to be the benefits of making it explicit to the student when he is being rewarded for increased effort and when he is being rewarded for mastery. It was also observed that the teachers in this school did not give immediate reinstruction as often as the teachers in the higher achieving predominantly black school. If a student was struggling with a problem or an assignment, as a rule, the teacher would call on another student. More often than not, the student called upon was one of the "brighter" students in the class.

Behaviors which are rewarded tend to be repeated; those which are not rewarded tend to be extinguished. In the classroom setting, teachers have a variety of means at their disposal either to positively reinforce or to punish student behaviors. Teachers in the four observed schools used different kinds and types of reinforcement patterns which appear to have had an impact upon students' academic behavior.

In the higher achieving black and white schools there was little evidence of either confusing or inappropriate reinforcement messages. That is, teachers in these schools for the most part did not give positive reinforcement messages to their students for inappropriate behavior. The general practice in these schools was for a teacher to make immediate corrections and provide reinstruction to students giving incorrect answers and immediate positive reinforcement to those giving correct answers.

In the lower achieving black and white schools, there is some evidence that students identified as slow learners are positively reinforced for incorrect answers or answers that are only partially correct. Further, there is some evidence that "slow learners" are negatively rewarded when they exceed the teachers' academic expectations. In general, teachers in the lower achieving black and white schools tended to accept poor academic performances as being natural and expected and did not use techniques such as reinstruction to improve students' performance.

In sum, our observations suggest that teachers in the high achieving black and white schools were more likely to use reinforcement practices conducive to higher student achievement than were teachers in the lower achieving black and white schools.

The Principal's Role

The principal in the White A school assumed the role of educational leader as well as that of administrator. His concern for student achievement was reflected in his interaction with students, teachers and other staff. He "dropped in" on classrooms frequently—each class was to be visited approximately 30 times over the school year. The principal here was very innovative in terms of presenting his teachers with "new" programs, interaction techniques, and so on. During the three-month observation period in this school, the principal ran teacher group meetings to discuss books such as *Schools Without Failure* (Glasser 1969), tried to organize teacher effectiveness training and held many meetings with small groups of teachers to discuss their students' achievement. Although he served as disciplinarian when necessary, this did not seem to be a major part of his role. In total, the principal in White A seemed to have a positive effect on the academic climate of the school. His concern for achievement was known to both students and teachers. He not only expressed high expectations for the students' achievement to the observers but to his teachers as well. In addition to holding and expressing high expectations, he exhibited a commitment to insuring that their students could and should be achieving at relatively high levels, but worked closely and shared the responsibility for student achievement with the teachers.

The principal at White B also served as principal at another school in the district. His time at White B was limited to alternating mornings and afternoons. His "role" seemed to consist primarily of handling administrative duties and discipline problems in the school. He did not spend time in the classrooms or in special meetings with the teachers. While he did analyze achievement results and provide them to the teachers, these findings were not discussed with them. He seemed satisfied with student achievement results because they were in line with the achievement levels of other schools in the district. His expectations for student achievement were low, and were communicated to the teaching staff. On several occasions he was observed urging his teachers not to demand more from their students than the students could handle given their family backgrounds and limited ability.

On the whole, the principal in White B seemed to have negative impact on the academic climate in the school. He did not exhibit those characteristics such as commitment to improvement, high expectations, and so on, which we believe to be related to higher student achievement.

The principal of the predominantly black higher achieving school exhibited behaviors and voiced certain attitudes that, we feel may have had direct influence on the academic climate that prevailed in this school. The principal indicated that he was proud of the fact that his teachers for the most part were experienced because he could demand more of experienced teachers in the classroom, particularly in terms of maintaining discipline. While he allowed that less experienced teachers could be innovative in the classroom, he felt that maintaining discipline was a necessary condition for higher achievement. This attitude was made known to the teachers both verbally and through written memos. These messages indicated that teachers were to assume the major responsibility for discipline in the school.

The principal maintained that his job was to see that the day-to-day educational and business functions of the school ran smoothly. He felt that he did this best by assuming responsibility for the business aspects of running the school and delegating responsibility to his teachers regarding the more directly educational aspects of the school, which, he felt, included maintaining discipline. He critiqued his teachers periodically by observing them in the classroom. Teachers were called into his office individually to discuss his observations. He was supportive of teachers regularly attending seminars that were designed to help them improve their effectiveness in the classroom. In general, our observations suggest that the major role of the principal here was that of administrating the day-to-day business functions of the school and delegating the major responsibility for discipline and achievement to his teachers.

Our observations of the role of the principal in the lower achieving predominantly black school lead us to classify this person as primarily an administrator of the day-to-day functions of the school, as well as a disciplinarian. The major responsibility for overseeing academic affairs was assigned to the assistant principal. While the assistant principal appeared to have made a conscious and determined effort to oversee the mechanics of classroom instruction, very little emphasis was placed on the attitudes and expectations that were held by the teachers concerning their students.

In general, disciplinary problems were referred to the principal's office. Dealing with these problems plus administrative duties appeared to consume most of the principal's school day. During our period of observation at this school, it was brought to the attention of the observer by the principal and several teachers that their most immediate goal of the present academic year was to show a significant improvement in achievement. This goal was reiterated at one of the staff meetings attended by the observer. While the statement of this goal was concrete and clear, strategies for improving achievement were not readily apparent. Thus observations suggest that the principal was not actively involved in the development of strategies for improving achievement at this school.

Our observations suggest that the kind of role assumed by the principal varied considerably among the four schools studied. While basic administrative duties were required of and performed by each of the principals, the amount of time devoted to these activities varied considerably. In the higher achieving white school the principal was as, if not more, involved in activities relating to the instructional programs as he was in those relating to administration. Many of the more routine aspects of administration were handled by his secretary, who also filled the function of administrative assistant. This principal maintained frequent communication with the teachers regarding student achievement and spent a good deal of time on in-service training, and development of instructional programs.

The principal in the higher achieving black school spent most of his time in activities relating to administration. While he did seem very interested in the strictly instructional activities going on in the school, he reported that primary responsibility for these activities belonged to the teachers. He was more likely than the principal in White A to evaluate his teachers on their performance but less likely to spend time with the teachers devoted to improving their instructional programs.

The principals of the lower achieving black and white schools, like the principal in the higher achieving predominantly black school, were perceived primarily as administrators of the business aspects of the school, but the principal of the lower achieving black school did demonstrate an interest in improving achievement at this school. She indicated to the teachers and to the observers that increased reading achievement was a priority goal for that present academic year. The lack of emphasis on increased achievement demonstrated in the classrooms, however, indicated that the teachers did not feel pressured to respond to this stated goal. This lack of pressure relative to teacher performance appeared to be the primary difference in the academic roles demonstrated by the principals in the higher and lower achieving predominantly black schools.

The principal of the lower achieving predominantly white school did not indicate at any time that higher achievement could be expected of the students in the school. As such, the principal's role appears to have been characterized as lacking almost any emphasis on increased achievement.

SUMMARY

The initial phase of this research sought to identify factors associated with academic climate which could account for the variance in achievement levels in a random sample of Michigan elementary schools. The guiding hypothesis of this research was that climate variables would account for variance in achievement over and above that accounted for by SES and racial composition. Fourteen climate variables were identified from the survey data. Taken together, these variables significantly accounted for variance in achievement beyond that accounted for by the composition variables, race and socio-economic status.

The case study phase of this research was conducted in order to provide us with a first-hand look at the possible differences in climate that exist between two sets of schools located in similar communities and with similar student bodies, but displaying differences in mean school achievement. More specifically, through the case studies we hoped to develop a profile of at least relatively successful, low SES predominantly black and predominantly white schools. Our observation data, then, were to serve several purposes. First, the observations would serve as a "check" on the survey data. Secondly, school social system characteristics which may impact upon achievement, but were not identified in the survey data could be recognized. Finally, it was hoped that the statistical relationships found in the initial phase of this research could be translated into meaningful behavorial relationships.

In contrasting the observed differences in the factors that appear to have been related to academic climate, our reporting could be misconstrued as suggesting that the higher achieving schools studied were perfect examples of how low SES black and white schools should be, and that the lower achieving schools studied are perfect examples of how schools should not be. This is not the case, however, and in fairness to the teachers who were observed, we must point out that not all teachers in the higher achieving schools appeared to have contributed to the relatively positive factors that existed in these schools, just as not all of the teachers in the lower achieving schools contributed to the negative factors that were observed in these schools. Perhaps the most important finding is, that the majority of the staff members in the higher achieving schools within each pair studied seemed to demonstrate attitudes and behaviors that were conducive to higher achievement, and the majority of the staff members in the lower achieving schools did not.

The presentation and discussion of those factors that appear to have been related to the achievement levels maintained in the schools observed is not intended to suggest that simply incorporating one of these factors will cause an increase in achievement. These factors appear to have been highly interrelated, and shared one common factor—whether or not higher achievement was considered a real and attainable goal. Within the pairs of low SES white and black schools studied, it appears that the harder the respective staff members worked at attaining this goal, the higher the achievement. Thus, the two higher achieving schools studied are not presented as models to which others should conform but rather as evidence that race and (or) SES are not the invariable cause of high and low academic achievement. Those teachers and administrators who are willing to accept the notion that the attitudes they hold, and the behaviors they exhibit, are primary determinants of achievement, and that these attitudes and behaviors can be conducive to high achievement, are likely to produce higher achievement in their schools. Simply put, we believe that the more the teachers and administrators believe that their students, regardless of race and family background, are capable of higher achievement, and the more this belief is translated into real and observable classroom and school behavoir, the higher the resulting mean achievement is likely to be.

Students' academic achievement is not determined by their race, their neighborhood, or their economic status, although such factors may predispose educators to have different levels of expectation. Academic achievement is the end product of a composite of human variables. Perhaps the most important of these variables is the belief, on the part of the teachers, principals, and the students themselves, that they can be academic "successes". Teachers and principals who believe that poor and (or) minority students are capable of high achievement are more likely to assume responsibility for seeing to it that the students do achieve at high levels. Once adverse out-of-school environmental factors are viewed as inhibitors of, not determinants of, higher academic achievement, academic success for poor and minority students becomes an attainable and realistic goal. What the successful schools studied had in common were teachers and principals who believed that their students could achieve at high levels and who accepted the responsibility for seeing that their students' potential for high achievement became a reality.

6

Summary
and
Interpretation

The conclusion of some scholars (Jencks, et al., 1972, and Hauser, Sewell and Alwin, 1976) that schools do not and (or) cannot make a difference in the achievement outcomes has been based on inadequate evidence. The studies of the social context of the school have devoted little or no attention to the nature of the social interaction which occurs within the school social system. The measures of family origins of the students and some other inputs into the social system such as teachers' qualifications, expenditures, and other personnel characteristics have been the primary variables used to examine the impact of schools on achievement outcomes. Since family background and the associated composition of the student body have been the only social input-type variables that contribute significantly to an explanation of differences in achievement between schools or between individuals within schools, many have concluded that nothing about the school social system can affect the learning which occurs in the social unit. This study rejects that conclusion. It was undertaken to examine the possible effects of other social and social-psychological characteristics of the school social system on the student learning outcomes in school.

The general hypothesis that guided this research is that the cultural or

135

social-psychological normative climate and the student status-role definitions which characterized the school social system explain much of the variance in achievement and other behavioral outcomes of the schools. This general guiding hypothesis indicated that the norms, expectations, kinds of evaluations made of students and the definitions of appropriate student role behavior are the crucial characteristics of the school social system that affect the socialization of the students in that social system. The teachers' salaries, their experience and some proxy measures of others' attitudes did not seem adequate as indices of the social-cultural norms, expectations, behavioral definitions which characterize a school social system. We, therefore, sought to identify the social climate and structural characteristics of the school and some of the specific behaviors associated with these characteristics of the social system to investigate the extent to which they explain the differences in outcomes between schools.

Since the social unit in which the student interacts directly is centered in a school building, we have focused our attention on the social system which exists within the school. Unlike most of the studies of the school social context, we have examined elementary school social systems. Although there are variations between classrooms and among different smaller groupings within the school social system that may explain within-school variance in student outcomes, we have examined the school rather than the subordinate units as a relevant unit of student socialization and achievement. This does not obviate the importance of either the classroom or other formal or informal groups as contributors to the learning of students in school. Students, however, move through several classrooms during their elementary school experience and perhaps several significant other social groups. The norms, expectations, and role behavior definitions vary with each of these. But some common characteristics of the school as a social unit may also contribute to the outcomes. It is the common characteristics of the school as a social unit which we examine in this research.

We, of course, recognize that individual background characteristics which may result from family socialization may affect the way in which the school system socializes the students. These individual background characteristics may explain much of the within-school variance in outcomes. Potentially, however, all children, regardless of individual differences, may be affected by the patterns of interaction, norms, expectations, evaluations, and other characteristics of the school social unit.

This research is based on the general theory of socialization. Human beings come to behave in the ways that they perceive others around them expect and define as appropriate for them. Students thus learn to behave in mathematics or reading as well as other areas of human behavior through interaction with others in the social systems of which they are a part. We hypothesize that the social climate, structure and student role definitions which characterize a school social system will affect the cognitive and other behavior acquired in that social system.

THE VARIABLES STUDIED

The variables which we have used to characterize the school social system are described and explained in detail in earlier sections of this report. For convenience we review them briefly. First of all, we have identified the social-economic-status and racial composition of the school student body. The former is measured by the mean rating of the occupations of the fourth- and fifth-grade students' parents; the latter is determined by the percentage of white students in the school student body. Other characteristics of the school student body may be relevant in determining the nature of the school social system. We believe, however, that the mean socio-economic status and racial composition broadly define how the adults and other students see the students and thus how they affect the norms and expectations of the school social system. In addition to the composition of the student body, we have examined a number of other personnel inputs. These include mean teacher salary, teachers' qualifications as measured by experience and advanced education, the number of students in the school, their average daily attendance, the ratio of students to professional personnel, and the average length of teacher tenure in the school. These other personnel inputs have been included because they often have been considered crucial determinants of outcomes. We therefore checked their impact on student outcomes and controlled them as we examined the impact of other social system variables on outcomes.

The second set of variables were designed to characterize some aspects of the school social structure. Two measures described some of the student status-role definitions. One of these measures is the extent to which students are differentiated and grouped for different instructional programs. The other is designed to identify the extent to which students are permitted to move about and vary their locations in the classroom social structure. The latter is identified as the degree of openness in the school organization. Other characteristics of the social structure are the extent to which the parents are known to the teachers and principal and are involved in the school social system; the amount of time, on the average, devoted to instructional activities as reported by the principal; and the teachers' satisfaction with their relationships with other teachers, principal, and students.

The final set of variables which we have used to characterize the social system may be identified as school climate. These are designed to describe the school cultural, or normative social-psychological environment. One subset of these variables is based upon the students' perception of their ability to function successfully in the system, their perception of others' expectations and evaluations of them, and the norms of the school social system. Another subset of climate variables is based upon the teachers' own and their perceptions of others' expectations, evaluations, commitment, and norms of the social system. The third subset of climate variables is based upon the principal's perception of others and his behavior with regard to student expectations, norms, and efforts to improve.

The students, teachers, and the school principal provide information about the nature of the school social climate. The fourteen variables identified from the data provided by these three sets of members of the school social system described the school climate.

The outcome variables which we have examined are the mean level of achievement in mathematics and reading at the fourth-grade level, the mean self-concept of academic ability of the students and the mean self-reliance. The latter two variables are measured by fourth- and fifth-grade students' responses to scales designed to measure these variables. The math and reading achievement are measured by objective referenced tests administered to fourth-grade students by the Michigan State Department of Education.

THE METHODS OF ANALYSIS

The focus of our attention is on the school as a social system, not on the characteristics of the individual students. We sought, therefore, to identify the characteristics of the school social system and not the characteristics of three hundred to a thousand unrelated human beings. Our thesis is that each school has some common norms, expectations, and beliefs about students and definitions of appropriate behavior which affect the behavior of the students.

This study is based upon random samples of public elementary schools in the state of Michigan with fourth- and fifth-grade students. The analyses are based on a random representative state sample of 68 schools and several sub-samples in which the majority racial characteristics and socio-economic characteristics of the student body are controlled.

We have analyzed the relation of the various sets of independent variables—personnel inputs, school social structure, and school climate—to the three dependent variables—mean school achievement in reading and math, mean student self-concept, and mean student self-reliance. These analyses involve simple correlation, multiple regression analysis, and the partitioning of the effects of the three sets of variables identified in the multiple regression analysis.

In addition to the analysis of data obtained from the fourth- and fifth-grade students, their teachers, and principals in random samples of Michigan elementary schools, we have participant observations of four selected low socio-economic schools. Two of these are majority black schools, two are majority white schools, and in each pair one is a relatively high achieving school and the other is a low achieving school.

SCHOOL EFFECTS ON MEAN ACHIEVEMENT

Although not specifically derived from this study, it is important to recognize that the public elementary schools in Michigan vary greatly in the level of achievement in reading and mathematics. The mean percentage of 49 objectives in reading and math mastered in 1974 ranged from 28 to 100. The schools in our random samples varied from 42 percent to 88 percent. The standard deviation in the representative state sample was 9.5 percent. The variances in mean self-concept of academic ability and in mean student self-reliance are significant but decidedly less so than the variance in mean cognitive achievement.

Perhaps the most significant finding of this research is that the combination of the three sets of social system variables—social composition and other personnel inputs, social structure of the school, and the school social climate—explain most of the variance between schools in all three of the dependent variables. More that 85 percent of the between-school variance in mean reading and math achievement in the representative state sample of schools is explained by this combination of social system variables. In the sample of majority black schools, nearly 90 percent of the variance in achievement is explained. Somewhat less of the variance in achievement among the white schools is explained, but 66 percent of the variance in achievement between schools with predominantly white students is explained by the same combination of variables. More than 90 percent of the difference in mean self-concept of academic ability is explained by the same set of variables. The proportion of the variance in mean self-reliance between schools explained by these three sets of variables ranges from 38 percent to 80 percent in the various samples. It is clear from these findings that a major portion of the differences between schools in reading and mathematics achievement and mean student academic self-concept may be explained by the combination of social system variables. The major portion of the explained variance in mathematics and reading achievement can be attributed to either the socio-economic and racial composition of the student body or to the school climate variables. The social composition and other personnel input variables, however, contribute little to the explanation of differences in mean self-concept of academic ability or mean self-reliance. The variance explained in each of the latter outcome variables is largely attributable to the school social climate variables.

It is essential to recognize that the several aspects of the school social system which we have examined do not operate independently. The expectations and evaluations of students, their feelings of futility, and the academic norms of the school are all interrelated in varying degrees with the racial and socio-economic composition of the student body. The adult members of the school social system, who are certainly critically important in creating the characteristic climate of the school, are probably influenced by their perceptions of the student body composition. Racial composition is more highly related to the climate variables, particularly the students' sense of futility, than are the socio-economic characteristics of the student body. Typically, the expectations and evaluations which characterize the school are decidedly lower in schools composed of majority black and Chicano students. Similarly, schools composed of largely poor and lower socio-economic students are typically characterized by lower expectations and evaluations. Most schools that are predominantly black also have a high mean sense of futility. There are, however, significant exceptions. Some low SES and minority schools have favorable school climates. As reflected in the four case studies reported in Chapter 5, both predominantly black and predominantly white low SES schools may have social systems that produce significantly higher achievement than typical schools with such student bodies.

Observations in the four low SES schools also indicated that the patterns of reinforcement and other instructional activities are related to the social system variables of structure and climate as well as to achievement. Schools in which the teachers believe that students are able to learn and in which they expect them to learn seem more likely to commit themselves to the instructional tasks and provide appropriate reinforcement for learning behavior.

Although some social structure variables are related to student body composition and to climate, our analysis indicates that the student status-role definitions identified by the grouping and differentiation variable and the open and closed school variable are less related to student body composition and to the normative school climate variables than the latter are to each other. Although neither of these student-status role variables make a high contribution to the explanation of outcomes, their limited effect is quite independent of both composition and climate.

The original purpose of the research recorded here was to examine the possible contribution of the normative social-psychological characteristics of school social system to the between-school variance in academic achievement. Both the preliminary study (Brookover et al., 1973) and this study demonstrate that the normative social-psychological variables identified as climate in this study explain much of the between-school variance in school achievement. Although the measures of climate are highly correlated with the measures of socio-economic and racial composition of the student bodies which reflect family background of students, it is clear that the proportion of variance explained by climate, .720, is essentially the same as that explained by the combined composition variables, .744, in the representative state-wide sample. When the student body composition variables, SES and racial composition, are in part controlled in the analysis of the three sub-samples, the contribution of the climate variables to achievement is more sharply identified. In the three sub-samples, high SES white, low SES white, and majority black schools, the climate variables explain decidedly more of the between-school variance in achievement when entered into regression analysis first than does the combined input variables including student body composition (see Table 14). Furthermore, in each of these sub-samples, climate variables explain an additional 25 percent or more of the variance in achievement after the effect of both the inputs and structural variables are removed. Also, when the contribution to variance in achievement in the three sub-samples is partitioned, the proportion uniquely attributable to climate variables is clearly greater than that attributable to either input or structure except in the high SES white sample. In the latter, the structural variables explain the same proportion as climate. These analyses clearly indicate that variance in climate does exist within the sub-samples with SES and racial composition controlled and that this climate variance explains significant proportions of the differences in achievement within those sub-samples. Although it is not sufficient proof, these analyses suggest that school climate rather than family background as reflected in student body composition has the more direct impact on achievement.

Observation of low SES black and white schools with differential levels of achievement further reinforces the conclusion that climate variables are significant contributors to the different levels of achievement when race and socio-economic composition are controlled. The differences between high and low achieving schools with similar composition are most observable with regard to the level of expectations and evaluations that the staff makes of the students and their commitment to seeing that reading and mathematics are learned. All of these, of course, rest on the assumption that it is possible for students to learn and that they will learn if provided appropriate instruction. When this assumption is not characteristic of the school, as is frequently true in the lower achieving low SES schools, there is evidence that a large proportion of the students are "written off" as unable to learn. Associated with this assumption and practice is the tendency to provide positive reinforcement for behavior that does not demonstrate achievement in the basic skills. The low expectations and evaluations, the assumption that students can't learn, and the classification of the students as slow or non-learners are all associated with feelings of futility on the part of the students.

The fact that some low SES white and black schools do demonstrate a high level of academic achievement suggests that the socio-economic and racial variables are not directly causal forces in the school social system. We, therefore, conclude that the school social climate and the instructional behaviors associated with it are more direct causal links in the production of achievement behavior in reading and mathematics.

Although the set of social structure variables which we have identified do not consistently contribute highly to the variance in mean school achievement, some summary observations concerning these variables are in order. Except in the majority black school sample, parent involvement does not explain a significant proportion of variance in mean school achievement between schools. In the high SES white school sample the relationship between parent involvement and achievement is actually negative. Although the degree of openness in the classrooms is not highly related to mean school achievement, it is worthy of note that the direction of the relationship is negative in the white school samples and positive in the black school samples. There is little variation in the degree of openness in the latter. The patterns of differentiated student-role definitions as reflected in the differentiated programs variable is not highly related to mean school achievement but the direction of the relationship, like that of open classrooms, is positive in the black school samples and negative in the white school samples. There is a greater range of differentiation in programs among the white schools than among the black schools. The negative relationship in the white schools, particularly in the high SES white school sample, suggests that teachers' and principal's expectations and evaluations of some students in differentiated programs are lower. Students may develop a greater sense of futility in the schools where there is extensive grouping in differentiation in programs.

The personnel inputs other than socio-economic and racial composition of the student body contribute very little to an explanation of the between-school variance in achievement. In fact, these variables contribute essentially nothing after the effect of student body composition has been removed except in the black school sample. In the latter, teachers' salary, teacher experience, percent of teachers with graduate degrees and smaller school size all contribute positively to achievement. These findings confirm earlier indications that staff personnel inputs do explain some of the difference in cognitive outcomes among minority-group schools.

Perhaps the most effective way to summarize the relationship of the social system variables to mean school achievement is to describe briefly the nature of the climate and structure of the high achieving schools in contrast with the low achieving schools. Although the various characteristics may be present in different degrees and combinations in high achieving schools in contrast to low achieving schools, the descriptions of the general social climate and patterns of interaction provide some basis for understanding the social system associated with higher achievement.

Our data indicate that high achieving schools are most likely to be characterized by the students' feeling that they have control, or mastery of their academic work and the school system is not stacked against them. This is expressed in their feelings that what they do may make a difference in their success and that teachers care about their academic performance. Teachers and principals in higher achieving schools express the belief that students can master their academic work, and that they expect them to do so, and they are committed to seeing that their students learn to read, and to do mathematics, and other academic work. These teacher and principal expectations are expressed in such a way that the students perceive that they are expected to learn and the school academic norms are recognized as setting a standard of high achievement. These norms and the teachers' commitment are expressed in the instructional activities which absorb most of the school day. There is little differentiation among students or the instructional programs provided for them. Teachers consistently reward students for their demonstrated achievement in the academic subjects and do not indiscriminately reward students for responding regardless of the correctness of their response.

In contrast, the schools that are achieving at lower levels are characterized by the students' feelings of futility in regard to their academic performance. This futility is expressed in their belief that the system functions in such a way that they cannot achieve, that teachers are not committed to their high achievement, and that other students will make fun of them if they actually try to achieve. These feelings of futility are associated with lower teacher evaluations of their ability and low expectations on the part of teachers and principals. The norms of achievement as perceived by the students and the teachers are low. Since little is expected and teachers and principals believe that students are not likely to learn at a high level, they devote less time to instructional activity, write off a large proportion of students as unable to learn, differentiate extensively among them, and are likely to praise students for poor achievement.

These characteristics of low achieving schools are more frequently found in schools whose student bodies are black or poor, or both. The exceptions to this rule, however, demonstrate that high achievement is possible in schools composed of minority or poor white students. In such schools the climate is much like that of the high achieving schools. Although having a minority or low socio-economic student body may predispose teachers and principals to tolerate low levels of achievement, a favorable academic climate and high achievement can be developed for such students.

SCHOOL EFFECTS ON MEAN
SELF-CONCEPT OF ACADEMIC ABILITY

Much has been written in recent decades concerning the importance of student self-concept. Extensive research has indicated that individual student's self-concept of academic ability is positively associated with individual academic achievement. There is no significant prior evidence indicating the relationship between school mean self-concept of academic ability and school mean achievement. This relationship does not hold when this relationship is clearly affected by the very significant difference between the mean self-concept of students in predominantly black schools as compared with that of students in predominantly white schools. As some previous evidence indicates (Hara, 1972, and Henderson, 1973), the mean self-concept of academic ability of students in predominantly black schools is significantly higher than of students in predominantly white schools. Since students in predominantly black schools generally achieve at lower levels than students in predominantly white schools, there is a significant negative relationship between the school mean self-concept of academic ability and school mean achievement. This relationship does not hold when the socio-economic and racial composition is controlled. There is essentially no correlation between mean self-concept and mean academic ability among the schools in the sub-samples except for a slight negative relationship in the low SES white school sample. The positive relationship between individual self-concept of academic ability and school achievement is, therefore, an in-school phenomenon. One cannot generalize from the individual relationship to a similar relationship between aggregates of students in various schools.

An analysis of the relationship between the three sets of social system variables—input, social structure, and social climate—clearly demonstrates that two climate variables—the students' perception of others' present evaluations and expectations of them, and their perceptions of others' future evaluations and expectations—explain most of the between-school variance in mean self-concept of academic ability. The three sets of social system variables together explain most of the between-school variance in mean self-concept of academic ability in the representative sample and the several sub-samples. The vast majority of this is attributable to the climate variables and particularly to the two student variables concerned with their perception of others' evaluations and expectations of them. Except for the percentage of white students among the schools in the representative state sample, none of the other social system variables contribute significantly to the variance in mean self-concept of academic ability.

One final comment concerning self-concept of academic ability: there have been wide-spread assumptions among behavioral scientists and educators that students' sense, or locus, of control is essentially synonymous with student self-concept. Our data indicate that this is clearly not the case. The variable which we have identified as student sense of futility, which includes a series of items generally identified as measuring sense of control, is not to any extent positively related to mean student self-concept of academic ability. In fact, in the state representative sample, including both black and white schools, there is a significant negative relationship, -.43. This reflects the fact that students in predominantly black schools have high self-concept of academic ability and at the same time low sense of control, or high sense of futility.

SCHOOL EFFECTS ON MEAN STUDENT SELF-RELIANCE

The measure of student self-reliance used in this research is a new one and primarily oriented toward the students' preference for solving problems and doing things alone rather than in groups. All items are oriented toward the school. This measure of self-reliance should probably be identified, therefore, as self-reliance in the classroom situation. Since the instrument has not been previously validated, all the observations concerning self-reliance should be highly tentative.

The mean student self-reliance in these elementary schools is not highly related to the cluster of input variables which we have identified. The student body composition variables contribute only slightly to that variance, and none of the other personnel inputs contribute significantly to the variance in mean self-reliance in any of the samples. The cluster of social structure variables also makes little contribution to the variance in mean student self-reliance. Contrary to popular assumption, the degree of openness in these samples of schools explains little of the variance in mean self-reliance. Only in the black school sample is the relationship between openness and mean self-reliance a positive one. In the high SES white sample schools, the relationship between openness and mean self-reliance is negative and significant to the 5-percent level of probability. This casts considerable doubt on the common conclusion that patterns of open-classroom organization will produce self-reliant student behavior.

The major contributors to the explanation of differences in mean self-reliance are the school climate variables. The students' perception of others' evaluations and expectations of them, particularly for later years, the teachers' evaluations and expectations for further education, and the teachers' current evaluations and expectations for school completion are all consistently and positively associated with mean self-reliance. A much larger proportion of the total variance in mean self-reliance is explained in the low SES white school sample, 83 percent, and the majority black school sample, 75 percent in the combined social system variables, than in the high SES white sample. The major portion of this explained variance is contributed by the school climate variables. The greater amount of explained variance in the low SES white and black school samples suggest that the schools are greater contributors to self-reliant behavior among children in these types of schools. Perhaps children from higher SES white families are more affected by the family social systems and the school has a lesser impact.

A RECONCEPTUALIZATION OF THE SCHOOLS' ROLE IN LEARNING

Schools can make a difference in what students learn. This is the primary conclusion of this study of 91 randomly selected public elementary schools in Michigan. The persistent belief that the socio-economic and racial identity of students' families and the resultant socio-economic and racial composition of the schools explains all the differences in school achievement that can be currently explained has led to the belief that school social environment can make little or no difference in what students learn. This belief associated with one that all children's abilities to learn are widely different and that many do not have the ability or are not yet ready to learn what is taught in school has produced schools that make little difference in what the students learn. Many schools are characterized by the assumption that their low SES and minority group students do not have the ability to learn and it would be inappropriate to demand that they do so. Such schools are characterized by a high sense of futility among the students. Thus they come to believe that whatever they do is of little consequence in determining their success as learners in the academic arena.

The fact that school climate variables identified in this study explain the differences in mathematics and reading achievement as well as schools' student body composition and the major portion of the differences in mean self-concept and mean self-reliance all indicate that such characteristics of the schools can make a difference in student outcomes. The evaluations made of students' ability, the students' role definitions and expectations and the normative climate characterizing the patterns of interaction in the school provide the foundation for a social-psychological conception of school learning which we believe explains much of the differences in outcomes. Briefly, the characteristics of the school social system which we hypothesize will produce high achievement and other desired outcomes may be summarized as follows: First of all, assume that all children can and will learn whatever the school defines as desirable and appropriate. Expect all children to learn these patterns of behavior rather than differentiate among those who are expected and those who are not expected to learn. Have common norms that apply to all children so that all members of the school social system expect a high level of performance by all students. With these evaluations, expectations, and norms characterizing the school social system, the patterns of interaction between teacher and pupil should be characterized by consistently appropriate and clearly recognized reinforcement of learning behavior. Failure should be followed by immediate feedback and reinstruction rather than positive reinforcement. Positive reinforcement should be given only when correct responses are made. This type of school environment is best characterized by what has come to be known as the Mastery Model (Bloom, 1976). Mastery of each unit of instruction by all should be the goal and the total school social system should be mobilized to achieve that goal. Thus students, teachers, and all associated in the school social system should assume that all students can and will learn, should provide appropriate norms and expectations, and practice the appropriate patterns of reinforcement and instruction for all students. This may be facilitated by having students work in teams and compete with other teams rather than as individuals competing with each other.

Evidence from this study and experiments in mastery learning clearly indicate that schools can produce whatever behavior the school social system is designed to produce. It currently produces highly differentiated outcomes for different individuals, including academic failure for many. Unfortunately these differentiated outcomes and failure to read are highly associated with the family background of the student. We believe that the social system of the school explains these differences in outcomes and these failures, and further, that the school social systems currently provided are designed to produce exactly this range of outcomes. If we disregarded the bell-shaped curve which is used to justify the differentiations and failure of student outcomes and substituted the concept of the "J" curve with its assumptions that all can and will learn and develop a mastery model of instruction and reinforcement, the results would conform to the "J" curve distribution. In schools characterized by high evaluations of students, high expectations, high norms of achievement, with the appropriate patterns of reinforcement and instruction, the students will acquire a sense of control over their environment and overcome the feelings of futility which now characterize the students in many schools.

The school social system is no different from the family or other social organizations in that children learn to behave in the ways that the social system defines as appropriate and proper for them. Current evidence that schools do not make a difference results from the fact that research is not identifying the characteristics of the school that determine behavioral outcomes. School climates and organizations that promote and perpetuate non-learning are unlikely to produce high levels of achievement. But schools designed to produce high levels of achievement can function as well as any other social system.

APPENDIX A

Questionnaires

STUDENT QUESTIONNAIRE

School Social Climate Study

a b c

sponsored by
Michigan State University

Dr. Wilbur Brookover, Project Director

DIRECTIONS: We are trying to learn more about students and their work in schools. We would, therefore, like for you to respond to the following questions. This is not a test of any sort and will not affect your work in school. Your teacher and your principal *will not* see your answers. There are no right or wrong answers; we simply want you to tell us your answer to each question.

1. Name _____

PLEASE ANSWER THE FOLLOWING QUESTIONS BY CIRCLING THE NUMBER ON THE RIGHT OF YOUR BEST ANSWER TO THE QUESTION. PICK ONLY ONE ANSWER FOR EACH QUESTION!!!

2. How old were you on your last birthday?

9 years old — 1.
10 years old — 2.
11 years old — 3.
12 years old — 4.
13 years old — 5.

3. Are you a boy or girl?

boy — 1.
girl — 2.

4. What grade are you in?

3rd grade — 1.
4th grade — 2.
5th grade — 3.
6th grade — 4.
7th grade — 5.

5. Please write your teacher's name.

_____

6. Please write the name of your school.

_____

7. How many years have you been at this school?

Less than 1 year—1.
2 years — 2.
3 years — 3.
4 years — 4.
5 years — 5.
6 years — 6.
7 years or more — 7.

8. What type of work does your father do? (Give a short description of his job.)

_____

_____

_____

_____

THE FOLLOWING QUESTIONS ARE TO BE ANSWERED BY CIRCLING THE NUMBER ON THE RIGHT OF THE CORRECT ANSWER. REMEMBER, NO ONE WILL SEE YOUR ANSWERS EXCEPT THOSE OF US FROM MICHIGAN STATE UNIVERSITY, SO PLEASE TELL US JUST WHAT YOU THINK. (Pick only one answer for each question.)

9. If you could go as far as you wanted in school, how far would you like to go?

Finish grade school — 1.
Go to high school for a while — 2.
Finish high school — 3.

Go to college for a while — 4.

Finish college — 5.

10. Sometimes what you *want* to happen is not what you *think* will happen. How far do you *think* you will go in school?

Finish grade school — 1.

Go to high school for a while — 2.

Finish high school — 3.

Go to college for a while — 4.

Finish college — 5.

11. How many students in this school try hard to get a good grade on their weekly tests?

Almost all of the students — 1.

Most of the students — 2.

Half of the students — 3.

Some of the students — 4.

Almost none of the students — 5.

12. How many students in this school will work hard to get a better grade on the weekly tests than their friends do?

Almost all of the students — 1.

Most of the students — 2.

Half of the students — 3.

Some of the students — 4.

Almost none of the students — 5.

13. How many students in this school don't care if they get bad grades?

Almost all of the students — 1.

Most of the students — 2.

Half of the students — 3.

Some of the students — 4.

Almost none of the students — 5.

14. How many students in this school do more studying for weekly tests than they have to?

Almost all of the students — 1.

Most of the students — 2.

Half of the students — 3.

Some of the students — 4.

Almost none of the students — 5.

15. If most of the students here could go as far as they wanted in school, how far would they go?

Finish grade school — 1.

Go to high school for a while — 2.

Finish high school — 3.

Go to college for a while — 4.

Finish college — 5.

16. How important is it to you to be a good student?

Very important — 1.

Important — 2.

Somewhat important — 3.

Not very important — 4.

Not important at all — 5.

17. How important do most of the student in this *class* feel it is to do well in school work?

They feel it is very important — 1.

They feel it is important — 2.

They feel it is somewhat important — 3.

They feel it is not very important — 4.

They feel it is not important at all — 5.

18. How important do you think most of the students in this *school* feel it is to do well in school work?

They feel it is very important — 1.

They feel it is important — 2.

They feel it is somewhat important — 3.

They feel it is not very important — 4.

They feel it is not important at all — 5.

19. How many students in this *class* think reading is a fun thing to do and read even when they don't have to?

Almost all of the students — 1.

Most of the students — 2.

About half of the students — 3.

Some of the students — 4.

None of the students — 5.

20. How many students in this *school* make fun of or tease students who get real good grades?

Almost all of the students — 1.

Most of the students — 2.

About half of the students — 3.

Some of the students — 4.

None of the students — 5.

21. How many students don't do as well as they could do in school because they are afraid *other students* won't like them as much?

Almost all of the students — 1.

Most of the students — 2.

About half of the students — 3.

Some of the students — 4.

None of the students — 5.

REMEMBER, PLEASE ANSWER THE FOLLOWING QUESTIONS BY CIRCLING THE NUMBER WHICH BEST ANSWERS THE QUESTION FOR YOU. PICK ONLY ONE ANSWER FOR EACH QUESTION.

22. How many students don't do as well as they could do in school because they are afraid *their friends* won't like them as much?

Almost all of the students — 1.

Most of the students — 2.

About half of the students — 3.

Some of the students — 4.

None of the students — 5.

23. How many students in this school would study hard if their work wasn't graded by the teachers?

Almost all of the students — 1.

Most of the students — 2.

About half of the students — 3.

Some of the students — 4.

None of the students — 5.

24. People like me will not have much of a chance to do what we want to in life.

Strongly agree — 1.

Agree — 2.

Disagree — 3.

Strongly disagree — 4.

25. People like me will never do well in school even though we try hard.

Strongly agree — 1.

Agree — 2.

Disagree — 3.

Strongly disagree — 4.

26. I can do well in school if I work hard.

Strongly agree — 1.

Agree — 2.

Disagree — 3.

Strongly disagree — 4.

27. In this school, students like me don't have any luck.

> Strongly agree — 1.
> Agree — 2.
> Disagree — 3.
> Strongly disagree — 4.

28. You have to be lucky to get good grades in this school.

> Strongly agree — 1.
> Agree — 2.
> Disagree — 3.
> Strongly disagree — 4.

29. Think of your friends. Do you think you can do school work better, the same or poorer than your friends?

> Better than all of them — 1.
> Better than most of them — 2.
> About the same — 3.
> Poorer than most of them — 4.
> Poorer than all of them — 5.

30. Think of the students in your class. Do you think you can do school work better, the same or poorer than the students in your class?

> Better than all of them — 1.
> Better than most of them — 2.
> About the same — 3.
> Poorer than most of them — 4.
> Poorer than all of them — 5.

31. When you finish high school, do you think you will be one of the best students, about the same as most or below most of the students?

> One of the best — 1.
> Better than most of the students — 2.
> Same as most of the students — 3.
> Below most of the students — 4.
> One of the worst — 5.

32. Do you think you could finish college?

> Yes, for sure — 1.
> Yes, probably — 2.
> Maybe — 3.
> No, probably not — 4.
> No, for sure — 5.

33. If you went to college, do you think you would be one of the best students, same as most or below most of the students?

One of the best — 1.
Better than most of the students — 2.
Same as most of the students — 3.
Below most of the students — 4.
One of the worst — 5.

34. If you want to be a doctor or a teacher, you need more than four years of college. Do you think you could do that?

Yes, for sure — 1.
Yes, probably — 2.
Maybe — 3.
No, probably not — 4.
No, for sure — 5.

35. Forget how your teachers mark your work. How good do you think your own work is?

Excellent — 1.
Good — 2.
Same as most of the students — 3.
Below most of the students — 4.
Poor — 5.

36. What kind of grades do you think you really can get if you try?

Mostly A's — 1.
Mostly B's — 2.
Mostly C's — 3.
Mostly D's — 4.
Mostly E's — 5.

37. How far do you think your best friend believes you will go in school?

Finish grade school — 1.
Go to high school for a while — 2.
Finish high school — 3.
Go to college for a while — 4.
Finish college — 5.

38. How far do you think your best friend believes you will go in school?

Finish grade school — 1.
Go to high school for a while — 2.
Finish high school — 3.
Go to college for a while — 4.
Finish college — 5.

NOW WE WOULD LIKE TO ASK SOME QUESTIONS ABOUT THE TEACHERS IN THIS SCHOOL. ANSWER THESE QUESTIONS AS YOU ANSWERED THE OTHER ONES BY CIRCLING THE NUMBER. REMEMBER, **NO** TEACHER WILL SEE YOUR ANSWERS, SO BE AS HONEST AS YOU CAN.

39. Of the teachers that you know in this school, how many tell students to try hard to do better on tests?

Almost all of the teachers — 1.
Most of the teachers — 2.
Half of the teachers — 3.
Some of the teachers — 4.
Almost none of the teachers — 5.

40. How many teachers in this school tell students to try and get better grades than their classmates?

Almost all of the teachers — 1.
Most of the teachers — 2.
Half of the teachers — 3.
Some of the teachers — 4.
Almost none of the teachers — 5.

41. Of the teachers that you know in this school, how many don't care if the students get bad grades?

Almost all of the teachers — 1.
Most of the teachers — 2.
Half of the teachers — 3.
Some of the teachers — 4.
Almost none of the teachers — 5.

42. Of the teachers that you know in this school, how many tell students to do extra work so that they can get better grades?

Almost all of the teachers — 1.
Most of the teachers — 2.
Half of the teachers — 3.
Some of the teachers — 4.
Almost none of the teachers — 5.

43. Of the teachers that you know in this school, how many make the students work too hard?

Almost all of the teachers — 1.
Most of the teachers — 2.
Half of the teachers — 3.

Some of the teachers — 4.

Almost none of the teachers — 5.

44. Of the teachers that you know in this school, how many don't care how hard the student works, as long as he passes?

Almost all of the teachers — 1.

Most of the teachers — 2.

Half of the teachers — 3.

Some of the teachers — 4.

Almost none of the teachers — 5.

45. How far do you think *the teacher you like the best* believes you will go in school?

Finish grade school — 1.

Go to high school for a while — 2.

Finish high school — 3.

Go to college for a while — 4.

Finish college — 5.

46. How good of a student does *the teacher you like the best* expect you to be in school?

One of the best — 1.

Better than most of the students — 2.

Same as most of the students — 3.

Not as good as most of the students — 4.

One of the worst — 5.

47. Think of your teacher. Would your teacher say you can do school work better, the same or poorer than other people your age?

Better than all of them — 1.

Better than most of them — 2.

Same as most of them — 3.

Poorer than most of them — 4.

Poorer than all of them — 5.

48. Would your teacher say that your grades would be with the best, same as most or below most of the students when you graduate from high school?

One of the best — 1.

Better than most of the students — 2.

Same as most of the students — 3.

Below most of the students — 4.

One of the worst — 5.

49. How often do teachers in this school try to help students who do badly on their

school work?

They always try to help — 1.
They usually try to help — 2.
They sometimes try to help — 3.
They seldom try to help — 4.
They never try to help — 5.

50. Compared to students in other schools, how much do students in this school learn?

They learn a lot more in this school — 1.
They learn a little more in this school — 2.
About the same as in other schools — 3.
They learn a little bit less in this school — 4.
They learn a lot less in this school — 5.

51. Compared to students from other schools, how well will most of the students from this school do in high school?

They will be among the best — 1.
They will do better than most — 2.
They will do about the same as most — 3.
They will do poorer than most — 4.
They will be among the worst — 5.

52. How important is it to teachers in this school that their students learn their school work?

It is the most important thing to the teachers — 1.
It is very important to the teachers — 2.
It is somewhat important to the teachers — 3.
It is not very important to the teachers — 4.
It is not important at all to the teachers — 5.

53. Think about the teachers you know in this school. Do you think the teachers in this school care more, or less, than teachers in other schools about whether or not their students learn their school work?

Teachers in this school care a lot more — 1.
Teachers in this school care a little more — 2.
There is no difference — 3.
Teachers in this school care a little less — 4.
Teachers in this school care a lot less — 5.

54. Does your teacher think you could finish college?

Yes, for sure — 1.
Yes, probably — 2.
Maybe — 3.

Probably not — 4.

No, for sure — 5.

55. Remember you need more than four years of college to be a teacher or doctor. Does your teacher think you could do that?

Yes, for sure — 1.

Yes, probably — 2.

Maybe — 3.

Probably not — 4.

No, for sure — 5.

NOW WE WOULD LIKE YOU TO ANSWER SOME QUESTIONS ABOUT YOUR PARENTS. ANSWER THEM THE SAME WAY YOU ANSWERED THE OTHER ONES.

56. How far do you think your parents believe you will go in school?

Finish grade school — 1.

Go to high school for a while — 2.

Finish high school — 3.

Go to college for a while — 4.

Finish college — 5.

57. How good of a student do your parents expect you to be in school?

One of the best — 1.

Better than most of the students — 2.

Same as most of the students — 3.

Not as good as most of the students — 4.

One of the worst — 5.

58. Think of your parents. Do your parents say you can do school work better, the same or poorer than your friends?

Better than all of them — 1.

Better than most of them — 2.

Same as most of them — 3.

Poorer than most of them — 4.

Poorer than all of them — 5.

59. Would your parents say that your grades would be with the best, same as most or below most of the students when you finish high school?

One of the best — 1.

Better than most of the students — 2.

Same as most of the students — 3.

Not as good as most of the students — 4.

One of the worst — 5.

60. Do your parents think you could finish college?

Yes, for sure — 1.
Yes, probably — 2.
Maybe — 3.
No, probably not — 4.
No, for sure — 5.

61. Remember, you need more than four years of college to be a teacher or doctor. Do your parents think you could do that?

Yes, for sure — 1.
Yes, probably — 2.
Maybe — 3.
No, probably not — 4.
No, for sure — 5.

READ EACH STATEMENT BELOW. CIRCLE THE NUMBER OF THE ANSWER THAT TELLS HOW OFTEN THE STATEMENT IS TRUE FOR YOU.

62. I can talk to other students while I work.

Always — 1.
Often — 2.
Sometimes — 3.
Seldom — 4.
Never — 5.

63. In class, I can move about the room without asking the teacher.

Always — 1.
Often — 2.
Sometimes — 3.
Seldom — 4.
Never — 5.

64. In class, I have the same seat and I must sit next to the same students.

Always — 1.
Often — 2.
Sometimes — 3.
Seldom — 4.
Never — 5.

65. When I am working on a lesson, the other students in my class are working on the same lesson.

Always — 1.
Often — 2.

Sometimes — 3.
Seldom — 4.
Never — 5.

66. In most of my classes, the teacher tells me what I must work on; I have no choice.

Always — 1.
Often — 2.
Sometimes — 3.
Seldom — 4.
Never — 5.

67. In class, the teacher stands in front of the room and works with the class as a whole.

Always — 1.
Often — 2.
Sometimes — 3.
Seldom — 4.
Never — 5.

68. If your teacher gave you a hard assignment, would you rather figure out how to do it by yourself or would you want your teacher to tell you how to do it?

I almost always prefer figuring it out for myself — 1.
I usually prefer figuring it out for myself — 2.
Sometimes I prefer figuring it out for myself — 3.
I usually like the teacher to tell me how to do it — 4.
I always like the teacher to tell me how to do it — 5.

69. When your teachers give you difficult assignments, do they usually give you too much help or not enough?

They almost always give too much help — 1.
They usually give too much help — 2.
They give just enough help — 3.
They usually don't give enough help — 4.
They almost never give enough help — 5.

70. Suppose you had some free time and wanted to do something fun but all your friends were busy and couldn't play with you. Do you think you could find something fun to do all by yourself?

Yes, it would be easy — 1.
Yes, if I tried hard — 2.
Maybe — 3.
No, probably not — 4.
No, it is never fun to be alone — 5.

71. Sometimes we are faced with a problem that at first seems to difficult for us to handle. When this happens, how often do you try to solve the problem all be yourself instead of asking someone for help?

Always — 1.

Most of the time — 2.

Sometimes — 3.

Not very often — 4.

Never — 5.

72. Some people enjoy solving problems or making decisions all by themselves, other people don't enjoy it. Do you like to solve problems all by yourself?

I almost always like to — 1.

I usually like to — 2.

I like to sometimes — 3.

I usually don't like to — 4.

I almost never like to — 5.

TEACHER QUESTIONNAIRE

School Social Climate Study
sponsored by
Michigan State University
and
Michigan Department of Education
directed by
Dr. Wilbur B. Brookover, Professor
Urban and Metropolitan studies, Sociology and Education
Michigan State University

(Teacher Questionnaire continued on page 163.)

Directions: The information which you give us on this questionnaire is completely *confidential*. *No one* will see your answers except the members of our research staff. Reports will be made with aggregate data, and no one person will be identified with his or her data. After your questionnaire has been completely coded and punched on IBM cards, your questionnaire will be destroyed. *Complete confidentiality is assured*. It is very important that you be as candid as possible in your answers. Do not respond to any question that you feel is too "personal" or that you for any other reason prefer to leave unanswered.

1. Name _____

2. Please write the name of this school.

   _____

3. Are you male or female (circle the number of the correct answer)?

   female — 1.
   male — 2.

4. What is your race or ethnic group?

   Black — 1.
   Chicano — 2.
   Other Spanish Speaking — 3.
   Native American — 4.
   Oriental Origin — 5.
   White — 6.

5. How long have you taught school (circle the number of the correct answer)?

   This is my first year — 1.
   1 - 4 years — 2.
   5 - 9 years — 3.
   10 years or more — 4.

6. How long have you taught in this school?

   This is my first year — 1.
   1 - 4 years — 2.
   5 - 9 years — 3.
   10 years or more — 4.

7. What grade level(s) are you teaching:

4th grade — 1.
5th grade — 2.
6th grade — 3.
Combination 4th & 5th — 4.
Combination 5th & 6th — 5.
Combination 4th, 5th & 6th — 6.

8. How much formal preparation do you have?

Less than a Bachelor's degree — 1.
Bachelor's degree — 2.
Some graduate work but less than Master's degree — 3.
Masters degree — 4.
More than Master's degree but not Doctorate — 5.
Doctor's degree — 6.

9. How did you feel about your assignment to this school before coming here?

Very happy about the assignment — 1.
Somewhat happy about the assignment — 2.
No feelings one way or the other — 3.
Somewhat unhappy about the assignment — 4.
Very unhappy about the assignment — 5.

10. Which best describes the students in your class(es)?

All children of professional and
white collar workers — 1.
Mostly children of professional and
white collar workers — 2.
Children from a general cross section
of society — 3.
Mostly children of factory and
other blue collar workers — 4.
All children of factory and
other blue collar worders — 5.
Children of rural families — 6.

11. If you had your choice of school settings, which would you select from among the following?

All children of professional and
white collar workers — 1.
Mostly children of professional and
white collar workers — 2.
Children from a general cross section

of society — 3.

Mostly children of factory and
other blue collar workers — 4.

All children of factory and
other blue collar workers — 5.

Children of rural families — 6.

12. What kind of school do you prefer to work in as far as racial composition is concerned?

An all white school — 1.

A mostly white school but with some
non-white students — 2.

A school that has about half white and half
non-white students — 3.

A mostly non-white school but with
some white students — 4.

A school with all non-white students — 5.

I have no preference — 6.

13. In your judgment, what is the general reputation of this school among teachers outside the school?

Among the best — 1.

Better than average — 2.

About average — 3.

Below average — 4.

A poor school — 5.

14. If you had to choose a single one, which of the following sources of information do you think best predicts a pupil's success or failure in higher education?

Teacher recommendations — 1.

Group or individual intelligence
or scholastic aptitude test scores — 2.

Other standardized test scores
(e.g., personality and vocational
inventories, etc.) — 3.

School grades — 4.

Other — 5.

WE WOULD LIKE TO ASK YOU SOME QUESTIONS ABOUT GROUPING PRACTICES AND USE OF STANDARDIZED TESTS IN THIS SCHOOL.

PLEASE FEEL FREE TO WRITE ANY ADDITIONAL COMMENTS AFTER EACH QUESTION.

15. In general, how are students in the same grade level assigned to different classes?

Homogeneous grouping according to ability
in all subjects — 1.
Homogeneous by ability in some subjects — 2
Heterogeneous grouping according to ability — 3.
Random grouping — 4.
No intentional grouping — 5.
Other (indicate) _____ — 6.

16. In general, how do you group the students within your class?

Homogeneous grouping according to ability in all subjects — 1.
Homogeneous by ability in some subjects — 2.
Heterogeneous grouping according to ability — 3.
Random grouping — 4.
No intentional grouping — 5.
Other (indicate)_____ — 6.

17. How important do you think standardized intelligence test scores of your students are?

Very important — 1.
Somewhat important — 2.
Not very important — 3.
Not important at all — 4.
We do not give intelligence tests in this school — 5.

18. How often do you refer to or consider the I.Q. test scores of your students when you plan their work?

Very often — 1.
Often — 2.
Sometimes — 3.
Seldom — 4.
Never — 5.

19. On the average, what level of achievement can be expected of the students in this school?

Much above national norm — 1.
Slightly above national norm — 2.
Approximately at national norm — 3.

Slightly below national norm — 4.
Much below national norm — 5.

20. On the average, what level of achievement can be expected of the students in your class?

Much above national norm — 1.
Slightly above national norm — 2.
Approximately at national norm — 3.
Slightly below national norm — 4.
Much below national norm — 5.

21. What percent of the students in this *school* do *you* expect to complete high school?

90% or more — 1.
70% to 89% — 2
50% to 69% — 3.
30% to 49% — 4.
Less than 30% — 5.

22. What percent of the students in your *class* do *you* expect to complete high school?

90% or more — 1.
70% to 89% — 2.
50% to 69% — 3.
30% to 49% — 4.
Less than 30% — 5.

23. What percent of the students in this *school* do *you* expect to *attend* college?

90% or more — 1.
70% to 89% — 2.
50% to 69% — 3.
30% to 49% — 4.
Less than 30% — 5.

24. What percent of the students in your *class* do *you* expect to *attend* college?

90% or more — 1.
70% to 89% — 2.
50% to 69% — 3.
30% to 49% — 4.
Less than 30% — 5.

25. What percent of the students in this *school* do *you* expect to *complete* college?

90% or more — 1.
70% to 89% — 2.

50% to 69% — 3.
30% to 49% — 4.
Less than 30% — 5.

26. What percent of the students in your *class* do *you* expect to *complete* college?

90% or more — 1.
70% to 89% — 2.
50% to 69% — 3.
30% to 49% — 4.
Less than 30% — 5.

27. How many of the students in this *school* are capable of getting mostly A's and B's?

90% or more — 1.
70% to 89% — 2.
50% to 69% — 3.
30% to 49% — 4.
Less than 30% — 5.

28. How lmany of the students in your *class* are capable of getting mostly A's and B's?

90% or more — 1.
70% to 89% — 2.
50% to 69% — 3.
30% to 49% — 4.
Less than 30% — 5.

29. How would you rate the academic ability of the students in this *school* compared to other schools?

Ability here is much higher — 1.
Ability here is somewhat higher — 2.
Ability here is about the same — 3.
Ability here is somewhat lower — 4.
Ability here is much lower — 5.

30. What percent of the students in this *school* would you say *want* to complete high school?

90% or more — 1.
90% or more — 1.
70% to 89% — 2.
50% to 69% — 3.
30% to 49% — 4.
Less than 30% — 5.

31. What percent of the students in your *class* would you say *want* to complete high school?

90% or more — 1.
70% to 89% — 2.
50% to 69% — 3.
30% to 49% — 4.
Less than 30% — 5.

32. What percent of the students in this *school* would you say *want* to go to college?

90% or more — 1.
70% to 89% — 2.
50% to 69% — 3.
30% to 49% — 4.
Less than 30% — 5.

33. What percent of the students in your *class* would you say *want* to go to college?

90% or more — 1.
70% to 89% — 2.
50% to 69% — 3.
30% to 49% — 4.
Less than 30% — 5.

PLEASE REMEMBER, YOUR ANSWERS TO ALL OF THESE QUESTIONS ARE COMPLETELY **CONFIDENTIAL**. NO ONE BUT OUR RESEARCH STAFF WILL SEE YOUR ANSWERS.

34. How much do you enjoy teaching in this school?

Very much — 1.
Much — 2.
Average — 3.
Little — 4.
Not at all — 5.

35. If someone were to offer you an interesting and secure non-teaching job for $1,000 more a year, how seriously would you consider taking the job?

Very seriously — 1.
Somewhat seriously — 2.
Not very seriously — 3.
Not at all — 4.

36. If someone were to offer you an interesting and secure non-teaching job for $3,000 more a year, how seriously would you consider taking the job?

Very seriously — 1.
Somewhat seriously — 2.
Not very seriously — 3.
Not at all — 4.

37. What percent of the students in this school do you think the principal expects to *complete* high school?

90% or more — 1.
70% to 89% — 2.
50% to 69% — 3.
30% to 49% — 4.
Less than 30% — 5.

38. What percent of the students in this school do you think the principal expects to *attend* college?

90% or more — 1.
70% to 89% — 2.
50% to 69% — 3.
30% to 49% — 4.
Less than 30% — 5.

39. What percent of the students in this school do you think the principal expects to *complete* college?

90% or more — 1.
70% to 89% — 2.
50% to 69% — 3.
30% to 49% — 4.
Less than 30% — 5.

40. How many students in this school do you think the principal believes are capable of getting A's and B's?

90% or more — 1.
70% to 89% — 2.
50% to 69% — 3.
30% to 49% — 4.
Less than 30% — 5.

41. How do you think your principal rates the academic ability of the students in this school, compared to other schools?

Rates it much better — 1.
Rates it somewhat better — 2.
Rates it the same — 3.
Rates it somewhat lower — 4.
Rates it much lower — 5.

42. Completion of *high school* is a realistic goal which you set for what percentage of your students?

> 90% or more — 1.
> 70% to 89% — 2.
> 50% to 69% — 3.
> 30% to 49% — 4.
> Less than 30% — 5.

43. Completion of *college* is a realistic goal which you set for what percentage of your students?

> 90% or more — 1.
> 70% to 89% — 2.
> 50% to 69% — 3.
> 30% to 49% — 4.
> Less than 30% — 5.

44. How often do you stress to your students the necessity of a post high school education for a good job/or a comfortable life?

> Very often — 1.
> Often — 2.
> Sometimes — 3.
> Seldom — 4.
> Never — 5.

45. Do you encourage your students who do not have sufficient economic resources to aspire to go to college?

> Always — 1.
> Usually — 2.
> Sometimes — 3.
> Seldom — 4.
> Never — 5.

46. Do you encourage your students who do not have sufficient academic ability to aspire to go to college?

> Always — 1.
> Usually — 2.
> Sometimes — 3.
> Seldom — 4.
> Never — 5.

47. How many teachers in this school feel that all their students should be taught to read well and master other academic subjects, even though some students may not appear to be interested?

> Almost all of the teachers — 1.

Most of the teachers — 2.
Half of the teachers — 3.
Some of the teachers — 4.
Almost none of the teachers — 5.

48. It would be unfair for teachers in this school to insist on a higher level of achievement from students than they now seem capable of achieving?

Strongly agree — 1.
Agree — 2.
Not sure — 3.
Disagree — 4.
Strongly disagree — 5.

49. If I think a student is not able to do some school work, I son't try to push him very hard?

Strongly agree — 1.
Agree — 2.
Not sure — 3.
Disagree — 4.
Strongly disagree — 5.

50. I am generally very careful not to push students to a level of frustration.

Strongly agree — 1.
Agree — 2.
Not sure — 3.
Disagree — 4.
Strongly disagree — 5.

51. How many teachers encourage students to seek extra school work so that the students can get better grades?

Almost all of the teachers — 1.
Most of the teachers — 2.
About half of the teachers — 3.
Some of the teachers — 4.
Almost none of the teachers — 5.

52. How many students in this *school* try hard to improve on previous work?

Almost all of the students — 1.
Most of the students — 2.
About half of the students — 3.
Some of the students — 4.
Almost none of the students — 5.

53. How many students in your *class* try hard to improve on previous work?

Almost all of the students — 1.
Most of the students — 2.
About half of the students — 3.
Some of the students — 4.
Almost none of the students — 5.

54. How many students in this *school* will try hard to do better school work than their friends do?

Almost all of the students — 1.
Most of the students — 2.
About half of the students — 3.
Some of the students — 4.
Almost none of the students — 5.

55. How many students in your *class* will try hard to do better school work than their classmates do?

Almost all of the students — 1.
Most of the students — 2.
About half of the students — 3.
Some of the students — 4.
Almost none of the students — 5.

56. How many students in your *school* will try hard to do better school work than their classmates do?

Almost all of the students — 1.
Most of the students — 2.
About half of the students — 3.
Some of the students — 4.
Almost none of the students — 5.

57. How many students in your *class* are content to do less than they should?

Almost all of the students — 1.
Most of the students — 2.
About half of the students — 3.
Some of the students — 4.
Almost none of the students — 5.

58. How many students in this *school* will seek extra work so that they can get better grades?

Almost all of the students — 1.
Most of the students — 2.
About half of the students — 3.
Some of the students — 4.
Almost none of the students — 5.

59. How many students in your *class* will seek extra work so that they can get better grades?

>Almost all of the students — 1.
>Most of the students — 2.
>About half of the students — 3.
>Some of the students — 4.
>Almost none of the students — 5.

60. The parents of students in this school regard this school primarily as a "baby-sitting" agency:

>Strongly agree — 1.
>Agree — 2.
>Not sure — 3.
>Disagree — 4.
>Strongly disagree — 5.

61. The parents of students in this school are deeply concerned that their children receive a top quality education.

>Strongly agree — 1.
>Agree — 2.
>Not sure — 3.
>Disagree — 4.
>Strongly disagree — 5.

62. How many of the parents of students in this school expect their children to complete high school?

>Almost all of the parents — 1.
>Most of the parents — 2.
>About half of the parents — 3.
>Some of the parents — 4.
>Almost none of the parents — 5.

63. How many of the parents of students in this school expect their children to complete college?

>Almost all of the parents — 1.
>Most of the parents — 2.
>About half of the parents — 3.
>Some of the parents — 4.
>Almost none of the parents — 5.

64. How many of the parents of students in this school don't care if their children obtain low grades?

>Almost all of the parents — 1.
>Most of the parents — 2.

About half of the parents — 3.

Some of the parents — 4.

Almost none of the parents — 5.

65. How many of the parents of students in this school want feedback from the principal and teachers on how their children are doing in school?

Almost all of the parents — 1.

Most of the parents — 2.

About half of the parents — 3.

Some of the parents — 4.

Almost none of the parents — 5.

66. For each of the following aspects of your job, please indicate in the first column how important it is for your job satisfaction and in the second column, how well satisfied you are with that aspect of your job.

	I Degree of Importance for Your Job Satisfaction	II Present Level of Satisfaction with Job
A. Salary:	Very important — 1. Important — 2. Somewhat important — 3. Unimportant — 4. Very unimportant — 5.	Very satisfied — 1. Satisfied — 2. Somewhat satisfied — 3. Dissatisfied — 4. Very dissatisfied — 5.
B. Level of student achievement:	Very important — 1. Important — 2. Somewhat important — 3. Unimportant — 4. Very unimportant — 5.	Very satisfied — 1. Satisfied — 2. Somewhat satisfied — 3. Dissatisfied — 4. Very dissatisfied — 5.
C. Parent/teacher relationships:	Very important — 1. Important — 2. Somewhat important — 3. Unimportant — 4. Very unimportant — 5.	Very satisfied — 1. Satisfied — 2. Somewhat satisfied — 3. Dissatisfied — 4. Very dissatisfied —5.
D. Teacher/teacher relationships:	Very important — 1. Important — 2. Somewhat important — 3. Unimportant — 4. Very unimportant — 5.	Very satisfied — 1. Satisfied — 2. Somewhat satisfied — 3. Dissatisfied — 4. Very dissatisfied — 5.

E. Teacher/pupil
relationships:

Very important — 1.   Very satisfied — 1.
Important — 2.   Satisfied — 2.
Somewhat important — 3.Somewhat satisfied — 3.
Unimportant — 4.   Dissatisfied — 4.
Very unimportant — 5.   Very dissatisfied — 5.

F. Teacher/adminis-
tration
relationships:

Very important — 1.   Very satisfied — 1.
Important — 2.   Satisfied — 2.
Somewhat important — 3.Somewhat satisfied — 3.
Unimportant — 4.   Dissatisfied — 4.
Very unimportant — 5.   Very dissatisfied — 5.

G. The curricula in
your school:

Very important — 1.   Very satisfied — 1.
Important — 2.   Satisfied — 2.
Somewhat important — 3.Somewhat satisfied — 3.
Unimportant — 4.   Dissatisfied — 4.
Very unimportant — 5.   Very dissatisfied — 5.

H. Teacher autonomy:

Very important — 1.   Very satisfied — 1.
Important — 2.   Satisfied — 2.
Somewhat important — 3.Somewhat satisfied — 3.
Unimportant — 4.   Dissatisfied — 4.
Very unimportant — 5.   Very dissatisfied — 5.

I. Teacher authority
over students:

Very important — 1.   Very satisfied — 1.
Important — 2.   Satisfied — 2.
Somewhat important — 3.Somewhat satisfied — 3.
Unimportant — 4.   Dissatisfied — 4.
Very unimportant — 5.   Very dissatisfied — 5.

J. Teacher evlaluation
procedures in your
school:

Very important — 1.   Very satisfied — 1.
Important — 2.   Satisfied — 2.
Somewhat important — 3.Somewhat satisfied — 3.
Unimportant — 4.   Dissatisfied — 4.
Very unimportant — 5.   Very dissatisfied — 5.

K. Recognition for
teacher
achievement

Very important — 1.   Very satisfied — 1.
Important — 2.   Satisfied — 2.
Somewhat important — 3.Somewhat satisfied — 3.
Unimportant — 4.   Dissatisfied — 4.
Very unimportant — 5.   Very dissatisfied — 5.

L. Participation in
making decisions
within the

Very important — 1.   Very satisfied — 1.
Important — 2.   Satisfied — 2.
Somewhat important — 3.Somewhat satisfied — 3.

building: Unimportant — 4.   Dissatisfied — 4.
                     Very unimportant — 5.   Very dissatisfied — 5.

67. Administrative duties, counseling, handling of discipline problems, etc., are all
    time comsuming activities that teachers must assume in addition to their
    teaching responsibilities. Approximately what percentage of a typical school
    day is spent on each of these activities?

Parent-teacher contracts (notes to parents,
phone calls, conferences)_____%

Conferring with individual students about
academic progress_____%

Conferring with individual students about behavior
or personal and social growth_____%

Classroom or small groups instruction_____%

Establishing and maintaining order
in the classroom_____%

Administrative duties (attendance taking,
record keeping)_____%

Time between lessons (recess, moving children
from one activity to another)_____%

Other _____ _____%

TOTAL 100%

68. What do you consider to be your *primary* responsibility to students in your
    class (circle only one)?

Teaching of academic subjects — 1.
Enhancing social skills and social interaction — 2.
Personal growth and development — 3.
Encouraging educational/occupational aspirations — 4.
Other (please specify)_____ — 5.

69. How successful would you say your school has been with regard to student
    development in the following areas?
    A. Teaching of academic skills:

Very successful — 1.
Successful — 2.
Somewhat successful — 3.
Not very successful — 4.
Very unsuccessful — 5.

    B. Enhancing of social skills:

Very successful — 1.
Successful — 2.
Somewhat successful — 3.
Not very successful — 4.
Very unsuccessful — 5.

C. Personal growth and development (self- reliance, etc.)

Very successful — 1.
Successful — 2.
Somewhat successful — 3.
Not very successful — 4.
Very unsuccessful — 5.

D. Educational/ occupational aspirations:

Very successful — 1.
Successful — 2.
Somewhat successful — 3.
Not very successful — 4.
Very unsuccessful — 5.

70. How responsible do you feel for a student's academic achievement?

Very responsible — 1.
Responsible — 2.
Somewhat responsible — 3.
Not very responsible — 4.
Not responsible at all — 5.

71. To what extent do you think that teaching *methods* affect students' achievement?

They have a great deal of effect on
student achievement — 1.
They have substantial effect on student
achievement — 2.
They have some effect on student
achievement — 3.
They do not have much effect on student
achievement — 4.
They have no effect at all — 5.

72. To what extent do you think teachers' attitudes toward their students affect their students' achievement?

They have a great deal of effect on
student achievement — 1.
They have substantial effect on student
achievement — 2.

They have some effect on student
achievement — 3.
They do not have much effect on student
achievement — 4.
They have no effect at all — 5.

73. How do your academic expectations for boys compare with the expectations for girls?

I expect boys to do better — 1.
I expect both to do the same — 2.
I expect girls to do better — 3.

74. What effect do you think each of the following has on students' academic achievement?
    A. Parents:

They have a great deal of effect on
student achievement — 1.
They have substantial effect on student
achievement — 2.
They have some effect on student
achievement — 3.
They do not have much effect on student
achievement — 4.
They have no effect at all — 5.

B. Teachers:

They have a great deal of effect on
student achievement — 1.
They have substantial effect on student
achievement — 2.
They have some effect on student
achievement — 3.
They do not have much effect on student
achievement — 4.
They have no effect at all — 5.

C. Friends or peer group:

They have a great deal of effect on
student achievement — 1.
They have substantial effect on student
achievement — 2.
They have some effect on student
achievement — 3.

They do not have much effect on student
achievement — 4.

They have no effect at all — 5.

D. School Boards:

They have a great deal of effect on
student achievement — 1.

They have substantial effect on student
achievement — 2.

They have some effect on student
achievement — 3.

They do not have much effect on student
achievement — 4.

They have no effect at all — 5.

E. Principal:

They have a great deal of effect on
student achievement — 1.

They have substantial effect on student
achievement — 2.

They have some effect on student
achievement — 3.

They do not have much effect on student
achievement — 4.

They have no effect at all — 5.

F. Student himself:

They have a great deal of effect on
student achievement — 1.

They have substantial effect on student
achievement — 2.

They have some effect on student
achievement — 3.

They do not have much effect on student
achievement — 4.

They have no effect at all — 5.

75. How often does the principal and / or other administrators in this school assist
and give support to the teachers on ways to improve their students' academic
achievement?

Very often — 1.

Often — 2.

Sometimes — 3.

Seldom — 4.

Never — 5.

76. One important criterion for evaluating a teachers' performance should be how well his/her students achieve at a high level.

Strongly agree — 1.

Agree — 2.

Not sure — 3.

Disagree — 4.

Strongly disagree — 5.

77. In this school, there is really very little a teacher can do to insure that all of his/her students achieve at a high level.

Strongly agree — 1.

Agree — 2.

Not sure — 3.

Disagree — 4.

Strongly disagree — 5.

78. When you are trying to improve your instructional program, how easy or difficult is it to get the principals assistance?

Very easy — 1.

Easy — 2.

Varies from time to time — 3.

Difficult — 4.

Very difficult — 5.

79. What is your policy with regard to students talking to each other while they are working on class assignments? Students are:

never encouraged to talk with each other — 1.

seldom encouraged to talk with each other — 2.

sometimes encouraged to talk with each other — 3.

often encouraged to talk with each other — 4.

almost always encouraged to talk with

each other — 5.

80. How do you feel about students walking around in the classroom? Students are:

never allowed to move about the room without

first getting permission — 1.

seldom allowed to move about the room without

first getting permission — 2.

sometimes allowed to move about the room without

first getting permission — 3.

often allowed to move about the room without
first getting permission — 4.
almost always allowed to move about the room without
first getting permission — 5.

81. What kind of seating arrangement do you have in your class(es)?
Students always select their own seats — 1.
Generally students select their own seats — 2.
Some students select their seats;
some are assigned — 3.
Generally teacher assigns seats — 4.
Teacher always assigns seats — 5.

82. In your class(es), how often are students' seats changed?
Several times a day — 1.
Daily — 2.
Periodically during the semester — 3.
They keep the same seats throughout
the semester — 4.

83. How often do you work with your class *as a whole*?
Always — 1.
Often — 2.
Sometimes — 3.
Seldom — 4.
Never — 5.

84. How often are all of your students working on the same lesson?
Always — 1.
Often — 2.
Sometimes — 3.
Seldom — 4.
Never — 5.

85. How would you characterize your teaching objectives?
They are the same for all students — 1.
They are the same for most of the students — 2.
They are the same for some of the students — 3.
They are different for most of the students — 4.
They are different for each student — 5.

86. How important are each of the following in determining teaching ofjectives for
your students?
A. School policy:

Very important — 1.
Important — 2.
Somewhat important — 3.
Not very important — 4.
Very unimportant — 5.

B. Student interest:

Very important — 1.
Important — 2.
Somewhat important — 3.
Not very important — 4.
Very unimportant — 5.

C. Individual student ability:

Very important — 1.
Important — 2.
Somewhat important — 3.
Not very important — 4.
Very unimportant — 5.

D. Your personal preference:

Very important — 1.
Important — 2.
Somewhat important — 3.
Not very important — 4.
Very unimportant — 5.

87. Do you have a teacher aide?

yes — 1.
no — 2.

88. What proportion of your students' parents do you know when you see them?

Nearly all — 1.
About 75% — 2.
About 50% — 3.
About 25% — 4.
Only a few — 5.

PRINCIPAL QUESTIONNAIRE

School Social Climate Study
sponsored by
Michigan State University
and
Michigan Department of Education
directed by
Dr. Wilbur B. Brookover, Professor
Urban and Metropolitan Studies, Sociology and Education
Michigan State University

Directions: The information you give us on this questionnaire is completely *confidential. No one* will see *your* answers except the members of our research staff. Reports will be made with aggregate data, and no one person will be identified with his or her data. After your questionnaire has been completely coded and punched on IBM cards (without your name), your questionnaire will be destroyed. *Complete confidentiality is assured.*

1. Name _____

2. Please write the name of this school.

   _____

3. Sex (circle the number of the correct answer)?

   female — 1.
   male — 2.

4. What is your race or ethnic group?

   Black — 1.
   Chicano — 2.
   Other Spanish Speaking — 3.
   Native American — 4.
   Oriental Origin — 5.
   White — 6.

5. How long have you been the principal of this school?

   Just this year — 1.
   1 to 4 years — 2.
   5 to 9 years — 3.

> 10 to 14 years — 4.
> 15 or more years — 5.

6. How long have you been a principal?

> Just this year — 1.
> 1 to 4 years — 2.
> 5 to 9 years — 3.
> 10 to 14 years — 4.
> 15 or more years — 5.

7. How long did you teach before becoming a principal?

> Never taught — 1.
> 1 to 4 years — 2.
> 5 to 9 years — 3.
> 10 to 14 years — 4.
> 15 years or more — 5.

8. How did you feel about your assignment to this school before you came here?

> Very happy — 1.
> Happy — 2.
> Somewhat happy — 3.
> Quite unhappy — 4.
> Very unhappy — 5.

9. Which best describes the location of your school?

> In a rural area — 1.
> In a residential suburb — 2.
> In an industrial suburb — 3.
> In a small town (5,000 or less) — 4.
> In a city of 5,000 to 50,000 — 5.
> In a residential area of a larger city (over 50,000) — 6.
> In the inner part of a larger city (over 50,000) — 7.

10. Which best describes the pupils served by this school?

> All children of professional and white collar workers — 1.
> Mostly children of professional and white collar workers — 2.
> Children from a general cross section of society — 3.
> Mostly children of factory and other blue collar workers — 4.
> All children of factory and other blue collar workers — 5.
> Children of rural families — 6.

11. How many families of your students are represented at a typical meeting of the PTA or similar parent group?

> We have no parents organization — 1.

Only a few — 2.
Less than half — 3.
About half — 4.
Over half — 5.
Almost all of them — 6.

12. About what is the average daily percentage of attendance in your school?

Over 98% — 1.
97% - 98% — 2.
95% - 96% — 3.
93% - 94% — 4.
91% - 92% — 5.
86% - 90% — 6.
85% or less — 7.

13. What percentage of your students this year are transfers from another school? (Do not count students who had completed the highest grade in this school from which they came.)

0 - 4% — 1.
5% - 9% — 2.
10% - 14% — 3.
15% - 19% — 4.
20% - 24% — 5.
25% or more — 6.

14. What is the lowest grade in your school?

Kindergarten — 1.
1st — 2.
2nd — 3.
3rd — 4.
4th — 5.

15. What is the highest grade in your school?

5th — 1.
6th — 2.
7th — 3.
8th — 4.
9th — 5.

16. What percent of students in your school receive free lunches each day?

None — 1.
9% or less — 2.
10% - 30% —3.
31% - 50% — 4.

51% - 70% — 5.
71% - 90% — 6.
More than 90% — 7.
There is no free lunch program — 8.

17. In your judgment, what is the general reputation of this school among educators?

Among the best — 1.
Better than average — 2.
About average — 3.
Below average — 4.
Inferior — 5.

18. With regard to student achievement, how would you rate this school?

Among the best — 1.
Better than average — 2.
About average — 3.
Below average — 4.
Inferior — 5.

19. With regard to student achievement, how good a school do you think this school *can* be?

Among the best — 1.
Better than average — 2.
About average — 3.
Below average — 4.
Inferior — 5.

20. What do you consider to be the school's primary reponsibility to the students?

Teaching of academic subjects — 1.
Enhancing social skills — 2.
Personal growth and development — 3.
Educational/occupational aspirations — 4.
Other (please specify)_____ — 5.

21. How successful would you say your school has been with regard to student development in the following areas?
    A. Teaching of academic skills:

Very successful — 1.
Successful — 2.
Somewhat successful — 3.
Not very successful — 4.
Very unsuccessful — 5.

B. Enhancing social skills (social interaction, etc.):

Very successful — 1.

Successful — 2.

Somewhat successful — 3.

Not very successful — 4.

Very unsuccessful — 5.

C. Personal growth and development:

Very successful — 1.

Successful — 2.

Somewhat successful — 3.

Not very successful — 4.

Very unsuccessful — 5.

D. Educational/occupational aspirations:

Very successful — 1.

Successful — 2.

Somewhat successful — 3.

Not very successful — 4.

Very unsuccessful — 5.

WE WOULD NOW LIKE TO ASK YOU SOME QUESTIONS ABOUT GROUPING PRACTICES, TEACHER CREDENTIALS AND TESTING PROCEDURES IN YOUR SCHOOL. PLEASE FEEL FREE TO WRITE ANY ADDITIONAL COMMENTS AFTER EACH QUESTION.

22. In general, what grouping procedure is practiced across sections of particular grade levels in this school?

Homogeneous grouping according to ability — 1.

Heterogeneous grouping according to ability — 2.

Random grouping — 3.

No intentional grouping — 4.

23. In general, what grouping procedure is practiced within individual sections of particular grade levels of this school?

Homogeneous grouping according to ability — 1.

Heterogeneous grouping according to ability — 2.

Random grouping — 3.

No intentional grouping — 4.

24. To what extent do the upper elementary teachers, 3 - 6 grades, individualize the instructional programs for their students?

All plan individual programs for most students — 1.

Most teachers have some individualized programs — 2.

Individualization varies from teacher to teacher and time to time — 3.
Most teachers have common instructional programs for their students — 4.
All teachers have common instructional programs for their students — 5.

25. Do you have any non-graded classrooms for children over eight years of age in this school?

Yes, all are non-graded — 1.
Yes, some are non-graded — 2.
No, we haven't any non-graded classrooms — 3.

26. What proportion of the 4th and 5th grade classrooms in your school has teacher aides?

All — 1.
Some — 2.
None — 3.

27. How many teachers in this school have at least a Bachelor's degree?

All — 1.
75% or more — 2.
50% - 74% — 3.
Less than 50% — 4.

28. How many teachers in this school have a provisional teaching certificate?

75% or more — 1.
50% - 74% — 2.
25% - 49% — 3.
Less than 25% — 4.

29. How many teachers in this school have a permanent teaching certificate?

75% or more — 1.
50% - 74% — 2.
25% - 49% — 3.
Less than 25% — 4.

30. How many teachers in this school have a graduate degree?

75% or more — 1.
50% - 74% — 2.
25% - 49% — 3.
Less than 25% — 4.

31. In what grade does your school give intelligence or aptitude tests to the students (circle all that apply)?

1st grade — 1.
2nd grade — 2.
3rd grade — 3.

4th grade — 4.
5th grade — 5.
6th grade — 6.
Do not give I.Q. or aptitude tests — 7.

32. In what grade does your school give standardized achievement tests to students? (Circle all correct answers. Do not include State Assessment.)

1st grade — 1.
2nd grade — 2.
3rd grade — 3.
4th grade — 4.
5th grade — 5.
6th grade — 6.
Do not give standardized tests — 7.

33. How often do teachers in this school refer to, or consider, a student's I.Q. or aptitude score when planning his work?

Always — 1.
Often — 2.
Sometimes — 3.
Seldom — 4.
Never — 5.

34. In this school, how often are students assigned to certain classes on the basis of their I.Q. or aptitude scores?

Always — 1.
Often — 2.
Sometimes — 3.
Seldom — 4.
Never — 5.

35. Which of the following do you think best predicts a pupil's success or failure in higher education?

Teacher recommendations — 1.
Group or individual intelligence or scholastic aptitude test scores — 2.
Other standardized test scores (e.g., personality and vocational inventories, etc.) — 3.
School grades — 4.
Other — 5.

PLEASE ANSWER EACH OF THE FOLLOWING QUESTIONS BY CIRCLING THE NUMBER OF THE CHOICE *WHICH MOST NEARLY ANSWERS THE QUESTION FOR YOU.*

36. On the average, what achievement level can be expected of the students in this school?

Much above national norm — 1.
Slightly above national norm — 2.
Approximately at national norm — 3.
Slightly below national norm — 4.
Much below national norm — 5.

37. What percent of the students in this school do you expect to complete high school?

90% or more — 1.
70% - 89% — 2.
50% - 69% — 3.
30% - 49% — 4.
Less than 30% — 5.

38. What percent of the students in this school do you expect to *attend* college?

90% or more — 1.
70% - 89% — 2.
50% - 69% — 3.
30% - 49% — 4.
Less than 30% — 5.

39. What percent of the students in this school do you expect to *complete* college?

90% or more — 1.
70% - 89% — 2.
50% - 69% — 3.
30% - 49% — 4.
Less than 30% — 5.

40. How many of the students in this school are capable of getting good grades?

90% or more — 1.
70% - 89% — 2.
50% - 69% — 3.
30% - 49% — 4.
Less than 30% — 5.

41. How would you rate the academic ability of the students in this school compared to other schools?

Ability here is much higher — 1.
Ability here is somewha higher — 2.
Ability here is about the same — 3.
Abilits here is somewhat lower — 4.
Ability here is much lower — 5.

42. The parents of students in this school regard this school as primarily a "baby-sitting" agency.

Strongly agree — 1.
Agree — 2.
Unsure — 3,
Disagree — 4.
Strongly disagree — 5.

43. The parents of students in this school are deeply concerned that their children receive a top quality education.

Strongly agree — 1.
Agree — 2.
Unsure — 3,
Disagree — 4.
Strongly disagree — 5.

44. How many of the parents of students in this school expect their children to complete high school?

Almost all of the parents — 1.
Most of the parents — 2.
About half of the parents — 3.
Some of the parents — 4.
Almost none of the parents — 5.

45. How many of the parents of students in this school expect their children to complete college?

Almost all of the parents — 1.
Most of the parents — 2.
About half of the parents — 3.
Some of the parents — 4.
Almost none of the parents — 5.

46. How many of the parents of students in this school don't care if their children obtain low grades?

Almost all of the parents — 1.
Most of the parents — 2.
About half of the parents — 3.
Some of the parents — 4.
Almost none of the parents — 5.

47. How many of the parents of students in this school want feedback from the principal and teachers on how their children are doing in school?

Almost all of the parents — 1.
Most of the parents — 2.

About half of the parents — 3.

Some of the parents — 4.

Almost none of the parents — 5.

48. What proportion of the teachers in this school would prefer to be teaching in another school?

About all — 1.

About 75% — 2.

About half — 3.

About 25% — 4.

Almost none — 5.

49. A typical teacher in this school has *some* contact with:

All of the parents — 1.

Most of the parents — 2.

Some of the parents — 3.

A few of the parents — 4.

None of the parents — 5.

50. How much contact does a typical teacher in this school have with most of the parents?

About once a month or more — 1.

About two times a semester — 2.

About once a semester — 3.

Once a year or less — 4.

51. Approximately what percentage of a typical school day does the average teacher spend on each of these activities?

Parent-teacher contacts (notes to parents, phone calls, conferences) _____%

Conferring with individual students (about academic progress) _____%

Conferring with individual students (about behavior, social growth, responsibility _____%

Administrative duties (attendance taking, noting pupil progress, filling out report cards) _____%

Establishing and maintaining order in the classroom _____%

Classroom and small group instruction _____%

Time between lessons (before and after recess, moving children from one activity to another) _____%

Other (specify)_____ _____%

TOTAL 100%

52. Evaluating teachers' performance is an important and often difficult task for principals. When evaluating a teacher's performance, how much importance

do you place on his/her students' *academic achievement?*

It is very important — 1.
It is quite important — 2.
It is somewhat important — 3.
It is not very important — 4.
It is not important at all — 5.

53. As a principal, how much effect do you think *you* have on students' academic achievement?

Very great effect — 1.
Substantial effect — 2.
Some effect — 3.
Very little effect — 4.
No effect at all — 5.

54. What percentage of the students in this school do you feel are capable of learning to read by the end of second grade?

100% — 1.
90% - 99% — 2.
80% - 89% — 3.
70% - 79% — 4.
50% - 69% — 5.
Less than 50% — 6.

55. What effect do you think each of the following has on students' academic achievement in this school?

A. Parents:

They have a great deal of effect on student achievement — 1.
They have substantial effect on student achievement — 2.
They have some effect on student achievement — 3.
They do not have much effect on student achievement — 4.
They have no effect at all — 5.

B. Teachers:

They have a great deal of effect on student achievement — 1.
They have substantial effect on student achievement — 2.
They have some effect on student achievement — 3.
They do not have much effect on student achievement — 4.
They have no effect at all — 5.

C. Friends or peer group:

They have a great deal of effect on student achievement — 1.
They have substantial effect on student achievement — 2.
They have some effect on student achievement — 3.

They do not have much effect on student achievement — 4.

They have no effect at all — 5.

D. School boards:

They have a great deal of effect on student achievement — 1.

They have substantial effect on student achievement — 2.

They have some effect on student achievement — 3.

They do not have much effect on student achievement — 4.

They have no effect at all — 5.

E. Principal:

They have a great deal of effect on student achievement — 1.

They have substantial effect on student achievement — 2.

They have some effect on student achievement — 3.

They do not have much effect on student achievement — 4.

They have no effect at all — 5.

F. Student himself:

They have a great deal of effect on student achievement — 1.

They have substantial effect on student achievement — 2.

They have some effect on student achievement — 3.

They do not have mu.ch effect on student achievement — 4.

They have no effect at all — 5.

56. How often do you suggest ways of improving student achievement to your teachers?

Very often — 1.

Often — 2.

Sometimes — 3.

Seldom — 4.

Never — 5.

57. How often do you meet with the teachers as a group to discuss ways of improving student achievement?

Very often — 1.

Often — 2.

Sometimes — 3.

Seldom — 4.

Never — 5.

58. To what extent do you think teaching *methods* affect students' academic achievement?

They have a great deal of effect on student achievement — 1.

They have substantial effect on student achievement — 2.

They have some effect on student achievement — 3.

They do not have much effect on student achievement — 4.

They have no effect at all — 5.

59. To what extent do you think that a teacher's *attitude* towards his/her students affects students' academic achievement?

They have a great deal of effect on student achievement — 1.

They have substantial effect on student achievement — 2.

They have some effect on student achievement — 3.

They do not have much effect on student achievement — 4.

They have no effect at all — 5.

60. To what extent do you think the degree to which their students achieve grade level in learning should be considered in evaluating a teachers' competence?

Very much — 1.

Some — 2.

Not much — 3.

Not at all — 4.

61. If the teachers and other staff members in this school were all doing their job well, nearly all of the students would achieve at grade level.

Strongly agree — 1.

Agree — 2.

Not sure — 3.

Disagree — 4.

Strongly Disagree — 5.

62. It is the principal's responsibility to work with the teachers to insure that their students achieve at a high level.

Strongly agree — 1.

Agree — 2.

Not sure — 3.

Disagree — 4.

Strongly Disagree — 5.

63. It is possible for a principal, with the cooperation of the teachers, to change a low achieving school into a high achieving school.

Strongly agree — 1.

Agree — 2.

Not sure — 3.

Disagree — 4.

Strongly Disagree — 5.

64. How would you characterize the achievement objectives in this school?

Same for all students — 1.
Same for most students — 2.
Different for most students — 3.
Different for all students — 4,

65. About what proportion of teachers in this school assign seats to their students?

Almost all of the teachers — 1.
Most of the teachers — 2.
About half of the teachers — 3.
Few of the teachers — 4.
Almost none of the teachers — 5.

66. About what proportion of teachers in this school allow their students to move about the classroom without first asking permission?

Almost all of the teachers — 1.
Most of the teachers — 2.
About half of the teachers — 3.
Few of the teachers — 4.
Almost none of the teachers — 5.

67. What proportion of the classrooms in your school have teacher aides?

All — 1.
Most — 2.
About half — 3.
Less than half — 4.
None — 5.

68. What percentage of your time in a typical week is devoted to each of the following activities?

Long range curriculum planning _____%
Supervision of instructional staff _____%
Supervision of non-instructional staff _____%
Parent and community concerns _____%
Discipline _____%
Other administrative duties _____%
TOTAL 100%

69. What proportion of the students' parents do you know when you see them?

Nearly all — 1.
About 75% — 2.
About 50% — 3.
About 25% — 4.
Only a few — 5.

70. In general, how do your students' parents feel about the achievement of their children?

> Nearly all feel they are doing well — 1.
> Most think students are achieving as well as they should — 2.
> Most think their children are NOT achieving high enough — 3.
> Nearly all think they are NOT achieving high enough — 4.

71. In general, how do you feel about the achievement of the students in this school?

> Nearly all students are achieving as well as they can — 1.
> Most students are achieving as well as they can — 2.
> Less than half the students are achieving as well as they can — 3.
> Only a few of the students are achieving as well as they can — 4.

Items Included in Each Set of Variables Used in Analysis

I. Combined School Input
   A. Social composition of student body
      1. Mean school socio-economic status based on Duncan rating of father's (or other main breadwinner) occupation of fourth and fifth grade students.
      2. Percent white students in the school.
   B. Other inputs into the school
      1. Mean teachers salary in the school.
      2. Number of professional personnel per 1000 students in the school.
      3. Size of the student body.
      4. Mean years of teaching experience of the teachers in the school.
      5. Mean years of teachers' tenure in this particular school.
      6. Average daily attendance in the school.
      7. Percent of teachers with graduate degrees.
II. School Social Structure
   A. Staff satisfaction with social system
      1. Mean difference between preference for white or black schools and the percent white in the school.
      2. Mean teacher satisfaction with student achievement.
      3. Mean teacher satisfaction with parent-teacher relationships.
      4. Mean teacher satisfaction with teacher-teacher relationships.
      5. Mean teacher satisfaction with teacher-administrator relationships.
      6. Mean teacher satisfaction with teacher autonomy.
      7. Principal's report of the percent of teachers that would prefer to teach elsewhere.
   B. Parent involvement in the school social system
      1. Mean teacher report of the percent of parents who want feedback on pupil progress.
      2. Mean teacher report of the percent of parents known by them.
      3. Principal's report of the percent of parents with whom teachers

have contact.

    4. Principal's report of the amount of teacher-parent contact.

C. Grouping and differentiation of student programs

    1. Mean teacher's report of the extent to which their teaching objectives are the same for all or different for each student.

    2. Mean teachers report of the frequency with which the teacher refers to IQ in planning student work.

    3. Mean teacher's report of the importance of student's interests in determining teaching objectives for students.

    4. Principal's report of the extent of homogeneous grouping according to ability.

    5. Principal's belief that students IQ best predicts success or failure in higher education.

    6. Principal's belief that other standardized test results best predict student's success or failure in higher education.

    7. Principal's report of the extent to which the school has the same or different objectives for all students.

D. Staff time allocation to instruction and parent concerns

    1. Principal's report of the percent of the average teacher's time devoted to conferring with individual students about academic progress.

    2. Principal's report of the percent of the average teacher's time devoted to classroom or small group instruction.

    3. Percent of the principal's time devoted to supervision of instruction.

    4. Percent of the principal's time devoted to community and parent concerns.

E. Open or closed characteristics of the classrooms in the school

    1. Mean teacher report of the extent to which students are encouraged to talk to each other while working on assignment.

    2. Mean teacher report of the extent to which students are permitted to move about the room without permission.

    3. Mean teacher's report of extent to which students select own seats or are assigned by the teacher.

    4. Mean teacher's report of the frequency with which students' seats are changed.

    5. Mean teacher's report of the frequency with which the teacher works with the class *as a whole*.

    6. Mean teacher's report of the frequency with which the students are all working on the same lesson.

    7. Principal's report of the proportion of teachers in the school who

assign seats to students.

8. Principal's report of the proportion of teachers who permit students to move about the classroom without permission.

9. Mean student response to "I can talk to other students while I work."

10. Mean student response to "In class I can move about the room without asking the teacher."

11. Mean student response to "In class I have the same seat and I must sit next to the same student.

12. Mean student response to "When I am working on a lesson, the other students in my class are working on the same lesson."

13. Mean student response to "In most of my classes, the teacher tells me what I must work on; I have no choice."

14. Mean student response to "In class the teacher stands in front of the room and works with the class as a whole."

III. School Academic Climate
    A. Student climate variables
        1. Student Sense of Academic Futility. Mean student response to the following questions:
            a. How many students in this school don't care if they get bad grades?
            b. How many students in this school make fun of or tease students who get real good grades?
            c. How many students don't do as well as they could do in school because they are afraid other students won't like them as much?
            d. How many students don't do as well as they could do in school because they are afraid their friends won't like them as much?
            e. People like me will not have much of a chance to do what we want to in life.
            f. People like me will never do well in school even though we try hard.
            g. I can do well in school if I work hard.
            h. In this school, students like me don't have any luck.
            i. You have to be lucky to get good grades in this school.
            j. How many teachers in this school tell students to try and get better grades than their classmates?
            k. Of the teachers that you know in this school, how many don't care if the students get bad grades?
            l. Of the teachers that you know in this school, how many don't care how hard the student works, as long as he passes?

2. Student Future Evaluations and Expectations. Mean student response to following questions:

a. If you could go as far as you wanted in school, how far would you like to go?

b. Sometimes what you *want* to happen is not what you *think* will happen. How far do you *think* you will go in school?

c. If most of the students here could go as far as they wanted in school, how far would they go?

d. How far do you think your best friend believes you will go in school?

e. How far do you think *the teacher you like best* believes you will go in school?

f. Does your teacher think you could finish college?

g. Remember you need more than four years of college to be a teacher or doctor. Does your teacher think you could do that?

h. How far do you think your parents believe you will go in school?

i. Do your parents think you could finish college?

j. Remember you need more than four years of college to be a teacher or doctor. Do your parents think you could do that?

3. Student Preceived Present Evaluations and Expectations. Mean student response to the following questions:

a. How good a student does *the teacher you like the best* expect you to be in school?

b. Think of your teacher. Would your teacher say you can do school work better, the same or poorer than other people your age?

c. Would your teacher say that your grades would be with the best, same as most or below most of the students when you graduate from high school?

d. How good of a student do your parents expect you to be in school?

e. Think of your parents. Do your parents say you can do school work better, the same or poorer than your friends?

f. Would your parents say that your grades would be with the best, same as most or below most of the students when you finish high school?

4. Student Perception of Teacher Push and Teacher Norms. Mean student response to the following questions:

a. Of the teachers that you know in this school, how many tell students to try hard to do better on tests?

b. How often do teachers in this school try to help students who do badly on their school work?

c. How important is it to teachers in this school that their students learn their school work?

d. Think about the teachers you know in this school. Do you think the teachers in this school care more, or less, than teachers in other schools about whether or not their students learn their school work?

5. Student Academic Norms. Mean student response to the following questions:

a. How many students in this school try hard to get a good grade on their weekly tests?

b. How many students in this school will work hard to get a better grade on the weekly tests than their friends do?

c. How important do most of the students in this *class* feel it is to do well in school work?

d. How important do you think most of the students in this *school* feel it is to do well in school work?

e. Compared to students in other schools, how much do students in this school learn?

f. Compared to students from other schools, how well will most of the students from this school do in high school?

B. Teacher climate variables

1. Ability, Evaluations, Expectations and Quality of Education for College. Mean teacher response to the following questions:

a. What percent of the students in this *school* do *you* expect to *attend* college?

b. What percent of students in your *class* do *you* expect to *attend* college?

c. What percent of the students in this *school* do *you* expect to *complete* college?

d. What percent of the students in your *class* do *you* expect to *complete* college?

e. How many of the students in this *school* are capable of getting mostly A's and B's?

f. How many of the students in your *class* are capable of getting A's and B's?

g. How would you rate the academic ability of the students in this *school* compared to other students?

h. What percent of the students in this *school* would you say *want* to go to college?

   i.   What percent of the students in your *class* would you say want to go to college?

   j.   Completion of *college* is a realistic goal which you set for what percentage of your students?

   k.   The parents of students in this school are deeply concerned that their children receive a top quality education.

   l.   How many of the parents of students in this school expect their children to complete college?

2. Present Evaluations and Expectations for High School Completion. Mean teacher response to the following questions:

   a.   On the average, what level of achievement can be expected the students in this school?

   b.   On the average, what level of achievement can be expected of the students in your class?

   c.   What percent of the students in this *school* do *you* expect to complete high school?

   d.   What percent of the students in your *class* do *you* expect to complete high school?

   e.   What percent of the students in this *school* would you say want to complete high school?

   f.   What percent of the students in your *class* would you say want to complete high school?

   g.   Completion of *high school* is a realistic goal which you set for what percentage of your students?

   h.   How often do you stress to your students the necessity of a post high school education for a good job and/or a comfortable life?

   i.   How many of the parents of students in this school expect their children to complete high school?

3. Teacher-Student Commitment to Improve. Mean teacher response to the following questions:

   a.   Do you encourage your students who do not have sufficient economic resources to aspire to go to college?

   b.   Do you encourage your students who do not have sufficient academic ability to aspire to go to college?

   c.   How many teachers in this school feel that all their students should be taught to read well and master other academic subjects, even though some students may not appear to be interested?

   d.   How many teachers encourage students to seek extra work so that the students can get better grades?

e. How many students in this *school* try hard to improve on previous work?

f. How many students in your *class* try hard to improve on previous work?

g. How many students in this *school* will try hard to do better school work than their friends?

h. How many students in your *class* will try hard to do better school work than their classmates do?

i. How many students in this *school* will seek extra work so that they can get better grades?

j. How many students in your *class* will seek extra work so that they can get better grades?

4. Teacher Perception of Principal's Expectations. Mean teacher response to the following questions:

a. What percent of the students in this school do you think the principal expects to complete high school?

b. What percent of the students in this school do you think the principal expects to *attend* college?

c. What percent of the students in this school do you think the principal expects to *complete* college?

d. How many students in this school do you think the principal believes are capable of getting mostly A's and B's?

e. How do you think your principal rates the academic ability of the students in this school, compared to other schools?

5. Teacher Academic Futility. Mean teacher response to the following questions:

a. It would be unfair for teachers in this school to insist on a higher level of achievement from students than they now seem capable of achieving.

b. If I think a student is not able to do some school work, I don't try to push him very hard.

c. I am generally very careful not to push students to a level of frustration.

d. How many students in this *school* are content to do less than they should?

e. How many students in your *class* are content to do less than they should?

f. The parents of students in this school regard this school primarily as a "baby-sitting" agency.

g. How many of the parents of students in this school don't care if their children obtain low grades?

h. In this school, there is really very little a teacher can do to insure that all of his/her students achieve at a high level.

C. Principal climate variables

1. Parent Concern and Expectations for Quality Education. Principal's response to the following questions:

   a. The parents of students in this school regard this school as primarily a "baby-sitting" agency.

   b. The parents of students in this school are deeply concerned that their children receive a top quality education.

   c. How many of the parents of students in this school expect their children to complete high school?

   d. How many of the parents in this school don't care if their children obtain low grades?

   e. How many of the parents of students in this school want feedback from the principal and teachers on how their children are doing in school?

2. Principal's Efforts to Improve. Principal's response to the following questions:

   a. How often do you suggest ways of improving student achievement to your teachers?

   b. How often do you meet with the teachers as a group to discuss ways of improving student achievement?

3. Principal and Parent Evaluation of Present School Quality. Principal's response to the following questions:

   a. In your judgment, what is the general reputation of this school among educators?

   b. With regard to student achievement, how would you rate this school?

   c. In general, how do your students' parents feel about the achievement of their children?

   d. In general, how do you feel about the achievement of the students in this school?

4. Principal's Present Expectations and Evaluations of Students. Principal's response to the following questions:

   a. With regard to student achievement, how good a school do you think this school *can* be?

   b. On the average, what achievement level can be expected of the students in this school?

   c. What percent of the students in this school do you expect to complete high school?

    d. What percent of the students in this school do you expect to *attend* college?

    e. What percent of the students in this school do you expect to *complete* college?

    f. How many of the students in this school are capable of getting good grades?

    g. How would you rate the academic ability of the students in this school compared to other schools?

    h. How many of the parents of students in this school expect their children to complete college?

    i. What percentage of the students in this school do you feel are capable of learning to read by the end of the second grade?

IV. Outcome Variables

    A. Mean School Achievement: The school mean percent of 49 reading and mathematics objectives mastered by the fourth grade students.

    B. Mean Student Self-Concept: The mean student response to self-concept of academic ability scale items as follows:

        1. Think of your friends. Do you think you can do school work better, the same or poorer than your friends?

        2. Think of the students in your class. Do you think you can do school work better, the same or poorer than the students in your class?

        3. When you finish high school, do you think you will be one of the best students, about the same as most or below most of the students?

        4. Do you think you could finish college?

        5. If you went to college, do you think you would be one of the best students, same as most or below most of the students?

        6. If you want to be a doctor or a teacher, you need more than four years of college. Do you think you could do that?

        7. Forget how your teachers mark your work. How good do you think your own work is?

        8. How good of a student do you think you can be in this school?

    C. Mean Student Self-Reliance: The mean student response to the following items:

        1. If your teacher gave you a hard assignment, would you rather figure out how to do it by yourself or would you want your teacher to tell you how to do it?

        2. When your teachers give you difficult assignments, do they usually give you too much help or not enough?

        3. Suppose you had some free time and wanted to do something fun

but all your friends were busy and couldn't play with you. Do you think you could find something fun to do all by yourself?

4. Sometimes we are faced with a problem that at first seems too difficult for us to handle. When this happens, how often do you try to solve the problem all by yourself instead of asking someone for help?

5. Some people enjoy solving problems or making decisions all by themselves, other people don't enjoy it. Do you like to solve problems all by yourself?

APPENDIX C

Simple Correlation Matrices of Variables Analyzed

TABLE 1: Mean school composition, combined inputs, social structure, school social climate, and outcome variables in representative state sample, Michigan Elementary School.

TABLE 2: Mean school input variables, combined social structure, combined social climate and outcome variables in representative state sample on Michigan Elementary Schools.

TABLE 3: Social composition, social structures, climate and outcome variables in random samples of Black and White Elementary Schools in Michigan.

APPENDIX C, TABLE 1*

Correlation Matrix for Mean School Social System and Outcome Variables in Representative Sample of 68 Michigan Elementary Schools.

		Ach74	SCAB	SSLR	SES	%wh	AO1	AO2	AO3	AO4	AO5	AO6
Mean sch. ach74	Ach74											
Mean s-concept acad. abil.	SCAB	-.55										
Mean stud. s-reliance	SSLR	.06	.29									
Mean stud. SES	SES	.68	-.18	.33								
% wh. stud.	%wh	.87	-.70	-.01	.58							
Comb. SES & % wh	AO1	.86	-.49	.18								
Comb. other person. inputs	AO2	.53	-.21	.14			.53					
Teach. satis. w soc. struc.	AO3	.55	-.40	-.06			.62	.41				
Parent involvement	AO4	.45	-.25	.22			.62	.48	.59			
Differentiated stud. prog.	AO5	-.14	.03	.07			.01	-.06	-.06	.07		
Prin. report instr. time	AO6	.45	-.16	.02			.56	.23	.36	.20	-.03	
Open-closed classroom	AO7	.16	-.17	-.13			.29	.09	.33	.30	.20	.22
Comb. social structure	CS	.48	-.31	.04	.59	.63	.69	.37	.72	.71	.39	.57
Stud. sense of fut (Fut=low)	Scl 1	.77	-.43	.16	.79	.76	.87	.43	.48	.51	-.01	.40
Perceived future eval. & exp.	Scl 2	.22	.38	.34	.59	.05	.36	.22	.10	.22	-.11	.32
Perceived present eval. & exp.	Scl 3	-.57	.88	.12	-.31	-.65	-.54	-.18	.29	-.31	-.02	-.19
Percep. of teach. push & norms	Scl 4	-.09	.35	.08	.08	-.10	-.01	.11	-.02	.01	.10	.09
Student academic norms	Scl 5	-.08	.28	.04	.06	-.06	.00	.05	.13	.02	-.08	.03
Teach. eval. & exp. for college	Tcl 1	.23	.21	.27	.50	.12	.35	.09	.31	.42	.09	.17
Teach. eval. & exp. for H.S.	Tcl 2	.66	-.25	.20	.17	.65	.74	.43	.56	.53	-.07	.50
Teach./Stud. commitment	Tcl 3	-.11	.34	.14	-.14	-.25	-.22	.00	.06	.10	-.12	-.33
Teach. percept. of prin. exp.	Tcl 4	.20	.08	.26	.30	.09	.21	.00	.26	.32	.00	.10
Teach. acad. futility	Tcl 5	-.13	.25	.17	-.05	.17	-.07	-.03	.02	.13	.21	-.14
Prin. concern & exp. for qual.	Pcl 1	.32	-.10	.31	.39	.27	.38	.35	.27	.57	-.03	.14
Prin. efforts to improve	Pcl 2	-.24	.20	-.03	-.08	-.16	-.13	-.07	-.07	-.08	-.21	.20
Prin. & parents eval. of qual.	Pcl 3	.37	-.13	.18	.40	.34	.42	.26	.39	.38	-.11	.22
Prin. present eval. & exp.	Pcl 4	.38	-.11	.23	.61	.37	.55	.32	.38	.53	-.05	.16
Comb. climate	Clim.	.29	.28	.37	.58		.49	.28	.39	.50	-.06	.25

*Table continued on next page.

APPENDIX C, TABLE 1 (continued)

AO7	CS	Sc11	Sc12	Sc13	Sc14	Sc15	Tc11	Tc12	Tc13	Tc14	Tc15	Pc11	Pc12	Pc13	Pc14
.67															
.20	.52														
.10	.21	.44													
.20	.33	.49	.20												
.00	.06	.06	.31	.40											
.04	.02	.11	.20	.36	.60										
.23	.40	.34	.63	.13	.19	.21									
.39	.63	.70	.46	.28	.20	.11	.55								
.10	.13	.19	.11	.31	.04	.02	.34	.02							
.01	.23	.18	.33	.01	.05	.01	.72	.40	.37						
.21	.14	.20	.22	.22	.03	.15	.05	.13	.17						
.15	.36	.25	.24	.20	.07	.02	.39	.34	.18	.40	.01				
.04	.07	.17	.16	.25	.25	.09	.00	.12	.05	.16	.16	.06			
.15	.34	.40	.17	.16	.09	.36	.21	.43	.10	.18	.00	.39	.03		
.21	.40	.52	.42	.17	.19	.22	.43	.51	.03	.29	.05	.55	.02	.45	
.19	.42	.47	.72	.22	.51	.47	.77	.63	.30	.52	.30	.53	.21	.50	.65

APPENDIX C, TABLE 2

Correlation Matrix of Mean School Input Variables, Combined Climate, and School Outcomes in State Sample of 68 Michigan Elementary Schools.

		Ach 74	SCAB	SSLR	SES	%wh	AOI	SBS	ADA	P/P	MTS	T.Exp.	T.Ten	%AD	A02	CS
Mean school achv. 74	Ach 74	1.00														
Mean s.-concept of acad. abil.	SCAB	-.55	1.00													
Mean student s.-reliance	SSLR	.06	.29	1.00												
Mean SES	SES	.68	-.18	.33	1.00											
% White students	%wh	.87	-.70	-.01	.58	1.00										
Comb. SES & % White	AOI	.86	-.49	.18			1.00									
Student body size	SBS	-.43	.44	-.05	-.31	-.56		1.00								
Ave. daily atten.	ADA	.39	.15	.13	.36	.36		-.41	1.00							
Prof. personnel per 1,000 students	P/P	.10	-.03	.02	.12	.12		-.32	.24	1.00						
Mean teach. salary	MTS	.28	-.07	.14	.33	.23		-.12	-.04	-.02	1.00					
Mean teach. Exp.	T.Exp	.31	-.06	.15	.27	.25		.03	.10	-.22	.56	1.00				
Mean teach. Ten.	T.Ten	.29	-.15	.01	.19	.17		.06	.01	-.03	.29	.68	1.00			
% teach. w/adv. degrees	%AD	.18	.13	.04	.22	.03		.03	.02	.09	.51	.34	.27	1.00		
Comb. other personnel inputs	AO2	.53	-.21	.14			.53								1.00	
Comb. social struct.	CS	.48	-.31	.04	.59	.63	.69	.47	.48	.04	.20	.06	-.02	.12	.37	1.00
Comb. climate	Clim	.29	.28	.37	.58		.44	-.23	.40	.10	.15	.03	-.14	.25	.28	.42

APPENDIX C, TABLE 3*

Correlation Matrix of Mean School Social Composition, Social Structure and Climate Variables in 30 Black and 61 white Public Michigan Elementary Schools (black, top, white, bottom)

		Ach74	SCAB	SSLR	SES	%wh	AO1	AO2	AO3	AO4	AO5	AO6
Mean sch. ach74	Ach74	1.00	.00	.20	.60	.40	.64	.67	.13	.59	.13	.16
Mean s-concept acad. abil.	SCAB	.04	1.00	.34	.34	-.25	.20	-.04	-.10	.12	.12	-.12
Mean stud. s-reliance	SSLR	.21	.37	1.00	.13	.33	.22	.04	-.14	.07	.11	-.10
Mean stud. SES	SES	.56	.27	.45	1.00	.29						
#wh. stud.	%wh	.56	-.08	.22	.44	1.00						
Comb. SES & % wh.	AO1	.63	.20	.44			1.00	.40	.04	.50	.16	.19
Comb. other person. inputs	AO2	.39	.13	.26			.39	1.00	.32	.61	.04	.18
Teach. satis. wh. soc. struc.	AO3	.07	.11	.12			.23	.12	1.00	.26	-.18	.08
Parent involvement	AO4	.21	.06	.33			.53	.33	.47	1.00	.21	.11
Differentiated stud. prog.	AO5	-.17	.05	.05			.07	.06	.03	.12	1.00	.14
Prin. report instr. time	AO6	.27	.27	.06			.45	.04	.15	.06	-.06	1.00
Open-closed classroom	AO7	-.14	.08	-.14			.10	.09	.28	.21	.20	.10
Comb. social structure	CS	.07	.19	.14	.45	.35	.48	.10	.61	.64	.51	.43
Stud. sense of fut (Fut=low)	Scl 1	.51	.11	.34	.74	.49	.76	.25	.03	.33	.06	.25
Perceived future eval. & exp.	Scl 2	.38	.53	.41	.69	.15	.62	.23	.05	.24	-.08	.36
Perceived present eval. & exp.	Scl 3	-.17	.79	.12	-.02	-.26	-.10	.11	.13	-.10	-.03	.13
Percep. of teach. push & norms	Scl 4	.01	.36	.09	.17	.06	.16	.15	.06	.17	.10	.14
Student academic norms	Scl 5	-.08	.33	.05	.11	.02	.09	.03	.25	.04	-.08	.15
Teach. eval. & exp. for college	Tcl 1	.28	.39	.33	.53	.13	.48	.03	.34	.44	.10	.12
Teach. eval. & exp. for H.S.	Tcl 2	.42	.29	.38	.57	.40	.59	.20	.24	.38	-.07	.42
Teach./Stud. commitment	Tcl 3	.09	.26	.14	-.06	-.21	-.11	.04	.23	.18	-.11	-.32
Teach. percept. of prin. exp.	Tcl 4	.34	.13	.30	.34	.19	.35	-.04	.34	.36	-.02	.05
Teach. acad. futility	Tcl 5	-.09	.21	.22	-.12	.20	.04	.00	.13	.21	.25	-.05
Prin. concern & exp. for qual.	Pcl 1	.32	.07	.32	.38	.29	.40	.20	.29	.50	-.07	-.04
Prin. efforts to improve	Pcl 2	-.26	.19	-.04	-.04	-.23	-.10	-.05	.02	-.03	-.23	.21
Prin. & parents eval of qual.	Pcl 3	.23	.12	.23	.32	.22	.34	.18	.35	.32	-.13	.15
Prin. present eval. & exp.	Pcl 4	.22	.16	.29	.56	.22	.53	.19	.23	.45	.03	.02
Comb. climate	Clim.	.30	.55	.45	.62	.17	.56	.21	.38	.50	-.05	.21

*Table continued on next page.

APPENDIX C, TABLE 3 (continued)

AO7	CS	Sc11	Sc12	Sc13	Sc14	Sc15	Tc11	Tc12	Tc13	Tc14	Tc15	Pc11	Pc12	Pc13	Pc14	Clim
.33	.45	.69	.40	.02	.20	.35	.52	.26	.39	.55	.07	.19	.23	.25	.41	.54
.07	.00	.28	.70	.86	.24	.34	.22	.37	.06	.04	.20	.01	.18	.12	.19	.42
.30	.01	.09	.22	.23	.40	.40	.08	.18	.16	.01	.05	.03	.13	.17	.14	.23
	.38	.80	.55	.18	.22	.09	.45	.36	.11	.36	.10	.08	.39	.48	.50	.46
	.22	.38	.04	.32	.16	.15	.10	.01	.08	.19	.13	.20	.13	.24	.20	.20
.30	.39	.81	.48	.04	.24	.13	.41	.30	.07	.37	.13	.14	.29	.49	.49	.46
.19	.50	.39	.27	.07	.21	.35	.35	.29	.41	.41	.08	.29	.16	.12	.27	.45
.20	.61	.12	.10	.05	.16	.16	.49	.25	.53	.22	.12	.25	.09	.06	.28	.39
.23	.54	.60	.41	.05	.38	.56	.42	.39	.33	.49	.04	.43	.19	.43	.35	.65
.27	.45	.25	.26	.16	.03	.05	.11	.05	.05	.16	.10	.41	.07	.20	.15	.20
.20	.53	.12	.09	.08	.05	.18	.12	.01	.10	.00	.13	.09	.12	.11	.08	.04
1.00	.57	.17	.15	.16	.31	.17	.45	.50	.18	.37	.14	.36	.02	.30	.29	.49
.65	1.00	.44	.35	.05	.31	.25	.58	.38	.39	.41	.01	.53	.05	.36	.30	.60
.02	.24	1.00	.52	.18	.06	.20	.55	.37	.06	.38	.01	.21	.27	.51	.45	.55
.12	.24	.64	1.00	.59	.27	.26	.44	.37	.11	.32	.18	.29	.06	.13	.37	.63
.01	.03	.15	.24	1.00	.17	.31	.22	.36	.01	.06	.25	.13	.17	.01	.01	.34
.02	.14	.22	.28	.43	1.00	.71	.37	.25	.37	.47	.05	.14	.16	.26	.22	.59
.03	.09	.17	.22	.40	.61	1.00	.22	.13	.43	.36	.12	.09	.29	.30	.12	.55
.22	.41	.40	.62	.22	.16	.21	1.00	.72	.50	.74	.10	.40	.03	.28	.50	.82
.29	.43	.51	.59	.11	.30	.13	.62	1.00	.13	.43	.38	.37	.02	.18	.52	.71
.04	.05	.10	.08	.22	.12	.05	.35	.09	1.00	.49	.14	.27	.07	.21	.10	.46
.01	.23	.26	.33	.01	.09	.01	.71	.47	.38	1.00	.17	.34	.14	.41	.36	.70
.28	.30	.07	.20	.17	.15	.06	.15	.09	.11	.18	1.00	.05	.06	.02	.04	.24
.06	.28	.22	.26	.09	.06	.08	.39	.31	.21	.40	.07	1.00	.43	.31	.46	.59
.01	.23	.09	.12	.26	.23	.16	.01	-.04	.02	.16	.19	.09	1.00	.19	.08	.05
.07	.27	.29	.20	.02	.13	.38	.19	.32	-.05	.18	.01	.39	.04	1.00	.47	.46
.13	.48	.44	.44	.02	.22	.22	.41	.41	-.00	.00	.09	.53	.02	.40	1.00	.65
.16	.40	.53	.73	.39	.49	.48	.77	.68	.31	.51	.30	.54	.24	.50	.64	1.00

APPENDIX D

Stepwise Forward Regression Analysis of Mean School Achievement on 14 School Climate Variables in:

TABLE 1: A Representative Random Sample of Michigan Public Elementary Schools.

TABLE 2: A Random Sample of Majority Black Michigan Public Elementary Schools.

TABLE 3: A Random Sample of Majority White Michigan Public Elementary Schools.

APPENDIX D, TABLE 1

Summary of Multiple Regression Analysis of Mean School Achievement on Mean School Climate Variables in a Random Sample of 30 Majority Black Elementary Schools in Michigan

Variable	Beta	Multiple R	R^2	R^2 change	Signif-icance
Student Climate 1, Sense of Futility	.750	.69374	.48127		.000
Teacher Climate 3, Teacher-Student Commitment	−.023	.77891	.60670	.12543	.007
Teacher Climate 4, Perception of Principle's Expectations	.526	.79298	.62881	.02211	.224
Teacher Climate 1, Eval., Exp. for Col.	.094	.80613	.64985	.02104	.232
Principal Climate 3, Prin. & Par. Eval.	−.470	.81732	.66801	.01817	.263
Principal Climate 4, Eval & Exp.	.279	.82897	.68719	.09118	.247
Student Climate 5, Academic Norms	.289	.83407	.69568	.00849	.442
Student Climate 3, Present Eval. & Exp.	−.092	.84271	.71016	.01448	.317
Student Climate 4, Perception of Teacher Push Norms	−.104	.84599	.71521	.00555	.539
Teacher Climate 2, Present Eval. & Exp.	−.208	.84890	.72063	.00492	.570
Teacher Climate 5, Teacher Academic Fut.	−.106	.85150	.72792	.00443	.597
Student Climate 2, Future Eval. & Exp.	−.092	.85318	.72792	.00286	.678
Principal Climate 2, Efforts to Improve	−.017	.85329	.72810	.00018	.919

One climate variable, Principal Climate 1, was omitted because the F-level was insufficient for computation.

APPENDIX D, TABLE 2

**Summary of Multiple Regression of Mean School Achievement
on Mean School Climate Variables in a Representative
Random Sample of 68 Michigan Elementary Schools**

Variable	Beta	Multiple R	R^2	R^2 change	Signif-icance
Student Climate 1, Sense of Futility	.519	.76885	.59114		.000
Student Climate 3, Present Eval./Exp.	−.158	.80074	.64118	.05005	.004
Teacher Climate 2, Present Eval./Exp.	.340	.82561	.68164	.04046	.006
Teacher Climate 5, Teacher Academic Futility	.130	.82916	.68750	.00586	.281
Teacher Climate 3, Teacher-Student Commitment	.103	.83228	.69355	.00605	.273
Teacher Climate 4, Perception of Principal's Exp.	−.131	.83927	.70438	.01083	.143
Principal Climate 1, Parent Concern & Exp.	.116	.84226	.70940	.00503	.312
Student Climate 5, Academic Norms	−.100	.84582	.71541	.00600	.269
Principal Climate 4, Expectation & Eval.	−.086	.84807	.71922	.00381	.379
Principal Climate 3, Prin. & Par. Eval.	.061	.84974	.72205	.00284	.449
Principal Climate 2, Effort of Improve	.044	.85100	.72419	.00214	.512
Teacher Climate 1, Eval & Exp. for Col.	−037	.85150	.72505	.00085	.681
Student Climate 2, Future Eval. & Exp.	−.030	.85170	.72539	.00034	.796

One climate variable, Student Climate 4, was omitted because the F-level was
insufficient for computation.

APPENDIX D, TABLE 3

Summary of Multiple Regression Analysis of Mean School Achievement on Mean School Climate Variables in a Random Sample of 61 Majority White Elementary Schools in Michigan

Variance	Beta	Multiple R	R^2	R change	Significance
Student Climate 1, Sense of Academic Futility	.358	.51428	.26448		.000
Principal Climate 2, Efforts to Improve	−.169	.55476	.30776	.04328	.062
Principal Climate 1, Par. Concern & Exp.	.171	.58658	.34407	.03632	.081
Student Climate 5, Academic Norms	−.237	.60559	.36674	.02267	.162
Teacher Climate 2, Present Eval. & Exp.	.149	.62419	.38961	.02287	.157
Teacher Climate 5, Teacher Academic Fut.	.167	.63664	.40532	.01571	.238
Principal Climate 4, Eval. & Exp.	−.140	.64458	.41548	.01016	.341
Principal Climate 3, Prin. & Par. Eval.	.147	.65020	.42276	.00729	.421
Student Climate 2, Future Eval. & Exp.	.180	.65634	.43078	.00802	.401
Teacher Climate 3, Teacher-Student Com.	.131	.66079	.43665	.00586	.474
Student Climate 4, Perception of Teacher Push Norms	.096	.66406	.44097	.00433	.541
Teacher Climate 1, Eval., Exp. for Col.	−.060	.66578	.44327	.00230	.658
Student Climate 3, Present Eval. & Exp.	−.057	.66686	.44470	.00143	.729
Teacher Climate 4, Percept. of Prin. Exp.	−.035	.66723	.44519	.0049	.841

APPENDIX E

Summary of Stepwise
Multiple Regression Analyses

TABLE 1: Summary of Stepwise Multiple Regression Analysis of Mean School Achievement on School Social System Variables in Random Sample of 68 Michigan Elementary Schools.

TABLE 2: Summary of Stepwise Multiple Regression Analysis of Mean Student Self-Concept on School Social System Variables in Representative Sample of 68 Michigan Public Elementary Schools.

TABLE 3: Summary of Stepwise Multiple Regression Analysis of Mean Student Self-Reliance on School Social System Variables in a Random Sample of 68 Michigan Public Elementary Schools.

APPENDIX E, TABLE 1

Summary of Stepwise Multiple Regression Analysis of Mean School Achievement on School Social System Variables in Random Sample of 68 Michigan Elementary Schools.

Step	Variable Entered	F to Enter or Remove	Significance	BETA	Multiple R	R²	R² change
1	AOI Comb. SES & Rac. Comp.	192.27	.000	.815	.863	.744	.744
2	AO5 Diff. stud. programs	5.57	.021	-.158	.874	.765	.020
3	PSCL2 Prin. efforts to improve	7.42	.008	-.126	.888	.789	.024
4	PSCL4 Prin. eval. & exp.	4.73	.033	-.107	.897	.804	.015
5	TSCL3 Teach./stud. commit.	2.26	.138	.124	.900	.811	.007
6	SSCL3 Stud. perc. eval. & exp.	3.34	.073	-.143	.906	.821	.010
7	AO4 Parent involvement	3.38	.055	-.255	.912	.831	.011
8	AO2 Comb. other person. input	4.37	.041	.130	.918	.843	.012
9	PSCL3 Prin. & parent evaluation	.84	.362	.047	.919	.845	.002
10	SSCL4 Stud. percp. of teach. push & norms	.60	.441	.064	.920	.847	.002
11	SSCL2 Stud. percp. of future eval. & percp.	.64	.427	-.122	.921	.849	.002
12	SSCL5 Stud. academic norms	.67	.417	-.054	.922	.850	.002
13	AO7 Open-closed classroom	.52	.472	-.057	.923	.852	.001
14	TSCL2 Pres. eval. & expectation	.57	.453	.031	.924	.853	.002
15	TSCL5 Teach. academic futility	.55	.460	.067	.925	.855	.002
16	TSCL4 Teach percp. of princ. exp.	.56	.456	.040	.925	.856	.002
17	PSCL1 Prin. percp. of parent concern & exp.	.17	.683	.040	.926	.857	.000
18	SSCL1 Sense of futility	.23	.630	.084	.926	.858	.001
19	AO6 Prin. report of instructor time	.12	.734	.033	.926	.858	.000
20	TSCL1 Teach. eval. & exp. for college	.05	.821	.029	.926	.858	.000
21	AO3 Teach. satisf. w/soc. structure	.02	.891	.012	.926	.858	.000

APPENDIX E, TABLE 2

Summary of Stepwise Multiple Regression Analysis of Mean Student Self-Concept on School Social System Variables in Representative Sample of 68 Michigan Public Elementary Schools.

Step	Variable Entered	F to Enter or Remove	Significance	BETA	Multiple R	R^2	R^2 change
1	SSCL3 Stud. percp. eval. & exp.	223.74	0	.675	.879	.772	.772
2	SSCL2 Stud. percp. of future eval. & percp.	14.31	.000	.384	.902	.813	.041
3	AO3 Teach. satisf. w/soc. structure	13.56	.000	−.207	.920	.846	.033
4	SSCL1 Sense of futility	5.24	.025	−.215	.926	.856	.012
5	AO4 Parent involvement	3.09	.084	.117	.930	.866	.007
6	PSCL2 Prin. efforts to improve	2.07	.155	−.074	.932	.869	.004
7	AO5 Diff. stud. programs	1.36	.249	.072	.934	.872	.003
8	TSCL3 Teach./stud. commitment	1.71	.196	.118	.936	.875	.004
9	PSCL3 Prin. & parent evaluation	1.70	.197	.072	.938	.879	.004
10	TSCL1 Teach. eval. & exp. for college	1.07	.306	−.127	.939	.881	.002
11	AO2 Comb. other personnel input	1.82	.183	−.057	.941	.885	.004
12	AO6 Prin. report of instructor time	.52	.476	.052	.941	.886	.001
13	TSCL2 Pres. eval. & expectation	.29	.594	−.066	.942	.887	.001
14	TSCL4 Teach. percp. of princ. exp.	.17	.685	.065	.942	.887	.000
15	PSCL1 Prin. percp. of parent concern & exp.	.16	.695	−.033	.942	.887	.000
16	TSCL5 Teacher academic futility	.12	.735	.026	.942	.888	.000
17	SSCL5 Student academic norms	.16	.695	.032	.942	.888	.000
18	AO1 Comb. SES & Racial Composition	.10	.750	.052	.942	.888	.000
19	AO7 Open-closed classroom	.09	.761	.019	.943	.888	.000

APPENDIX E, TABLE 3

Summary of Stepwise Multiple Regression Analysis of Mean Student Self-Reliance on School Social System Variables in a Random Sample of 68 Michigan Public Elementary Schools

Step	Variable Entered	F to Enter or Remove	Significance	BETA	Multiple R	R^2	R^2 change
1	SSCL2 Stud. percp. of future eval. & percp.	8.80	.004	.270	.343	.118	.118
2	PSCL1 Prin. percp. of parent concern & exp.	4.12	.046	.180	.413	.170	.053
3	AO7 Open-closed classroom	3.27	.075	-.230	.457	.211	.040
4	TSCL5 Teacher academic futility	2.26	.137	.194	.488	.238	.027
5	AO5 Diff. student programs	1.40	.242	.172	.505	.255	.017
6	TSCL2 Pres. eval. & expectation	.76	.386	.269	.514	.264	.009
7	AO3 Teach. satisf. w/ soc. structure	2.03	.159	-.372	.537	.288	.024
8	SSCL4 Stud. percp. of teach. push & norms	1.01	.318	-.190	.548	.300	.012
9	SSCL3 Stud. percp. eval. & exp.	1.33	.253	.283	.562	.316	.016
10	AO1 Comb. SES & racial composition	1.49	.228	.649	.577	.333	.017
11	AO6 Prin. report of instructor time	.64	.426	-.185	.584	.341	.008
12	PSCL3 Prin. & parent evaluation	.56	.456	.085	.589	.347	.007
13	SSCL1 Sense of futility	.80	.376	-.309	.597	.357	.009
14	TSCL4 Teach. percp. of princ. exp.	.44	.510	.247	.602	.362	.005
15	TSCL1 Teach. eval. & exp. for college	1.15	.288	-.328	.613	.376	.014
16	SSCL5 Student academic norms	.32	.575	.114	.616	.380	.004
17	AO4 Parent involvement	.29	.591	.102	.619	.383	.004
18	TSCL3 Teach./stud. commitment	.14	.710	.047	.621	.385	.002
19	PSCL4 Prin. eval. & exp.	.08	.773	-.058	.622	.386	.001
20	PSCL2 Prin. efforts to improve	.05	.819	.032	.622	.387	.007
21	AO2 Comb. other personnel input	.03	.875	-.026	.622	.387	.000

REFERENCES

Anderson, Gary. "Effects of Classroom Social Climates on Individual Learning." *American Educational Research Journal*, 7:2 (March 1970).

Bloom, Benjamin. *Human Characteristics and School Learning.* New York: McGraw-Hill Book Company, 1976.

Brookover, Wilbur; Ann Paterson, Shailer Thomas. *Self-Concept of Ability and School Achievement.* East Lansing, Mich.: College of Education, Michigan State University (Cooperative Research Project 485), 1962.

————, Jean Lapere, Don Hamachek, Shailer Thomas, and Edsel Erickson. *Self-Concept of Ability and School Achievement II.* East Lansing, Mich.: College of Education, Michigan State University (Cooperative Research Project, 1636), 1965.

————, Edsel Erickson, M. Joiner. *Self-Concept of Ability and School Achievement III.* East Lansing, Mich.: College of Education, Michigan State University (Cooperative Research Project 2831), 1967.

————, and Edsel Erickson. *Sociology of Education.* Homewood, Ill.: Dorsey Press, 1975.

————, Richard Gigliotti, Ronald Henderson, and Jeffrey Schneider, *Elementary School Environment and School Achievement.* East Lansing, Mich.: College of Urban Development, Michigan State University, 1973.

————, and Jeffery Schneider, "Academic Environments and Elementary School Achievement" *Journal of Research and Development in Education*, 9:1, (Fall 1975).

Coleman, James (et. al.). Equality of Educational Opportunity, Department of Health, Education and Welfare, Washington, D.C.: U.S. Government Printing Office, 1966.

DeVries, David L., and Robert Slavin. *Team Games Tournament: A Final Research Report.* Baltimore: *The Johns Hopkins University Center for Social Organization of Schools* (Report 217), 1976.

Epstein, Joyce, and James M. McPartland, *The Effects of Open School Organization on Student Outcomes.* Baltimore: *The Johns Hopkins University Center for Social Organization of Schools* (Report 194), 1975.

Farkus, George. "Specifications, Residuals, and Context Effects". *Sociological Methods and Research*, 2:3 (1974); and reply by Robert Hauser, "Contextual Effects Revisited," same reference.

Fernandez, Celestine; Ruben W. Espinosa, and Sanford Dornbush. *Factors Perpetuating the Low Academic Status of Chicano High School Students.* Palo Alto, California: Stanford Center for Research and Development in Teaching. (R & D Memorandum 138), 1975.

Glasser, William. *Schools Without Failure.* New York: Harper and Row, Publishers, Inc., 1969.

Hara, Kimi T. *A Cross Cultural Comparison of Self-Concept and Value Orientations of Japanese and American Ninth Grades.* Ph. D. dissertation, Michigan State University, 1972.

Hauser, Robert. *Socio-Economic Background and Educational Performance.* Washington, D.C., American Sociological Association, 1971.

——, Wm. Sewell, and Duane Alwin. "High School Effects on Achievement," in Sewell, Hauser, and Featherman, *School and Academic Achievement in American Society.* New York: Academic Press, 1976.

Henderson, Grace. *An Analysis of Self-Concept of Academic Ability as Related to Social Psychological Variable Comprising School Climate in Black and White Elementary Children with Differential School Settings.* Ph. D. dissertation, East Lansing, Michigan State University, 1973.

Jencks, Christopher (et. al.). *Inequality.* New York: Basic Books, Inc., 1972.

Joiner, Lee. *The Reliability and Construct Validity of Academic Ability Scale Found for Hearing Impaired Students.* Ph. D. dissertation, Michigan State University, 1966.

Mayeske, George W. (et. al.). *A Study of Our Nation's Schools* (a working paper). Washington, D.C.: Office of Education, Department of Health, Education and Welfare, 1969.

McDill, Edward and Leo Rigsby. *The Academic Impact of Educational Climates — Structure and Process in Secondary Schools.* Baltimore: The Johns Hopkins University Press, 1973.

——, Leo Rigsby, and Edmund Meyers. "Institutional Effects on Academic Behavior of High School Students." *Sociology of Education* 40 (1967): 181-199.

McGhan, Barry. *A Survey and Analysis of Teachers' Use of Authority and Its Relation to Open Education and School Climate Variables in Michigan Elementary Schools,* Ph.D. dissertation, Michigan State University, 1977.

Michigan Department of Education. *Questions and Answers About Michigan Educational Assessment.* Lansing Michigan Department of Education, (Also other reports on Assessment.) (No date.)

Mood, Alexander. "Partitioning Variance in Multiple Regression Analysis as a Tool for Developing Learning Models." *American Educational Research Journal* 8:2 (March 1971), pp 191-202.

O'Reilly, R., "Classroom Climate and Achievement in Secondary School Mathematics Class," *Alberta Journal of Educational Research,* 21:3 (1975).

Passalacqua, Joseph. *An Analysis of the Ecological Phenomena of Self-Concept.* MA Thesis; (1979) Michigan State University. In Press.

Rosenthal, Robert and Lenore Jacobsen. *Pygmalion in the Classroom.* New York:

Holt, Rinehart and Winston, Inc., 1968.

St. John, Nancy H. *School Desegregation — Outcomes for Children*. New York, John Wiley and Sons, Inc., 1975.

Smith, Marshall. "Equality of Educational Opportunity: The Basic Findings." Reconsidered in Fredrick Mosteller and Daniel P. Moynihan. *On Equality of Educational Opportunity*. New York: Vintage Book Division, Random House, Inc., 1972.

Author Index

Subject Index

Academic achievement (*see* School achievement)

Academic climate, 4, 18
in high schools, 4
(*see also* School climate variables)

Academic futility (*see* Student sense of academic futility)

Achievement:
as attainable goal, 134
in low SES schools, 80, 111
in minority schools, 80, 111
and reinforcement practices, 127-132
and teacher commitment, 118-121
and teacher expectations, 122-124
and teaching games, 121-122
(*see also* School achievement)

Achievement variance, 2
explained by social system, 141

Atypical school study, 5

Average daily attendance as input measure, 13

Beliefs as school social climate, 19

Belief students can learn as crucial climate variable, 134

Bell-shaped curve, 148

Black school sample, 10

Black students:
self-concept of, 144-145

Case studies:
of Black A school, 94-101
of Black B school, 108-116
comparison of schools, 116-132
purpose of 80, 82, 116-177, 133
selection of schools for, 81-83
summary of, 132-134
as supplement to survey, 80
of White A school, 83-94
of White B school, 101-108

Center for study of school organization, 25

Climate variables (*see* School climate variables)

Combined school inputs, 14

Commitment to achievement:
in Black A school, 99-100
in Black B school, 115
comparison among schools, 118-121
and family background, 119-121
and instructional time, 121
and level of achievement, 119-120
as teacher responsibility, 118
in White A school, 93-94

About the Senior Author

Since receiving his Ph.D. in Sociology from the University of Wisconsin, Dr. Wilbur Brookover's longstanding research interest, as reflected in his extensive bibliography of books and journal articles, has been concerned with the social and the social psychological factors related to school learning. *School Social Systems and Student Achievement* is one of his most recent contributions in this area of research.

Among his other activities, Dr. Brookover was an expert witness at the Brown versus Topeka Board of Education case which was the lead case resulting in the landmark school desegregation decision of the Supreme Court in 1954. From 1971-1975 he served as Mayor of the city of East Lansing, Michigan.

Dr. Brookover is Professor, Sociology and Education, and Urban and Metropolitan Studies at Michigan State University.